THE
HEALING
PATH

DAN B. ALLENDER, PH.D.

THE
HEALING
PATH

HOW THE HURTS IN YOUR PAST CAN
LEAD YOU TO A MORE ABUNDANT LIFE

WATERBROOK
PRESS

THE HEALING PATH
PUBLISHED BY WATERBROOK PRESS
5446 North Academy Boulevard, Suite 200
Colorado Springs, Colorado 80918
A division of Random House, Inc.

Unless otherwise noted, Scripture quotations are from *The Holy Bible,
New International Version* (NIV) © 1973, 1984 by International Bible
Society, used by permission of Zondervan Publishing House. Scripture
quotations marked (NLT) are taken from the *Holy Bible, New Living
Translation,* copyright © 1996. Used by permission of Tyndale House
Publishers, Inc., Wheaton, Illinois 60189. All rights reserved.

Details in some anecdotes and stories have been changed to protect
the identities of the persons involved.

ISBN 1-57856-109-4

Copyright © 1999 by Dr. Dan B. Allender

Published in association with the literary agency of Alive
Communications, Inc., 1465 Kelly Johnson Blvd., Suite 320,
Colorado Springs, CO 80920

Printed in the United States of America

1999—First Edition

10 9 8 7 6 5 4 3 2 1

CONTENTS

115875

Some stupid people started the idea that because women obviously back up their own people through everything, therefore women are blind and do not see anything. They can hardly have known any women. The same women who are ready to defend their men through thick and thin are (in their personal intercourse with the man) almost morbidly lucid about the thinness of his excuses or the thickness of his head.

G. K. CHESTERTON

To four women who have walked the path with me, gentle and lucid:

Susan Berthiaume

Allyson Baker

Laura Wackman

Linda Busse

ACKNOWLEDGMENTS

This book was written largely on a journey between Denver and Seattle. It was the first year of the Mars Hill Forum's new seminary and counseling program at Western Seminary–Seattle and also my oldest daughter's senior year in high school. Instead of moving from our home in Denver and disrupting her year, our family allowed me to travel weekly to Seattle and endured my long absences. The cost has been great, but the book enabled me to focus on what is involved in being an alien and a stranger. But one can't exist as a stranger without the aid of kind patrons along the way.

I'm deeply grateful for my "apostolic" community in Seattle: Liam Atchison, Christie Lynk, Don Hudson, Kim Hutchins, Kirk and Heather Webb, and Ken Wilson. All bore additional burdens in my absence, opening their homes and hearts to our family. I'm also grateful for many friends who have read and commented on the manuscript as it has evolved: Deb Richards, Elizabeth Turnage, Suzzane and Don Hudson, Heather Webb, Kim Hutchins, Gail Foster, and Sharon Hersh.

To Tremper Longman, my friend and colleague who read the manuscript and suffered with me through each chapter: My work is always co-authored even when your name is not on the front.

To WaterBrook Press, my new friends Dan Rich and Rebecca Price: Your support for this book has been felt at many levels, and I am honored to be part of your new shop. Thank you.

To Kathy Yanni: Oh, how odd to have you go from editor to friend to agent. In all your manifestations, you serve with untold mercy and vision. Thank you.

To Traci Mullins: How sweet it is after nearly eight years to work with you again. Your willingness to offer me your scintillating mind and huge heart is a gift that has shaped this work from beginning to end. Thank you.

To my children, Anna, Amanda, and Andrew: You have endured a hard year, a difficult move, and the stress of your daft parents with unusual maturity and a minimum of outrageous outbursts. Thank you.

To Becky: I doubt a day goes by that I don't gaze at you in wonder. Your simple, kind, elegant love is the window I most look through to glimpse the face of God. I love you.

SAVORING JOY IN SPITE OF SORROW

The book you hold in your hands has taken me on a journey I didn't expect. What you read here first, I have waited till the end to write. I did this in large measure because I needed to see if the book turned out as I thought it might. It did, but in ways I could not have anticipated when I began. For each of us the healing path is surprising.

Originally this book was conceived as a ten-year follow-up to *The Wounded Heart.* So much of what I wrote about the damage and the process of healing for sexual-abuse victims is equally true for those who have not been abused. Why? Because we all live in a fallen world, are damaged, and need to be healed as we grow in our relationships with others and God.

The Healing Path is and is not about sexual abuse. It is about what happens to our soul when we suffer in a world that is at times dark and tragic. We lose faith: *How could God allow this to happen to me?* We lose hope: *How can I ever be the same after this hurt?* And we lose love: *How can I give and receive when so much has been lost?*

But great tragedies aren't the only things that snuff out faith, hope, and love. These precious assets are similarly smothered by nondramatic, routine suffering—the loss of a friendship, the misery of not getting ahead, the petty squabbles with one's kids or spouse, the frustration of remaining uncoupled or childless or out of work, the struggles with internal or external conflicts that simply don't go away after much prayer and effort. The wearisome battles of life drain us daily of faith, hope, and love.

Foundational principles like faith, hope, and love may seem elemental. What can be said that we don't already know? Isn't faith a matter of just believing and putting doubts away? Is hope any more than turning away from despair and being positive? We know that love involves being kind and not letting disappointment make us bitter. So why a whole book about basic Christian truths we've heard and tried to live all our lives?

Because I believe our understanding is shallow. The path that truly heals and redeems begins at the point when we realize we want more perspective, purpose, and passion in life. It passes through the dark terrain of the shadow of death, through the dry desert where little makes sense and where we lose most, if not all, that seems important to us. And then it takes us to a green, verdant valley that once was Baca, the place of tears, and is now a meadow of lush joy and inconceivable pleasure. My premise is that doubt, despair, and disappointment are not only a reality of daily life, they are also the tools God uses to grow faith, hope, and love in us. If we run from what we fear or find displeasureable, we actually rob ourselves of the joy God intends for us to experience as we walk through our past, play with our future, and live now with new passion.

This life has great suffering and sorrow woven into its fabric, but it also has an incandescent beauty and compelling call. For now, the beauty serves as a window through which we can glimpse the face of God, which we will one day see in its glorious fullness. *The Healing Path* is about how God redeems our doubt and betrayal, our despair and powerlessness, our disappointment and ambivalence. It calls us to move toward the great destination of this life: becoming a man or woman of faith, hope, and love.

The reward of following the healing path is simple: the capacity to savor greater joy in spite of inevitable sorrow. We can dance, eat, sing, drink, talk, and party with more joy if our hearts truly grasp God's perspective on our past, the purpose of our future, and the passion we are to embrace in our present.

Come walk with me on the healing path.

PART ONE

———

Suffering As a Sacred Journey

CHAPTER 1

THE LONG WALK

Opening our arms to a day is an act of faith. Even on the days when we feel the most optimistic about the course life is taking, our confidence can be shattered by events beyond our control. A morning that begins with a cheerful whistle can be sideswiped by the droning negativity of a spouse who gets up on the wrong side of the bed. A much-anticipated vacation can be cut short by a broken leg, a stolen wallet, or the death of a loved one back home. A pleasant Sunday morning can be shot to pieces by the cool rebuff of a friend sitting in an adjacent church pew. A single split-second decision can change the course of our lives forever.

I'll never forget the woman who told me about the morning that changed everything for her. She had put her son in the backseat of the car and buckled his seat belt, got into the front seat, and then realized she had left her purse in the house. She left the keys in the ignition, but did not start the car. She ran back into the house, and as she grabbed her purse, the phone rang. She hesitated but decided to answer it. The call lasted no more than three minutes. When she went back outside she witnessed a horror that would change everything about her life forever.

Apparently seconds after her son was left alone in the car, he escaped from the backseat, climbed to the front seat, started the car, and put it in reverse. When he felt the movement of the car, he panicked and tried to jump out. He must have caught his coat on the car door because he was dragged under the wheels and his skull was crushed. In a matter of seconds, his young life was extinguished, and his mother's heart was shattered.

Two years after the accident the woman was doing much better, but she still suffered waves of nausea and guilt that threatened to drown her. Her marriage was at grave risk, and she continued to take medication for depression. Her story and the sorrow embedded in her eyes shook me. But one comment in particular unnerved me. "Thank you," she said, "for letting me know it is not wrong to suffer." Everyone else wanted her to be "fine," she explained. They wanted her to "move on with her life." She said she used to have similar sentiments toward those who suffered tragic losses; she hadn't understood the depth of harm with which they wrestled. Now she did. Wistfully she commented, "I simply never thought that tragedy could really, I mean *really*, come to my door."

PAINFUL REALITIES

Most of us are spared such life-wrenching tragedy, but none of us escapes the heartache of living in a fallen world. To live is to hurt. We barely take our first breath and a wail is the first sound we utter. Seventy years later (if we're lucky) our exit is with a moan or a whimper, a last breath reminiscent of the first cry.

Negative? A downer? Unnecessarily pessimistic? Surely life is not that bad for most people. Of course we know suffering will visit us sometimes, but we don't want to think about it. What is the point of contemplating something that is out of our control? If we could prevent it, then we might briefly consider our stance toward suffering. But why bother when God "causes his sun to rise on the evil and the good, and sends rain on the righteous and the unrighteous" (Matthew 5:45)? We're all going to get our share of joy and sorrow, so let's just get on with our lives and hope for the best.

The problem with this position is that once the inevitable pain comes, it is too late to consider how we will allow ourselves to be shaped by it. If we fail to anticipate thoughtfully how we will respond to the harm of living in a fallen world, the pain may be for naught. It will either numb or destroy us rather than refine and even bless us.

Suffering need not destroy the heart; it has the potential to lead to life. But few people I know suffer deeply and profit. Instead, pain is seldom expected nor embraced when it comes. It is often denied or swept under the spiritual rug of "God's sovereignty." The apostle Paul tells us that as we "groan inwardly," we "wait eagerly" for our final redemption (Romans 8:23). But few of us enter the tragedy of living in a fallen world and simultaneously struggle with God until our hearts bleed with hope. We either give into pain with a hopeless cynicism, or we settle for an artificial resolution that insists that things really aren't too bad and we need not muck around in the "negatives" of life.

God's perspective on suffering is very different. He invites us on a healing journey through the valleys and over the cliffs of an evil world, but we often miss out on his redemptive path. Too many of us suffer for naught.

For the past fifteen years, I have spent countless hours with men and women who have suffered the ravages of childhood sexual abuse. In 1988 my book *The Wounded Heart* detailed the harm such abuse wreaks upon the soul and how it eats at the core of what makes us human beings in God's image: our capacity for faith, hope, and love. A decade later, sexual abuse continues to ravage lives even in a culture that has spent unprecedented time and energy talking about the subject. Cast the net even wider, and it becomes clear that many of us are carrying deep hurts simply because human beings inflict harm on each other, whether intentionally or unintentionally, provoked or unprovoked.

Ten years and far more reflection on these issues have made clearer to me what the evil in this world is doing to harm *all* of our hearts and darken our love for God and others. No matter how we have acquired our wounds, we all need the good news of the healing power of redemption: Evil meant our suffering for our destruction, but God meant it for our good.

Healing in this life is not the *resolution* of our past; it is the *use* of our past to draw us into deeper relationship with God and his purposes for our lives. We need a new understanding of how to deal with past hurts, one that acknowledges the damage to the human spirit while charting a path toward the abundant life God promises.

FROM ESCAPE TO EMBRACE

We hate suffering. (Of course we do.) At the first sign of a headache, we grab aspirin. At the first hint of tension with a friend, we try to patch things up—or if addressing the tension causes more conflict, then we are apt to get busy with other activities. We are escape artists.

Obviously, if pain has a clear cause and ready solution, there is no point in suffering for suffering's sake. But most pain cannot be erased by the simple decision to pick up a bottle of aspirin. We are called then to address it. And as followers of Christ, we are to consider the path of suffering a sacred journey: "To this you were called, because Christ suffered for you, leaving you an example, that you should follow in his steps" (1 Peter 2:21).

The way we approach suffering usually is determined by our basic attitude toward the struggles of this life. Many of us believe that God's commitment is to help us avoid or triumph over adversity—we are "more than conquerors." And we are. But that biblical belief can be cheapened to presume there is a way to completely eradicate our pain if we just find the right combination of prayer and action. If an illness does not succumb to medical care, then prayer, anointing with oil, and a deliverance service might do the trick. The bottom-line assumption is that pain "ought" to be relieved. If it isn't, then we tend to believe we're doing something wrong; after all, there has to be a cure if we are more than conquerors.

But pain plays an important role in the physical, spiritual, and relational realm. One of the most widely read modern-day allegories is Hannah Hurnard's *Hinds' Feet on High Places*. In this parable God calls Much-Afraid to make a journey to the high country with two companions, Suffering and Sorrow, who will help her on her sojourn. Stunned that God would call her to travel with such unattractive friends, she pleads with the Shepherd. "I can't go with them," she gasped. "I can't. I can't. O my Shepherd, why do you do this to me? How can I travel in their company? It is more than I can bear. You tell me that the mountain way itself is so steep and difficult that I cannot climb it alone. Then why, oh why, must you make Sorrow and Suffering my companions. Couldn't you have given Joy and Peace to go with me, to strengthen me, and encourage me and help me on this difficult way. I never thought you would do this to me!"[1]

Nor did I. I will never forget the night when the Shepherd introduced me to my traveling companions. My stepfather called to tell me he had lung cancer and would probably live less than a year. It was also my son's third birthday. We had balloons and decorations hanging all over the kitchen. We had served Andrew's favorite meal at that time: grilled cheese sandwiches and broccoli. Dinner was finished, and we were about to open presents when Dad called to inform me of his diagnosis.

After the phone call I felt as if I had been rubbed raw; my head was spinning in shock. I had gone from enjoying a great meal and reminiscing about my son's birth and his first few years of life to hearing that my father was about to die. Nausea came over me in waves. I could barely stand to go back to the party.

In that awful moment my spirit heard the voice of God say clearly, "Don't dread any moment that comes from me." It was a phrase that seared me with its gentle power. "Don't dread any moment." How was I to pull that off? How was I to travel nimbly from the painful phone call to the delight and joy my son would feel as he opened his presents?

We have all faced such moments—times when we recognize anew that we are called to a journey that will shape us and change us. The journey has the potential to heal us or harden us. It will harden us if we attempt to do an end run around the desert, valley, or craggy peak where God compels us to walk. It will soften, break, mold, and heal us if we choose to take sorrow and suffering by the hand and walk by faith into the damage of our past, the struggles of the present, and our fears of the future.

To make such a choice, we must consciously turn from paths that seem more reasonable and sure than a journey with those odd companions. After years of listening to survivors of childhood sexual abuse, I have identified four routes we *all* choose to take through the often barren, rocky, or wild terrain of life. Each route is logical to us, depending on our view of life, but each is a tangent from the truly healing path. When we choose the Paranoid, Fatalistic, Heroic, or Optimistic route, we might escape some of our pain, but we also miss our true destiny. Some of life's messiness is avoided, but so is its richness and joy.

PARANOID: "LIFE IS DIFFICULT, THEN YOU DIE"

One of the most popular forms of music in contemporary culture is what I call angst rock. Alanis Morissette's music typifies this angst-ridden hopelessness regarding relationships and the future. She has sold tens of millions of records with a good but not superb voice, intriguing but not compelling lyrics, and predictable orchestration. Why? She has tapped into the current nerve of nihilism and rage in our culture—especially among many teens and young adults.

Nihilism views life as *nada*, a nothing. Life is a long hard struggle, then you die. No one can offer a real escape from this mortal plane, so you are doomed. Hope is grounded in your next meal, sexual act, hallucinogenic high. What is the point in saving money? Having a family? Working hard for someone else's gain? It's all for *nada*.

The paranoiac lives by this gloomy philosophy. He sees a dark lining in every cotton-candy cloud. He lives on caffeine and irony. Cynicism is his calling card.

I have met many believers who operate in this sphere. They believe the gospel will pay off in heaven, but right now is a different story. This life is a Darwinian survival of the fittest, and they are going to be eaten if they don't kill and eat first. To escape the horror of hope in something they cannot control, they interpret life from the darkest possible eventuality. Often, these people live unconventional lives but refuse to take genuine risks. Others may behave inconsistently within their basic world-view and thus buy a house, invest in the stock market, get married, and send their kids to a good private school. Either way, they are rebels who never actually *live*. The risk of what might happen while they're simply embracing the day is too great.

A believer I met at a seminar lived in this safe gloom. He was confident that his evangelical church had been hoodwinked by the liberals and that his pastor was working against him because he was not granted the opportunity to teach a Sunday school class. He mentioned several other Christian leaders and ministries that had succumbed to the ways of the world, and he wanted me to know that I seemed to be moving in their direction. I walked away from the conversation battling cynicism and exhaustion.

Paranoiacs have a keen grasp of the tragedy of life. They overpredict misfortune, but they are eventually correct because nothing lasts and there is something wrong with everything in this imperfect world. They see the crucifixion as it is but fail to see what it will come to be: the resurrection.

As they become more entrenched in their stance toward life, paranoiacs do not merely wait to watch things turn tragic; instead, they actively produce decay by sabotaging good and twisting joy into the dramatic mask of sorrow. Paranoiacs predict and then create sorrow to avoid the far more penetrating sadness of unexpected and unexplained pain. When they set the scene for sorrow to come, they can describe in great detail why it has arrived. There is no surprise, no horror. Tragedy is a familiar and comforting friend to the paranoid.

FATALISTIC: "QUÉ SERÁ, SERÁ— ROLL WITH IT, BABY"

The television screen flickered with the smoldering remains of a plane that had fallen out of the sky. Forty perished and five survived. A survivor who was hardly scratched by the ordeal was being interviewed. He looked disheveled but serene as the interviewer asked, "Weren't you afraid? How did you handle the moments before the crash?" The survivor answered, "I knew if it was my time to go, then fine. If not, then it didn't matter what I did or didn't do. So I just relaxed and let things come."

It was hard to argue with his conclusion as the wreckage burned in the background. Why did he live and others equally deserving of life did not? Did he do anything different than those who perished? Was it explainable, or was it "fate"—simply the way things turned out?

Qué será, será. What will be, will be.

A pastor I worked with responded similarly to criticism from his congregation. *It is inevitable,* he told himself, *so just let it roll off your back.* He neither took offense nor took the feedback seriously. Many times the remarks were insensitive, but sometimes they were also well intended and could have been the basis for meaningful dialogue about personal and theological differences. Instead, no one profited from the input, and the "easygoing" pastor gained a reputation for being unwilling to interact in a significant way with those he worked with and led. Eventually the criticism went on behind his back because he didn't want to converse, learn from others, experience conflict, or confront those who harmed him unfairly.

A fatalistic view of life takes pain in stride. Suffering is inevitable, but it likely won't last, so hunker down and wait for better karma. Or, from a Christian perspective, God is in control, so just trust him, don't worry, get on with life. The fatalist handles suffering by minimizing it, shrugging his shoulders, refocusing on the good things in life, and waxing philosophical about real harm.

Fatalism anesthetizes desire, seeking to rise above the desire-disappointment cycle. Fatalists may appear serene, but their stance results in distance from others, lack of empathy, and a trivialization of their part in shaping the future. Fatalism is morally lazy, unimaginative, and leads to a spectator approach to life.

HEROIC: "WHAT DOES NOT KILL ME MAKES ME STRONGER"

Friedrich Nietzsche's definitive statement sums up the superhuman philosophy that despises weakness and hates vulnerability. The Nietzschean hero believes that living well means transcending the ordinary sufferings of this life by transforming them into challenges to overcome. Power—mastery of self and domination of others—becomes the goal. The heroic approach to pain goes beyond the notion that "all things work together for good" to "you are the master of your own destiny."

A friend who has suffered illness, family disasters, and many other debilitating setbacks told me, "I wake up every day knowing it will be a hard day, but I know that I can shape each event to a higher purpose and to a better end than most people. And so far I am a conqueror, not a victim."

There seems to be a growing disdain in our day for the language of victimization. If you are a member of a minority group, deal with it. If you have been the victim of gender discrimination or harassment, fight it or don't complain. If you were sexually abused as a child, stop whining and get on with life. The heroic slogan, borrowed from the Nike commercial, is a sweaty, swaggering shout: *Just do it!*

My friend is a survivor, not a victim. When something difficult confronts him, he strides into the middle of the problem and works as long and as hard as it takes to resolve it. Even though he has suffered a great deal, he seems stronger and better for his trials. His family, however, is rarely able to keep up with his pace. While he marches into battle, his wife is lonely and his kids are resentful. Like a good hero, he bears their burdens when they falter, but his family members live as second-class citizens because they can't run his race.

The heroic approach champions some good things, such as personal responsibility and a sense of individual destiny, but it leaves little or no place for dealing with real pain or experiencing community. At some point, we will be unable to finish the race without the sacrificial support of another person. But if our highest value is sweaty, gritty performance and perseverance that is both personal and private, then life is not a team sport but solely an individual endeavor.

This ethic leaves little opportunity for relationship other than a baton handoff in the race of life: a brief, utilitarian, and smooth or bobbled connection that ends as quickly as it began. The heroic philosophy leads to a disdain for any who cannot run ahead of the pack or, worse, who fall behind and need care to survive.

OPTIMISTIC: "JUST GRIN AND BEAR IT"

The paranoiac frowns. The fatalist grins. The hero grits his teeth. And the optimist laughs. Of all the options, this way of escaping deep engagement in a fallen world seems the most advantageous. When you smile, the world smiles with you; when you weep, by implication, you cry alone. Who wants to be alone? Why not grin and bear it and then climb up another rung to see the silver lining in the dark clouds?

Of all the other approaches, this one seems to be most in accord with living a life of faith. If we have faith in God, then we can "let go" and let him work things out. And given that he loves us, we can reason, it will all work out well in the end. If we are patient and trust him, then we can expect the best.

The best? Indeed, God loves us and has a wonderful plan for our lives. But that plan may be to labor for forty years with a recalcitrant, hard-hearted youth group that ages and dies in the wilderness, with only a few who make it into the Promised Land. How could God's best for Moses be to bring the man to the brink of what he'd worked his whole life to achieve, and then bar him from enjoying it before he died? The fact is, God's perfect plan might include untold suffering that has no clear purpose or meaning in this life. The optimistic path breaks down in the face of this kind of reality.

We all know someone who has suffered the weight of life at a level we fear but have not had to endure. The person who comes to my mind has suffered through many personal and family problems in the past five years. He has suffered an aneurysm, cancer, severe allergies, depression, plus insurance complications that make the physical challenges look easy. His kids have had severe struggles, including dating and peer-group issues, learning disabilities, and violations of the law. Three lawsuits have been brought against him, two of which merit his own suit. He has struggled with untold complications trying to get legal, medical, psychiatric, insurance, educational, and accounting professionals to resolve differences related to his various problems. It exhausts me just to ponder his nightmare; what would it be like to live it?

The hardest element in this man's life is the lack of care from other

Christians—optimists by "faith"—who have simply encouraged him to "hang in there" because "it will soon work out for the best." But his family's struggles have continued for years without relief. Some of his Christian associates have switched from offering shallow encouragement to helpful solutions. But when the solutions haven't mitigated the problems, they have presumed there is sin in the camp: Someone in his family needs to repent, and then all will be well.

Optimism is the comfort zone of those who want to distance themselves from pain. Like a guarded community, they lock out the undesirable and unsafe. But it is naive to think that once we lock out the world, safety is now ours to enjoy.

We embrace optimism only by turning our eyes from the poor, the marginalized, and the dying. The price of that turn is a walled-off heart that cannot afford to smell the decay or hear the sorrow of life. And such a busy, pressured, oblivious life creates its own wake of sorrow. To be sure, every optimist will eventually be pierced by the facts of life and forced to examine his presumptions of invulnerability and predictability.

All four routes—paranoid, fatalistic, heroic, optimistic—seek to avoid life's pain. The paranoiac avoids pain by seeing it everywhere and with everyone. He avoids disappointment by never being surprised by sorrow. The fatalist avoids pain by accepting it as normal and part of the impersonal "luck" of life. The hero avoids pain by seizing it as an opportunity to grow without ever acknowledging need or weakness. The optimist avoids pain by seeing all the good surrounding it in other areas of life. By avoiding pain, we might escape life's sorrow. But at what cost?

WRESTLING WITH SORROW

Suffering can move us toward God, or it can move us away from him and consequently away from being fully human and alive. If we are closed to sorrow, we will also be closed to true joy. If we see death, the loss of a job, an unwanted pregnancy, or a physical illness as nothing more than an event to be resolved as quickly and painlessly as possible, then we will miss the potential to grasp the true meaning of the event.

Too often we either focus exclusively on the event in order to resolve it, or we ask deep but angry existential questions: "Why me? What have I done to deserve this?" There is a time to concentrate on the problem; another time to cry out in a lament of heartache and confusion. But if we are to experience the good that God intends through our suffering, at some point it is crucial to ask: "What happens to me, deep down, at the core of my heart, when I face loss, suffering, and harm?" We can do little to control the pain that may come in the future, but we can make a heart decision now as to how we will view pain and how we will attempt to face it when it comes.

How we deal with loss and suffering will mostly depend on our ability to see what painful events do to our hearts. If we refuse to face the damage, the dysfunctional patterns set in motion to handle it will continue to exacerbate the wound. Like a broken arm that is not properly set, it may fuse and heal improperly. We may learn to adapt to the way the fissures set, but it is unlikely to provide us with the optimum opportunity to live the way we were meant to live.

Suffering changes the human heart—sometimes for good and often for ill. We are faced with the challenge of learning how to wrestle with sorrow so it can bring about the greatest good. If we want to become more like God wants us to be, we must consider what it means to live well in a fallen world rather than scramble to escape the veil of sorrow.

As men and women after God's own heart, we are called to walk the path Jesus walked. Jesus, "a man of sorrows, and familiar with suffering" (Isaiah 53:3), never once dealt with reality by turning to dark cynicism, blasé acceptance, angry strength, or empty hope. The route to Golgotha was strewn with temptations to sidestep death, yet Jesus learned obedience through suffering. Jesus' choice to embrace life to the point of death resulted in the healing of the greatest wound of our hearts: separation from God. As his followers, we are on the same journey, the same healing path.

CHAPTER 2

THE HEALING PATH

———

The computer stuttered and the screen slowly flickered to life. A shower and a cup of coffee behind me, I had turned to a familiar ritual: checking e-mail. The number of pieces of mail at 5 A.M. were only ten. I scanned the list and immediately erased three messages that looked like advertisements. I quickly answered four more in monosyllabic brevity. The last three took a few minutes. One ruined my day. A good friend wrote:

> Dan, can you bear some complaining? I was fired today. I finished the work for a contract that made the firm a lot of money. I turned the final papers in, and two hours later I was called to my boss's office. I was so foolish. I thought, "I wonder if I'm going to get a raise." I had done an excellent job. I had worked thoroughly and quickly and I made a number of revisions that saved the client money, made us look good, and set us up to be a player in a major deal with the same folks on another contract.
>
> I went to his office and in about ten minutes I realized I was cooked. He thanked me for my work and loyalty to the firm. He realized this would come as difficult news, but the firm needed to cut administrative costs. And I was no longer needed. I would get a month's severance for my high quality work. I

needed to be out of the office at the end of the day. I asked him if it was because of anything I had done or not done. He assured me it was a matter of simple downsizing.

I know he is lying. I had overheard a conversation a few days before that indicated the upper management did not like the fact that I'd saved the client money. They thought it might put too much pressure on us to do the same again and again. Frankly, without much effort we could, but it would rattle some of the big boys to make a significant change.

I'm not doing well. I agreed for the sake of my family to work as a consultant to the firm for a few months to finish the other projects I was involved in. To think they will get more work, for less money, and still be able to cut me loose any moment—and I agreed to it! I feel like such a fool. Please pray for me. John

Another day in corporate America. Another sad story of living in the '90s where life is good—very good—until it is bad. I felt sick for John. He had been extremely happy in his work. Like most everyone else who gives a lot to his job, John felt the frustration of not having enough time at home and with the kids, but he knew that while he was in his midthirties it was important to establish his career. In a flash, his dreams were shattered, his sacrifices taken for granted, and his career sideswiped.

THROUGH DESERTS AND VALLEYS

The characters change, but the plot remains the same. A marriage that seemed fine for years melts down and ends in divorce. A teenager who was a serious student and committed to the youth group turns away from the Lord and is soon pregnant. A healthy man discovers a few droplets of blood in his urine; after a visit to his doctor he learns he is fighting cancer.

The path of life runs in and out of darkness, confusion, uncertainty, loss, and heartache—not a path we would choose naturally. It compels us to walk as aliens and strangers through the desert and through the valley of the shadow of death.

But God has always called his people to a path that ends not in an arrival, but in anticipation. The author of Hebrews says,

> All these people were still living by faith when they died. They did not receive the things promised; they only saw them and welcomed them from a distance. And they admitted that they were aliens and strangers on earth. People who say such things show that they are looking for a country of their own. If they had been thinking of the country they had left, they would have had opportunity to return. Instead, they were longing for a better country—a heavenly one. Therefore God is not ashamed to be called their God, for he has prepared a city for them. (Hebrews 11:13-16)

This passage is rich in allusion to other stories and lives. Promise. Alien. Stranger. Country. City. The author of Hebrews alludes directly to the sojourn of God's chosen people. They were given a promise through Abraham, who set out on a journey that required leaving his home and country, but with a promise of becoming a great nation with descendants spread throughout the earth.

God promises us redemption, but his sacred path leads us away from safety, predictability, and comfort. Any attempt to fly over the dangerous terrain or make a detour to safer ground is doomed because it will not take us to God. Instead, it leads to a host of other idols that can't provide us with the confidence of faith, the dynamic of hope, or the passion of love we so deeply crave.

Each day we either live for God or for other gods. In each moment of hardship we fear either God or man. When we choose to worship gods and fear men our lives will suffer an emptiness and turmoil that is not much different than trying to fill our bellies with dirt. At first we may feel full, but in short order our violation of God's plan will lead to torment.

My friend John suffered an unpredictable but not uncommon assault in the corporate world. At first he fretted and ruminated, but he decided it was pointless and tried to pray instead. When his prayers brought him no comfort or direction, he remained externally faithful to God, but over time his heart became brittle and his spiritual passion dull. He stopped worrying, but he also walked away from the desperation that made him cling to God. Instead he pursued a path that seemed more immediately fulfilling: He found momentary passion through pornography. But God will not let his children wander in the realm of death without giving them some kind of wake-up call.

Relationship with God requires leaving, letting go, in order to pursue his promises. He calls his followers on a journey that takes them beyond the limits of their sight. Hosea tells us that God will woo us to the desert in order to win us back to himself. God says: "'Therefore I am now going to allure her; I will lead her into the desert and speak tenderly to her. There I will give her back her vineyards, and will make the Valley of Achor a door of hope. There she will sing as in the days of her youth, as in the day she came up out of Egypt. In that day,' declares the LORD, 'you will call me "my husband"; you will no longer call me "my master"'" (Hosea 2:14-16).

And what is the desert? It is the opposite of Eden, the garden green with luxury and life. The desert is brown, rocky, and desolate. It is not exactly the most romantic spot to renew a broken marriage between God and his bride. So why would God take his beloved to the desert in order to restore her? Because only there can he reveal to her the magnitude of his love.

The woman Gomer, who is a portrait of God's people in the book of Hosea, is a whore. She marries Hosea the prophet, and God uses their union as an allegorical tale of the heartache and mercy of God, who grieves the loss of his wife as she pursues other men and yet will not forsake her. God uses the desert to strip from her all other lovers. Her lovers are fair-weather suitors who want a dalliance in a nice climate and comfortable surroundings. They will not pursue Gomer to the ends of the earth. No false god will go that far. But God will. And in the desert, he strips his bride of her finery and her presumptions of independence in order to offer her a new beauty that leads not to pride and arrogance, but to praise and gratitude. Beauty with pride always leads to haughty eyes and contempt toward others, whereas beauty with humility invites others to join in a greater glory: the splendor of God.

The healing path must pass through the desert or else our healing will be the product of our own will and wisdom. It is in the silence of the desert that we hear our dependence on noise. It is in the poverty of the desert that we see clearly our attachments to the trinkets and baubles we cling to for security and pleasure. The desert shatters the soul's arrogance and leaves body and soul crying out in thirst and hunger. In the desert, we trust God or we die.

God not only leads us through the desert, but he calls us to walk through the valley as the sun sets and shadows spread across the land. To get to the table set for us by God we are called to walk through danger. Any valley is dangerous terrain. Not only can rocks roll down on us unexpectedly, but we are surrounded by higher ground on which an enemy can perch and rain down assault. No military tactician would willingly send his troops marching through a valley; it is a place of death. And if one must march through a valley, the worst possible time to do so is at sunset when shadows distort and make it impossible to pick out enemies hiding in wait.

Why would God have us walk through danger to get to him? Again, because valleys strip us of the presumption of independence; danger draws us to a greater dependence on the only one who can provide and protect. The desert brings us to our knees with craving; the valley calls us to cling to the hem of the one who leads us to safety. The psalmist says, "Even though I walk through the valley of the shadow of death, I will fear no evil, for you are with me; your rod and your staff, they comfort me" (Psalm 23:4).

God is with us. His rod and staff and his sure vision, steady balance, and infinite knowledge of the terrain will guide us as we walk through the shadowlands. But don't be fooled: His leading does not always guide us out of harm's way. Rather, God often leads us directly into the hottest and most perilous point of the battle.

In direct contrast to the psalmist's confidence in Psalm 23, the writer in Lamentations 3 describes his desolation when he says, "I am the man who has seen affliction by the rod of his wrath" (verse 1). *His rod and staff are not much of a comfort to me.* "He has driven me away and made me walk in darkness rather than light; indeed, he has turned his hand against me again and again, all day long" (verses 2-3). *He doesn't guide; he drives away. He doesn't lead through darkness; he drives me into the shadows!* "He has made my skin and my flesh grow old and has broken my bones" (verse 4). *What about restoring my soul? Instead, he makes me old and sick.* "He has filled me with bitter herbs and sated me with gall. He has broken my teeth with gravel; he has trampled me in the dust" (verses 15-16). *What about the table set before my enemies? Instead, God makes me a laughingstock, then feeds me food that sickens me and breaks my teeth.* "I remember my affliction and my wandering, the bitterness and the gall. I well remember them, and my soul is downcast within me" (verses 19-20). *I am at my wit's end and I can't deny I hate the path he has me on.*

But listen to the discouraged writer's final conclusion: "Yet this I call to mind and therefore I have hope: Because of the LORD's great love we are not consumed, for his compassions never fail. They are new every morn-ing; great is your faithfulness. I say to myself, 'The LORD is my portion; therefore I will wait for him.' The LORD is good to those whose hope is in him, to the one who seeks him; it is good to wait quietly for the salvation of the LORD" (verses 21-26). *I may be in pain, but I can't deny that his loving-kindness has hold of my heart. Even a new day brings the reminder that he has not abandoned me to darkness. I cannot kill the hope he has planted in me that is deeper than my suffering.*

The healing path is not a jaunt in the park. It is a life-rattling, heart-revealing journey that takes us through danger, harm, heartache—and ultimately to new trust, profound hope, and a love that can't be scorched by assault or destroyed by loss. The healing path is glorious, but the only way we will stay on course and resist the temptation to flee to safer ground is by comprehending more deeply the assaults and losses we will face on our journey. In the desert and valley we will pass through the dangers of betrayal, powerlessness, and ambivalence. These three reali-ties will pull faith, hope, and love right out from under us if we are not ready for them.

BETRAYAL AND THE LOSS OF FAITH

One of the great wounds in life is the shattering of a relationship—having a friend who turns on us and reverses shalom, or what the Bible calls peace. Betrayal is the experience of being set up, violated, and then discarded. It is being used by someone who violates our dignity and then is unmoved by our pain.

Such betrayal, for whatever reason, isolates us in loneliness, doubt, and shame. The connection we once assumed and enjoyed becomes a web of awkwardness. We don't know whether to speak to the estranged friend when our paths cross, or simply pass with eyes averted. To the degree there is avoidance, suspiciousness grows. If there is conversation, it is constrained and tight, marking the contrast to the way it once was. This is the soil where blame shifting and slander can grow like robust weeds.

The memory of how-it-once-was burns a deep and hollow spot in the heart. Memory haunts and self-doubt grips. *Why did it end? What did I do wrong? Why does my friend no longer like me?* The intense shifts between angrily blaming the other and cutting oneself with the shards of self-doubt are exhausting.

My friend John suffered for months with second-guessing himself about his strategy to save money for the client in order to secure a future contract. In the end, what he'd thought was good business may have cost him his job. All his hard work and the risk he took on behalf of the firm seemed to be worth nothing. He felt betrayed and he hated the way his mind chronically rehearsed the possibilities of what he could have done differently.

The exhaustion of this process is exponentially increased by envy. Invariably you will run into an ally of the estranged friend who looks at you with pity or disgust, and the envy over the fact that someone else enjoys a place in the other's heart that once was yours can be excruciating. As your heart spirals down into the dark, it seems that the pain can be handled only by cutting off the gangrenous limb and getting on without the one with whom you once enjoyed peace and goodwill.

Betrayal, whether the result of mutual failings or one party's error, leaves the heart sick over the past and fearful of future loss. When the past is littered with the rusted-out remains of broken friendships, the heart is robbed of the desire to trust—not only in the relationship that has suffered harm, but in all other relationships. Betrayal particularly throws into question our relationship with God. Does he rescue? Does he protect? Will he let the guilty go free?

As hope is a focus on the future, faith is a reflection on the past.

When we are betrayed, our trust in others is shaken. When the wound is profound, we often question why God allowed the harm to occur. The current blow often erases the memory of other times God has saved us, or if we do recall those moments, we are left with more confusion as to why he didn't rescue us this time.

Faith is founded on the memory of God's redemptive acts in the past. Faith dashed calls into question the veracity of God's past care. We think, *God may have saved Israel, and he may have raised Jesus from the dead and broken the bondage of sin and death, but what he did doesn't take away my pain today.* Without faith, we are foundationless and susceptible to the shifting winds of whim and fortune. When we lack a sturdy anchor of confidence in God, we are more easily cast into confusion about our identity and our place in the world.

The healing path plunges us into the depths of our doubt, where a new faith can be born. This faith, birthed in the desert and the valley, frees us to remember a past not only with loss, but with redemption. It leads to a perspective that is full of God, therefore deepening our trust that redemption will dawn tomorrow as it did once before. First, however, this process often confronts us with who or what we really have been trusting rather than God.

John struggled with trusting God. When he first got fired, he was angry with his boss and the man's inability to see what John's cost-saving measures might produce for the company. After a few weeks, his anger turned against God for not protecting him against the duplicity of his firm. The wound robbed him of his memory of how God had redeemed him, introduced him to his wife, and provided for his son after a near-fatal accident. Refusing to think about anything but the recent betrayal, John's memory of God clouded.

Walking by a newsstand one day, John saw the barely hidden pornographic magazines it held. He recalled in a flash the ecstasy he felt as a teenager sneaking glimpses of naked women. At that awkward stage of life he had felt empowered when he stole those glimpses. He picked up a magazine and felt guilty, but he thought, *This is better than feeling bad.*

POWERLESSNESS AND THE LOSS OF HOPE

Life often leaves us feeling powerless. John felt the powerlessness we experience when we become aware of our inability to shape the future. We feel helpless to effect change that will improve our situation. We can, but that won't change our circumstances. We may plead, but our anguish seems to fall on deaf ears.

Eventually such a sense of powerlessness results in apathy and despair. When there is nothing we can do to change our situation, then it is normal to give up. It is easier to quit trying and grow numb than to hope and be disappointed time and again.

The book of Proverbs speaks to this sense of futility: "Hope deferred makes the heart sick, but a longing fulfilled is a tree of life" (Proverbs 13:12). Hope is what propels us into the future. If hope is lost, then we are cast into a mechanical, rote existence that experiences each day as nothing more than a repetition of what has come before. When hope dies, vitality, passion, and creativity are lost.

Hope is by far one of the most dangerous commitments we make in life. Hope draws us to create and sacrifice without any guarantee of fulfillment. The more we hope, the more we lean into the future, risking the present to secure the dreams that entice us. No wonder a wound like a rape or the loss of a job sears us with the foolishness of anticipating the future. "Once burned, shame on you. Twice burned, shame on me." For many, the shame of hoping and being burned again and again has turned them against hope and solidified their commitment to find something in this life they can control.

John lost his consulting position soon after sending me his e-mail. As he searched for a comparable job over the next six months, he felt powerless, exhausted, and lifeless. After purchasing the pornographic magazine, he later turned to pornography on the Internet for a sense of pleasure and control. He could manipulate the computer quickly to gain access to pictures and conversation that he could direct; he was the one who decided when he went on-line and when he switched off the source of his relief. He could make up the dialogue and be whoever he wanted to be. When he clicked into a pornographic chat room, he was the master and he felt powerful. But as with any addiction, the first rush of recouped power John experienced eventually led to a deeper slavery, greater emptiness, and self-hatred. He knew this was not life. He was meant for more.

The healing path takes us into the depths of our despair in order for a new hope to be born through our walk in the desert and the valley. This hope enables us to envision a future that is full of God, thereby deepening a passion that will empower us to reach beyond deadness and the mindless repetition of the past.

One night long after his wife and kids had gone to bed, John turned to his favorite pornographic Internet site. He was so engrossed he did not hear his ten-year-old son walk in. Jason must have stood staring at the images for a few minutes because he said to his dad, "Why do you look at one and then look at another naked woman?" Startled and shocked, John hit his shins against the desk as he turned to see his son's innocent eyes peering at the raw scenes on the screen. He quickly turned the computer off. "Jason," he said, "don't ever come in here without knocking first. I'm doing some research and those pictures came up by accident."

Jason looked at his father with questioning eyes. "Dad, you always said computers will only do what you tell them to do. How could that happen by accident?" John cleared his throat, made an excuse, and shooed his son back to bed.

Afterward he sat in his office feeling nauseous. He remembered the first time his father found a pornographic magazine under his bed, and he felt a flush of shame. His dad had scorned him and then said nothing more. Now John wondered what his own son would remember. He feared it would be a shameful wound to Jason that not only did his dad look at pornography, but he lied and made excuses about it.

It is hard to explain how God works, but John's memory of his past shame and the image of his son's future—if not present—disappointment in him was used by God to take John into the desert. He felt the heat and the darkness surround him, but he heard the tenderness of God reminding him he was not alone nor hated. He was loved and forgiven. John wept.

In a moment of profound powerlessness, far deeper than he had experienced in the loss of his job, John found the relief that comes in being weak and needy. He turned back to God for an embrace that would restore not only his memory of God's love, but his ability to imagine what it would be like to be fully whole. He began to hope again.

AMBIVALENCE AND THE LOSS OF LOVE

All harm brings in its wake a sense of betrayal and powerlessness that shakes our willingness to trust and hope. Perhaps the deepest damage is done, however, through the experience of ambivalence. Ambivalence is feeling torn in two. It creates a divided sense of self that feels shame and self-hatred for once enjoying what is ultimately stained or stolen from us.

John had trusted and enjoyed the man who eventually fired him with no more thought or feeling than killing a fly. The boss had encouraged John throughout the project, and John had felt nourished and strengthened by the man's words. Now he felt like a fool for having allowed himself to delight in the boss's feedback. When the collapse came, he felt shame and contempt for being so gullible and naive.

Ambivalence exposes our heart's desire for what we are no longer free to enjoy. It causes us to question the sanity of giving and receiving pleasure in our work and relationships. What if it ends? What if I enjoy you more than you enjoy me? What if your delight in me is bogus? Or worse, what if it is mere manipulation to get from me what you want? What if I love you and then you die, divorce me, or turn against me? The risk is more than I can bear, and so I refuse to open my heart to another person who will arouse my desire and then might use me or dash me to the ground.

Such ambivalence is the enemy of love. The core of love is the capacity to offer ourselves to others—to bless them with our presence and our gifts. The dance of love calls us then to be open to receive from others gratitude and the gift of their presence in return. Ambivalence kills this reciprocal movement of praise and forgiveness that gives, receives, and glories in the wonder of our capacity to touch each other.

The night John's son caught him viewing pornography, John tossed and turned until morning. He debated all night about what to do: Should he simply stop looking at pornography and talking in the chat rooms and just hope his son didn't think about what he'd seen or mention it to anyone? What if Jason told his mom? Then John would be in deeper trouble. He feared his wife's disappointment. He knew she might forgive him, but she would probably hold it against him for a long time.

John was disturbed that one of the strongest reasons he felt for confessing to his wife was the fear not of God, but of his son's innocent revelation. Even in his desire to repent, John felt the division of mixed motives. He couldn't even repent with a godly heart! He felt caught between duplicity and humility.

When morning came, he awakened his wife and told her of his sin and the hardness of his heart over the months. He asked her forgiveness and told her he had harmed their son. They both wept. John felt the sting of sorrow and the balm of forgiveness. He hated his sin, and he felt awe and gratitude toward a God who had already started the party for both the prodigal who had used pornography and for the elder brother who was so prideful he couldn't repent well.

We feel torn so often in life. But when we are caught in the tension of ambivalence, we are compelled to cry out to God. The healing path takes us into the desert and the valley, deep into the heart's disintegration, where a new love can be born. This love frees us to encounter the presence of God with redeeming awe and gratitude. It leads to a new sense of purpose in living: to know and be known, to give and to receive the glory of love. All tastes of God's love increase our desire to follow and imitate him.

THE CRY OF HOPE

The harm of living in a fallen world leads to the destruction of human glory through the damage inflicted by powerlessness, betrayal, and ambivalence. Evil stands over its labor, content that many have succumbed to its power, or at least to its damage, and have relinquished faith, hope, and love. But it need not be that way. The quintessential cry of hope is found in the remark Joseph made after experiencing devastating physical, sexual, and emotional abuse: "God turned into good what you meant for evil" (Genesis 50:20, NLT).

Damage need not destroy us! The journey of life need not strip us of joy! The walk through the desert and the valley can actually redeem us— but not if our commitment is to flee from it. We live in a culture that is committed to escaping the veil of sorrow, but if we are willing to embrace the damage we can be saved.

Embrace the harm of living in a fallen world. But even more, embrace the God who invites you to find rest and comfort in his love. It is in embracing life and God that we are healed and transformed.

CHAPTER 3

EMBRACING LIFE

Most of us presume that if we work hard, play fair, and keep on doing what is required, life will work out well. And if it doesn't then we simply need to find out what we're doing wrong, correct it, and presto—life works. But that formula doesn't always get the predicted results, does it? While I'm tempted daily to find the angle that, once achieved, gives me an advantage over life, I have not found it.

Many of the abused men and women I've talked with have been stripped of the illusions that guide most of our lives. People who have survived abuse seem to know more deeply than others that life is unfair, heartache certain, tragedy normal, and change an inch-by-inch battle that is surprising and humbling. Many people I know bear stories with so much tragedy and horror that I have privately wondered how they have chosen to live another day. But what I have most often noted as I've listened to these people is their determined passion to embrace life. Although some people allow their hurts to make them bitter, I am amazed by the many who have suffered profoundly yet sing with both the deepest strains of sorrow and the most haunting melodies of hope. Let me show you what I mean.

Katrina was the oldest daughter of a prominent attorney and a socially well-connected mother. They were a religious family who attended church and the country club regularly. Katrina's mother directed her three daughters in the graces of the well-to-do, and at a young age Katrina had the responsibility to practice the piano, attend ballet lessons, and play tennis. Her mother had been a college athlete. Her father was tan, lean, and suave. Often the children were dressed in matching outfits. The whole family turned heads when they walked into a room. They glowed with an aura of grace and luster wherever they went.

But no one could see the terror that frequently visited the family when the father would rage and grab one of the girls and shake her like a rag doll. Katrina took the brunt of the abuse. It is hard to know why she attracted her father's fury, other than the fact that she exuded a defiant, passionate air that seemed to compel her dad to extinguish a radiance that was set against his own glory. She would never cry; she would never call out for her mother's help.

Her mother witnessed the father's paroxysms of rage, but she turned her eyes away and seldom offered Katrina solace. Katrina's older sister, Margaret, was the only person in the family who would come to Katrina's room after a "spell" and offer one of her dolls. Katrina and Margaret would sit on her bed and comb the doll's hair and change her clothes for hours. Speechless. Absorbed. Even at a young age, both knew that to talk about what was going on in their family was to make it more real than either could bear.

Katrina grew to be an elegant, striking twelve-year-old. I recall the day she brought to counseling a series of pictures of her transition from a child to an adolescent. The pictures reflected both a smoldering defiance and a wistful loneliness. When I asked how she saw herself, she said: "I was an ugly dork who didn't know how to smile." She was anything but ugly, but she did not know how to smile until her tennis coach began to zero in on this easy mark.

The pictures from ages twelve to thirteen showed a childish exuberance that came from this man's involvement in her life. The one picture of her with the coach showed him with boyish blond bangs, perfect white teeth, and a confidence that could make an adult woman swoon. He stood with three girls, but his body leaned toward Katrina. She looked into the camera but her eyes were taking in his presence.

I flinched when I saw the picture. It was so obvious. So clear and indelicate. It was in fact only a matter of days after the picture was taken that on a country club tennis tournament road trip, he sexually abused her for the first time. Her arm had tightened after a match, and he had given her a massage. Touch led to further touch and then, in a moment that lasted but a second and then marked her for a lifetime, he crossed the line from impropriety to outright fondling. She resisted but then relented to his explorations. That trip led to multiple occasions of abuse. Six months later he raped her.

Over the next four years Katrina became involved in a cycle of abuse, escape, entrapment, and repetition. She felt powerless to break free of the coach's trap, baited with kindness that led to abuse. Only once did she confide in a female teacher, who told her it was not uncommon for girls to experiment with older men. Katrina felt betrayed by her teacher's cavalier remark. When she was sixteen she got involved with a boy in college. Her mother disapproved but did nothing to stop the relationship. When she was seventeen, she got pregnant, and her mother told her she had to get an abortion. She complied because by that point she had stopped caring about life.

Soon after the abortion, Katrina experimented with drugs and alcohol. She drifted in and out of a number of sexual relationships and somehow made it through college. She eventually migrated into business and worked for six years until she got married. She married a man who was attractive and insipid. He was a hard worker and required little of her. She had two sons, gained forty pounds, and settled into a routine of preschool and carpools.

Katrina lived with a low-level depression and an apathy that only occasionally compelled her to consider taking her life. She never acted on the thought, but she caught herself losing large portions of her day to mindless tasks and daydreams that had no content or meaning. She was dozing away her waking hours in a quiet stupor punctuated by bursts of energetic caring for her boys. She was involved in her church. She was a regular at the PTA. All who knew her viewed her as an attractive, competent, caring helper in the community.

Katrina's life plodded along until she found out she was pregnant and was going to have a girl. She was shattered. She spiraled into a severe depression that brought her to my office. A friend, who sensed that her depression was more than the combined exhaustion of caring for two boys and being pregnant, asked her if her despair had anything to do with expecting a girl. Katrina wept bitter tears and answered, "I can handle boys, but I can't stand seeing a girl grow up in a world where I know what will happen to her." Her friend asked, "What? What will happen?" Katrina answered, "You know. She will walk into someone's arms and then be lost in the web. Lost—you know, used. Devoured." Her friend said gently, "Like you were."

Katrina was stunned. She had never put two and two together. After much encouragement and prayer, her friend convinced her to see a therapist and she began the long journey of facing the agony of her past and her terror of the future. It was a healing journey that brought her back to life.

The healing journey is as difficult to describe as trying to recount exactly how the Allies won World War II. But the process of change for Katrina, or for any of us, involves naming what is true and calling on the name of God. It involves facing and embracing the reality of living in a fallen world. In the process, God speaks. He joins our healing process by calling us to himself and receiving us as we take hold of life, no matter what it holds for us.

THE EMBRACE

Embrace is an accurate metaphor to encompass what is involved in walking the healing path to God. There are four elements to an embrace:[1]

opening the heart rather than cynically shutting down
waiting with anticipation rather than killing hope
encircling the other instead of standing alone
letting go of the moment

Opening the Heart

Embracing a person or reality requires openness. Our arms must reach out to the other, which requires a position of vulnerability. To be open, extended, and reaching out is to be easy prey to one who might do us harm. With an embrace, the hands are open and the arms ill-prepared for defense or attack.

Openness involves a hunger for life. We would not reach out unless we wanted something from the one who is approaching. We are made for the dance of intimacy, and the dance requires arms that open to receive the moment that has been given to us.

In opening our arms to another, we put out a welcome sign that implies we have made room for them inside ourselves. They are invited in as guests, not as strangers. For that reason, to the degree we open our arms, we are changed. We want, create space for, and welcome the other, not knowing whether our embrace will be desired or reciprocated.

We don't usually reach out to someone who may abuse us or make light of our vulnerability. If there is a threat, then we will usually become defensive or aggressive. As a consequence, we open our arms and hearts to few. And when those few hurt us, we close down and refuse to open our arms wide to others. In that soil—in that cynicism and suspiciousness—paranoia begins to grow.

Katrina lived for years with a heart that refused to participate in the dance of intimacy. She knew her father hated her intensity and spirit. She knew her mother would neither delight in her nor protect her. When the coach came along, something in her young heart blossomed. The petals opened to the rays of the sun. But he stung her in her prime and most innocent hope. He snaked through her desire and coiled himself around her heart. Predictably, she shut down. She stopped caring and surrendered to lust, drugs, and death. Eventually, she chose a lifeless, loveless, "safe" marriage, refusing to open her arms because of her steely doubt and cynicism.

Suspiciousness is fueled by memories of betrayal or rejection. The images of past harm are applied indiscriminately to moments in the present. Often we live out our past pain and betrayal in the present by looking at every interaction with others from the vantage point of utility and cost. *What do you want? What is it going to require of me?* This stance robs us of spontaneity and fun. Life becomes dark and lonely.

But at least hurt is minimized. Or is it? The answer is, of course not. Someone with a closed heart virtually guarantees a repetition of past harm by setting herself up in a Catch-22 present. Paranoia ultimately turns everyone into an enemy and every interaction into a threat. Eventually people withdraw or get angry with the suspicious person, proving what the paranoid feared all along: *I will be hurt and abandoned.*

The past repeats itself through a ritual of reenactment because the person is unwilling to open his or her arms to the agony, shame, and loss of the past. If we don't open our arms and hearts to the past, we will remain suspicious and closed in the present.

So what does opening our arms to the past require? Embracing life in a fallen world, especially as we face the past, means honoring the data of life by actively turning toward the whole truth, reaching out to meet it, while also making space in our heart to receive it. To open our arms to truth is to cry out with the psalmist, "Search me, O God, and know my heart; test me and know my anxious thoughts. See if there is any offensive way in me, and lead me in the way everlasting" (Psalm 139:23-24). To honor the data of life requires that we open ourselves to all the good as well as to what is disconcerting and difficult to face.

Having open arms implies looking into the eyes of the other with a welcoming delight. As odd or nearly impossible as it may seem, we are to welcome our times of trouble as we would greet a friend who has been gone a long time. We are to greet trials with joy (James 1:2) and to rejoice when suffering comes (Romans 5:3). Why? Because suffering sets into motion our will to find meaning; it compels us to honestly assess the facts of our lives and begin to order truth into a framework that has personal meaning to us. We cannot have a sense of purpose or a deep understanding of what we're created for unless we encounter the kind of pain that compels us to rise above the daily domain and recollect who we are. Pain enables us to discover ourselves.

It was pain that unsettled Katrina. A major breakthrough came one day when her seven-year-old son asked, "Mommy, if I were to learn to dance and sing, would it bring a smile to your face?" His innocent anguish was a lightning bolt to her mother-heart that set her pulse beating again. She didn't want her young son to feel the pressure of having to revive his mother's heart.

Oh, what a strange way for God to work! He used her son's poignant question to awaken Katrina's memory to the countless times she had wanted to shake her own mother out of her dissociative stupor. Her mother had ignored her and allowed her to be abused. Now Katrina could ignore her son and allow him to feel responsible for her despair—or she could break the cycle. God was saying, "Remember…remember. Remember me. Remember your life. Because it is by remembering your life that your sorrow and hunger for me will grow." Katrina could allow the memory of what she'd longed for and did not receive to transform her now and become the gift she gave her son.

In an instant, she knew she could not remain silent and dead. She had to wake up! Her son was asking her to dance, to be all she was meant to be as a mother. God welcomed his daughter back to life, to love, to meaning.

We will be willing to embrace life, including its disappointments, only to the degree we hear God's welcome and see his open arms in the midst of our struggle. But most of us don't see God with open arms; rather, we see him with his arms crossed and his face tense and irritated. Or we don't really see him at all. Openness to living honestly in a fallen world comes only as we are drawn to God as one who struggles with the same reality we do—struggles not only with our life and sorrow but with all the brokenness of his creation, past, present, and future. God's willingness to open his arms to the world's angst, in all its sorrow and potential for joy, is the basis of our joining him in the reckless act of opening our hearts to the truth of our lives.

Opening our arms must then be followed by a willingness to wait. We will never risk embracing life unless we feel the pulse of a hungering heart that beats for something outside the realm of sight. We are meant for an invisible presence, a mystery and a touch that draws our hearts to a higher love.

Waiting with Anticipation

Opening the heart to face the complexity of living in this world requires waiting for truth to come to us. We are to move toward reality, but we can't go the whole distance; truth must come to us. We are to work out our salvation in fear and trembling, but change—profound, unquestionably supernatural transformation—comes not from our will, but from God's mercy. We must stretch out our arms to life, but God arrives when he wills.

Waiting stirs the soul's deep struggle with hope. We think it pleasant to hope, but in fact, nothing is more difficult than to hope. Hope lifts us up and gives us a view of how much ground must still be traveled on our journey. It allows us to see the horizon, usually far beyond our reach.

Oddly, hope both illumines what we most want to achieve and distances us from it. If we run to the horizon, it recedes. Many run anyway, striving to fully comprehend, seeking an alternative to living with uncertainty. Others refuse to dream at all, fleeing the potential disappointment of having their desires dashed.

Katrina began to change as she allowed desire to grow in her heart. But as her longing increased for a heart of love toward her unborn daughter and her dull husband, she grew impatient with the process. She eventually sought a number of quick cures, from self-help books to spiritual panaceas.

God did not refuse to comfort her through her own efforts, but nothing she did erased her self-hatred or soothed the memories that often disturbed her sleep. God was simply not ready to remove her struggles. Instead, as Katrina faced her anger at her parents, she was left for a lengthy time with a rage that did not dissipate no matter how hard she tried to forgive them. As God opened her eyes to the horror of the abuse she had experienced and to what was stirred in her both personally and physically by her abuser, she could not find relief for her ambivalence. She wanted to be healed, but she refused to hope. She could not flee her newly resurrected desire; she could not find solace for her struggle.

We hate to wait. We hate to hope. It seems contradictory for Paul to say, "Not only so, but we ourselves, who have the firstfruits of the Spirit, groan inwardly as we wait eagerly for our adoption as sons, the redemption of our bodies" (Romans 8:23). How are we to groan inwardly and also wait expectantly? It seems that when we groan most deeply, we most urgently anticipate resolution for our pain. But we cannot hope unless we learn to wait, and we cannot learn to wait if we have put God on our schedule.

God met Katrina molecule by molecule, not universe by universe as she demanded. He met her through her son's question that awakened her to painful memories and ultimately to the conviction: *I will not do to my son what my mother did to me.* It started her on the healing path. In that moment, faith grew (a little), and when faith grows it sets us on the path toward hope.

Hope is not a comfortable companion on the journey because it seems to invite us to dream and to desire with ever greater intensity. As Katrina began to hope, her fears of disappointment grew even greater. For that reason she wanted a "quick fix," a step-by-step sure plan that would bring her the results she desired. Notice, however, that God does not simply capitulate to our demands; rather, he satisfies our ultimate desire: to know him. But even that fulfillment comes on his terms, according to his timetable, and for his own purposes.

God often traps us between our desire and our demands in order to satisfy our deepest hungers with himself alone. He will not lessen our hunger, nor will he feed us when his bread will be viewed as our rightful claim. He will be no one's butler, only our God.

Slowly but surely, God trapped Katrina in hope. Even when she tried to abort her journey by running back into fear and deadness, God continued to allure her to wait, to keep her arms open for when he would arrive.

An embrace requires not only open arms, but a heart that is willing to linger with no immediate promise of satisfaction. To walk the healing path, we must wrestle with our refusal to keep traveling between desire and satisfaction, where God neither answers our prayer for healing nor clearly illumines a path away from fear. God lets us wait—not to punish us, not because he has forgotten us, but because our waiting is the crucible he uses to purify our hope for him.

Encircling the Other

Hunger compels us to open our arms to reality. Anticipated joy enables us to wait for the arrival of our dreams. And what are we waiting for? We all wait for love. We live for an embrace. To receive and hold life in our arms is to feel its form and engage with its presence and be molded to its purpose.

Think of the last time someone embraced you with joy and strength. True love is pure and solid. It does not wrestle the other with a bear hug, nor does it offer an anemic embrace. Real, bold, embracing love offers a taste of life that is indescribable.

In contrast, consider the last time you hugged someone who either was uncomfortable or did not want to embrace you. I hugged a man who for whatever reason gave me a distant, stiff squeeze. He awkwardly patted my back from a great distance and ended the embrace as quickly as he could. Afterward, he could barely look into my face and moved away from interaction with me. I felt like a leper, a toxic being that had repulsed him.

If that is love, then give me hate. I'd rather he look me in the face and say, "I'm sorry, but I don't hug." Or, "Forgive me, but an embrace would feel dishonest given certain things we need to talk about." In either case, as uncomfortable as I might have felt, I would have had the sense of being more honored and enjoyed than I was by his awkwardness.

We are meant to encircle another, not with a vice grip that asserts our power or preeminence, nor with a limp squeeze that refuses to really hold the other in our arms. Encircling another calls us to both receive and to give through an interplay of honor, passion, and respect. The interplay is full of mystery in its process and outcome.

Through countless experiences of this mystery, Katrina began to change. As she felt the embrace of God, she came to realize that she had lived her life to avoid its agony; in fact, she had chosen a living death. She had wrestled with the demons of her past. She had begun to face the terror of her future. But she still knew little gratitude or joy.

One night, as she struggled with her past and contemplated her future, she heard the words form in her mind: *Choose life or choose death.* She read in her Bible:

Then the LORD your God will make you most prosperous in all the work of your hands and in the fruit of your womb, the young of your livestock and the crops of your land. The LORD will again delight in you and make you prosperous, just as he delighted in your fathers, if you obey the LORD your God and keep his commands and decrees that are written in this Book of the Law and turn to the LORD your God with all your heart and with all your soul. Now what I am commanding you today is not too difficult for you or beyond your reach. It is not up in heaven, so that you have to ask, "Who will ascend into heaven to get it and proclaim it to us so we may obey it?" Nor is it beyond the sea, so that you have to ask, "Who will cross the sea to get it and proclaim it to us so we may obey it?" No, the word is very near you; it is in your mouth and in your heart so you may obey it. See, I set before you today life and prosperity, death and destruction.... This day I call heaven and earth as witnesses against you that I have set before you life and death, blessings and curses. Now choose life, so that you and your children may live and that you may love the LORD your God, listen to his voice, and hold fast to him. For the LORD is your life, and he will give you many years in the land he swore to give to your fathers, Abraham, Isaac and Jacob. (Deuteronomy 30:9-15,19-20)

Finally Katrina heard God and felt the breath of his voice and the touch of his arms. He was near, not beyond her reach. He had put his love in her heart. Now it was time to choose: life or death?

In the twinkling of an eye, she prayed. She asked for and received an embrace that changed her. She could not describe the moment any more clearly than this: "I knew something a moment later that I did not know a moment before."

The change manifested the next morning as a playfulness she could not contain. Years before, her children had given her a pair of Minnie Mouse earrings for her birthday. She had accepted them but had never worn them. She could not explain why; she simply could not put them on. That morning, she retrieved them from her jewelry box and put Minnie on her ears. It was not a burdensome choice; it was an embrace of life, an obedience to her awakened instinct to play and rejoice.

Embracing reality and encircling another requires courage—not merely to accept pain, but to risk asking, seeking, and knocking on the door of God until he answers with the bread of life. And when he answers it takes more courage to move with him in the dance of joy, fearing neither the scrutiny of others nor the moment when the dance stops. And in this life, stop it will.

Letting Go

An embrace from God or from another is life-giving and heart changing. Once we receive it, we never want to let go. We want people to stay and moments to last. One of the hardest components of life is saying farewell and letting sweet moments fade. And the more meaningful the experience, the harder it is to open our arms and let the moment go. For that reason it is easy to let go too soon. Often we brush away the precious touch too quickly and refuse to let our desire grow. Or we grip the moment with frantic craving and end up crushing it in our arms.

In her novel *Jazz*, Toni Morrison tells of a man so consumed with his passion for a woman that he kills her for fear he will lose her: "He minds her death, is so sorry about it, but minded more the possibility of his memory failing to conjure up the dearness....Now he lies in bed remembering every detail of that October afternoon when he first met her, from start to finish, and over and over. Not just because it is tasty, but because he is trying to sear her into his mind, brand her there against future wear.

So that neither she nor the alive love of her will fade or scab over the way it had with Violet."[2]

But his efforts to hold on to the memories were futile. They had begun to fade soon after they occurred. Morrison writes, "You could replay in the brain the scene of ecstasy, of murder, of tenderness, but it was drained of everything but the language to say it in."[3]

We can't hold on to memory, nor can we hold captive love in the present. We can't will our dreams to come true. To do so is to try to possess what can thrive only with freedom. Jealousy is a death grip that strangles the life of the other. We fear the loss of the one who has given us life, but in our stifling clinch we end up destroying what we have loved.

What we can do to a person, we can also do to a moment, an idea, or a truth. I know some people who "love" the truth of the Bible so violently that their hold is a vice grip that refuses to learn from any person or tradition different from their own. Their dogmatism sucks the marrow out of the Bible and leaves it devoid of life-giving, soul-changing power.

The same is true when a parent refuses to let a child grow up. A clutching father who refuses to let his adolescent daughter leave his protective shadow chains her soul to him and invites rebellion or risks the loss of her identity. In no area of life can we grow unless we let go and open our arms to the next moment, person, truth.

After Katrina embraced God and felt his loving arms, she found herself inviting her husband to dance. But he simply would not hear the music. She resorted to defiance and scolding sneers to chasten him into change. In the process, the embrace she received from God was forgotten; her fear of foolishness exponentially multiplied. She hated me. God. Life. She hated her own heart.

But once the heart has melted, rarely can it freeze over forever. Katrina was hooked, and over time she remembered God's faithfulness. Her faith deepened, and she began to allow her dreams to die without killing hope for the future. The more hope she permitted to grow, the larger her soul became for her husband. She tenderly, boldly, wildly, wisely surrounded him with love while allowing him to depart when he got too scared. She was ready to meet him whenever he crept back to gaze at her changes.

In time, the surprise of the love that had embraced and transformed his wife allured him to join a glorious dance, even though he barely heard the music. The process was not easy, quick, or elegant, but over many months Katrina lured her husband not only to herself, but to God. She was kind and playful. She was strong and tender. She didn't let him bully her or easily flee to his sanctuary of silence. On the other hand, she didn't chase after him, nor did she demand that he change. She became a living paradox— losing her life in order to find it.

Katrina's husband told me of a time he wanted to make love and she said no. Normally he would turn away, pout, and go to sleep while she kept reading. This time she nudged him and said gently, "You can pout, or we can talk. If we talk, I still don't want to make love. But you can be sure that if we don't talk, I ain't gonna be ready to make love anytime soon."

When he turned to look at her, he saw a radiant, kind, playful smile. He still wanted to scream or hide in silence, but he was willing to talk instead. They talked for over an hour about why she felt so distant from him and how deeply she wanted to be intertwined with his soul and body. Months later he confessed to me that that conversation was better than any moment of sexual intimacy they had known before. It was the beginning of a brand-new dance of love in their marriage.

The path to God requires embracing reality with open arms, waiting in hope, encircling God and others tenderly and firmly, and then letting go as God waltzes us into a new experience of life. The dance will give us greater perspective through the eyes of faith, deeper passion through the heart of hope, and a more tender touch through the embrace of love.

FACING OUR ENEMY

Each human journey is utterly distinct and unique as a snowflake. It is an overworked observation, but no human life is comparable to another. We share common experiences, but we must walk alone, on a different path than all others, even when we join another in marriage, ministry, work, or any other endeavor.

What is common to us all is the goal God has placed before us: maturity. We are called to be like God. The apostle Paul refers to maturity as a life of faith, hope, and love, and it is these prizes that beckon us to embark on the healing path.

What is equally common to all of us is a pernicious enemy that seeks to disrupt our passage to God. Many may deny there is an enemy—singular, personal, and persistent. But no one doubts that enemies—even impersonal forces like multiple sclerosis, inflation, or global warming—influence our journey.

I believe we face not only impersonal hindrances on our path to healing, but a diabolical foe. The Bible calls this enemy the Accuser, the evil one—one who is committed to ruining our life. Evil hates us because we uniquely reveal the glory of God. It can't destroy God, but it can do terrible damage to human beings—those who in bearing the very image of God reveal the glory of the Almighty. Evil works to destroy that glory by stealing and marring what makes us most glorious: our memory, our imagination, and our capacity for sacrifice. In other words, evil wishes to destroy faith, hope, and love.

We can't stay on the healing path without coming to grips with how evil has worked to derail us. The next three chapters will examine what mars the solidity of faith, the movement of hope, and the joy of love.

PART TWO

EXPOSING THE INTENTIONS OF EVIL

CHAPTER 4

BETRAYAL AND THE
LOSS OF FAITH

riends who were once friends walked by my wife and me at church. They were in the flow of traffic, and we were waiting to merge. They held hands as he broke ground in front of them; she followed safely behind. As they passed us, our eyes met. The flow would not have permitted stopping, but a word, a greeting, some warmth from the terrain of our relationship past could have been offered. I wanted to look away and ignore the distance that seemed to exist between us, but instead I said, "Good morning, George."

George looked me in the face, his eyes silent and hurt. His head nodded and he said, "Morning." His wife looked at me, and her eyes burned with fury. She said nothing. They passed like moments in the stream of life, which one can either dive in and retrieve or allow to pass, lost forever. I felt helpless to stop their departure, so I let the moment pass and asked Becky where she wanted to go for lunch.

This was not what I expected from the journey of life when I became a Christian over two decades ago. I knew life could be painful, but I believed a follower of Christ could work through petty issues of difference or conflict with other equally committed Christians. The couple that walked by had been friends with us for two years. We had been in the same

Bible study. We had shared their struggle with infertility; they had supported us when travel took me away from home over extended periods.

Then a rift occurred. I'm not sure what originally brought the tension. In one of our first discussions after a crisp November air blew through our friendship, it seemed he was disappointed that we did not spend more time together as couples. The expression of disappointment was hard to hear, but he made little accusation or demand.

His wife eventually talked with Becky and me and asked us to pray for him because he was going through a tough time in his business. He was questioning whether to try to regain ground lost to new competitors or to cut back on family expenses to compensate for the decrease in his income. I asked a number of questions and then suggested she not hide her concerns from him. I told her I'd once gone through a similar struggle, and though I wanted to hide from the issues, I was thrilled when Becky had pursued my heart during my flight from what I perceived to be failure.

She said, "I don't know. He gets really, really mad and can take it out on me or the kids. I just can't handle it at this point." I didn't know if I should pursue the hint of significant anger or let her decide whether to say more. I didn't want to be pushy; neither did I want to abandon a friend. The conversation ended with her panicked, demanding that we not mention our talk to him. She feared he would feel betrayed. I shrugged in concession, but I felt uncomfortable with my decision.

At our next Bible study, another couple shared similar concerns about their finances and raised questions about ambition and risk versus gratitude and living a simple life. I offered a few thoughts, and my friend condescendingly pointed out where he differed from me. I looked at his wife, and she seemed embarrassed. On the way to our cars that night, I asked him if something was wrong. He looked genuinely surprised and said, "No, not at all. Were you offended that I differed with you?" Before I could answer, he jokingly said, "Maybe you need to set up an appointment to talk it out with a therapist." I laughed, but it seemed apparent that he had dismissed me and diverted us from the road to reconciliation.

Several weeks passed, and we were not able to attend the study. Our next encounter with the couple was at a church picnic. It was an awkward discussion that ended with Becky asking me, "What's going on? That was really uncomfortable." I made another phone call later to ask them what was going on. Again I felt dismissed.

When we returned to the Bible study, they weren't there. One person told Becky that the woman sensed the group was not truly committed to growing together and so they had decided not to attend. Another friend said that the couple had implied I'd broken their trust and as a result they could no longer talk freely about their lives in the group. A few weeks later the group ended for the summer. Everyone acknowledged it was time for a break. We never got back together, nor did we come to any closure about what had brought the group to an end.

Not long afterward, I met with the husband for breakfast. He was furious and hurt. The marks of his mistrust were pronounced. I asked him how I had offended him. I told him I didn't want tensions and distance to separate us. He told me, "I don't know if you are sincere or not. But even if you are, what has happened has happened. Neither of us has the time. Let's drop it." I told him I was busy—he was even more harried as he worked to shore up his business—but I didn't want to drop it.

The only indication of the cause for the rift was a remark he made at the end of our time: "I had hoped for more than an off-and-on-again friendship where you tell us what you think we ought to do." I didn't know if he was referring to the Bible study, the remarks offered to his wife in confidence, or something else. We parted, and I watched a friendship drive away.

This is the journey of life? If so, then it is no wonder so few "love one another deeply from the heart." Relationships, even good ones, ebb and flow, come and go with little rhyme or reason. But the loss of a friendship after walking together in worship, suffering, and support is a blow that knocks us off our feet. Such a bumpy, confusing ride can strip away our perspective, passion, and purpose.

THE ROOTS OF BETRAYAL

This story reflects what most of us experience in some fashion a number of times throughout our lives. It is the story of a loss that is neither clean nor clear and leaves all parties with questions: What happened? Who failed? Who is to repent?

The apostle James tells us why relationships break down. He says,

> What causes fights and quarrels among you? Don't they come from your desires that battle within you? You want something but don't get it. You kill and covet, but you cannot have what you want. You quarrel and fight. You do not have, because you do not ask God. When you ask, you do not receive, because you ask with wrong motives, that you may spend what you get on your pleasures. You adulterous people, don't you know that friendship with the world is hatred toward God? Anyone who chooses to be a friend of the world becomes an enemy of God. (James 4:1-4)

Why did the relationship with our friends break down? James tells us that desires not surrendered to God will always lead to murder and lust (covetousness). We absorb others, then we kill them for not providing what we demand. Ultimately, all friendships that break down are due to a friendship with the world that makes us an enemy or betrayer of God. When we betray God, we will inevitably betray and be betrayed by others.

We befriend the world whenever we demand that others be what only

God has promised to be: faithful and sure. All human relationships, even our most intimate alliances, are temporary and incomplete. When we demand that another person provide safety, certainty, and fulfillment of our deepest desires, we turn from God to an idol for the fulfillment of our needs.

When we turn from God, we inevitably demand of others the very things we miss in our relationship with God. If we don't know his deep care and protection, then we will insist another human being provide what we lack. That demand is the genesis of lust and murder. The couple who came to hate my wife and me felt betrayed by our lack of time or willingness to comply with their expectations. Were they truly betrayed? I don't believe so; they would likely differ. But after their anger flared and the distance between us grew, I nursed my own sense of betrayal and turned against them in a fit of self-righteousness, reciting all their sins to another good friend. The betrayal, whether real or perceived, soon spawned new sin, greater friendship with the world, betrayal of the betrayers, and ultimately betrayal of God.

But all betrayal is not the same. There are countless levels and differences of damage to the heart, depending on the nature of the betrayal. Essentially, betrayal is the breaking of an implied or stated commitment of care. We are to love the Lord our God with our whole heart, soul, strength, and mind and to love our neighbor as ourselves. We are to care—that is, internally orient our heart toward and act on behalf of others for their good. We are to care for God. We are to care for others. When we break covenant toward another and refuse to care, then we have betrayed ourselves, our God, and that person.

When we refuse to care, we close our hearts to believe in the other person and hope for his or her good. A closed heart is a barrier, erected without explanation and without desire to remove it if change occurs. Of course, there are times when a relationship divides due to geographical or schedule changes. We can't maintain every relationship at the same intensity through all the different phases of life. Nonetheless, some relationships end simply because the parties refuse to struggle well on each other's behalf, acknowledge mutual sin, seek forgiveness, and work toward the good of the other. When that is the case, some kind of betrayal has occurred.

A BLOW TO DIGNITY

Betrayal involves harming the dignity of the other. We do so when we efface, mar, mock, manipulate, or ignore a person's glory.

Effacing dignity. To efface is to erase or obliterate the glory of the other. It is to seduce, entrap, violate, torture, and destroy an individual's wholeness. Satanic ritualistic abuse attempts to efface the utter dignity of a person. Evil itself always works to efface even when its daily harm is less dramatic. The person who insidiously delights in ripping the gossamer soul to bits through sexual, physical, and emotional abuse is the most grotesque of all betrayers.

Marring dignity. To mar is to put a mark on a painting that ruins it without entirely erasing its presence. Marring dignity steals another's capacity for security and joy. The betrayer may or may not delight in inflicting the harm but often violates another's physical or emotional boundaries repeatedly. Any assault, like a sexual assault or infidelity, scars another's sense of dignity and sears his or her desire to be loved and to love.

Mocking dignity. To mock is to cast doubt upon or question the integrity and value of another through gossip, slander, contempt, and emotional abuse. Mockery demeans and belittles in order to separate the person from others. For example, a parent who demeans a child for not doing well on an exam and compares him to a sibling who has done well in school divides the two children by lowering one and raising the other.

Manipulating dignity. To manipulate is to use others for gain in position, power, place, or pleasure without regard for their good, and then to discard them once their usefulness has been attained or punish them if they don't "come through." Manipulation is the pretense of a multifaceted relationship that in reality has only a one-dimensional purpose: the fulfillment of the "user."

Ignoring dignity. To ignore the other is to fade from a relationship without honestly acknowledging the distance or fighting to recover it. It is breaking off a relationship because of a grudge nursed through self-righteousness rather than working toward reconciliation through honest dialogue, confession, and repentance.

In those terms, the relationship Becky and I shared with the other couple was divided due to mutual betrayal. At best, we came to ignore one another; at worst, there was a sense of manipulation on both sides that degenerated into gossip and mockery.

In most cases of ignoring or manipulating dignity, betrayal begets betrayal to the point where it is almost impossible to discern where one betrayal ends and the other begins. For example, in a relationship between two people where one depends on the other for encouragement and support, the one who is the "helper" may end up resenting the time required by the other person but never addressing the issue. The failure to give freely and with joy leads to irritation, but because the needy friend seems so troubled, the helper says nothing. Over time the helper cuts phone calls short, avoids the friend at church, and backs away from involvement. The tension increases, and the needy friend feels more rejected than if the issue had been faced much earlier. Now who has betrayed? Most likely, the needy person used his friend, and the helper refused to make difficult choices about his time and availability, eventually coming to ignore his needy friend. Betrayal begets betrayal.

We will all face betrayal in major and minor relationships—it is inevitable. What happens to the human heart when betrayal casts its dark shadow over our lives? And why is it important to know? Betrayal eventually hardens the arteries of trust and causes us to become cynical and suspicious. It darkens our memories of even the good moments in a relationship and cuts us off from the presence of God.

But the fruit of facing betrayal in others and ourselves is that we come to a new awareness of God's faithfulness in response to our betrayal of him. He is faithful. And if we look carefully at the stories of our past that are laced with betrayal, loss, and bitterness, we will find they are also marked by memories of his surprising protection.

THE CYCLE OF BETRAYAL

The truth is that every conflict has at least two points of view. As any relationship ends through the trauma of betrayal, it moves through a process that involves more than one lie, one affair, or one moment of slander. But in essence it begins with a failure to love that is neither confessed, forgiven, nor reconciled.

As the schism widens, others will be invited to share each person's perspective. If the tension is severe, a confidant is unlikely to remain a trusted friend unless he sides with the "hurt," "misunderstood," "innocent" party—that is, the person bringing him into confidence. If the confidant is also a friend of the other person, he will probably be unable to remain close friends with either party if he attempts to retain neutrality or an objective perspective of both parties' sins.

The friends of a divorcing couple will either distance themselves from both husband and wife or pledge allegiance to one. If they choose neutrality, they'll probably lose the friendship of both; on the other hand, if they rally behind one, they'll probably experience immediate growth in intimacy with that person while sensing greater antipathy toward the other.

The opposed party must be demonized in order to justify such a change in allegiance. This requires new data, stories that place the husband or wife in clear categories of good and evil, innocence and guilt. Then the spin that exonerates the "innocent" and vilifies the "guilty" is told to a growing group of people willing to join the jury. As the stories are disseminated and ultimately distorted, the gossip reaches critical mass, and the original parties know that truth has collapsed on itself. Now it is little more than a propaganda war with misinformation that cannot be separated from a few kernels of truth. All betrayal is a community affair; it is never merely a matter of a division between two people. Even when the betrayal is between two people and kept a secret, as in sexual abuse, it still touches others' lives, even without anyone's cognizance.

A dilemma occurs when the wife whose husband has had an affair knows somewhere in her heart that she is not guiltless. Perhaps she was passive and disengaged, or demanding and demeaning. No failure of a wife or husband ever causes or excuses an affair; nonetheless, the downward spiral that leads to an affair usually involves mutual failure. His affair, however, is more public and more easily vilified than her more subtle failures to love well. When her friends attack him, she is unlikely to talk about her sin. Even if she does, it will likely add to her friends' astonished respect for her rather than alter their perspective of her husband. She cannot and dares not stop the community's growing disdain for him. The community's support depends on her perpetuation of the easily understood black-and-white story.

Because betrayal begets betrayal, the betrayed must not only wrestle with the loss, heartache, doubt, and shame that comes with any division, but also with an even deeper struggle: The betrayed often becomes the betrayer. The one who is hurt often hurts, the one shamed often shames, and the cycle of harm continues. But it is possible to break this sick cycle, this incessant wheel of death, if one gets on the healing path. The healing path does not deny the agony of betrayal but instead uses it to marvel at the solid ground of God's faithfulness in contrast to our fickleness.

For many the cycle of betrayal diminishes over time. New problems take priority and pull the community of friends to new calamities. A divorce may be hot news in January, but by summer it is a sad but forgotten memory. We all get on. But the ones who have been betrayed, have struggled with betraying, and have felt the agony of tormenting memories are left behind with unredeemed heartache and shattered lives—wounds that never fully heal.

Ultimately, betrayal cuts to the heart of faith. Faith is trust that comes from repeated encounters with a person who is solid and sure. Over time we develop greater confidence and rest more deeply in the care of the one we trust. Betrayal severs the arteries that feed trust and make our memories of rest seem naive and foolish. When betrayal ends a relationship, we struggle with profound doubt about our desirability and discernment. It becomes easy to replace faith with suspicion.

THE TORMENT OF MEMORY

My friend George told me the story of a tragic and commonplace betrayal. He was an associate pastor at a growing church. His job was to help families grow and to develop small groups that ministered to a well-to-do, busy, high-powered suburban population. George is a caring, easygoing, and generous man. But the senior pastor was under pressure to develop a dynamic ministry, and George by demeanor and calling was not the one to make it happen.

When George arrived at work one day, an executive pastor told him he had two weeks to find a new position. There had been no review of his work that indicated concern or problems. There was no dialogue with the elders or the other staff. When George asked to see the senior pastor, he was told it would be at least a week before he could get an appointment.

George was devastated. He had worked with the senior pastor for more than a decade. He had been part of the church's transition from less than a hundred members to over a thousand. He had wept with many of the elders in the midst of their heartaches and rejoiced with them through births and business successes. Then one day he was out. He felt used and discarded, unable to hear his accusers or rebut their assessments. No one fought for him. No one remembered his sacrifices and what he had brought to the team. His dignity was manipulated and then ignored.

He cleared out his desk that day. He alternated between feeling numb and being heartbroken. His wife was furious and frightened. Over the course of a single day, he was jobless, his ministry terminated, and his family devastated. He sat for hours that night after his wife had gone to bed, assaulted by haunting memories.

First came the memories that might have indicated there was a problem. There was the time he was the only staff member not invited to a particular elders meeting in which they allocated space in a new building. He had dismissed that as the consequence of being more interested in people than plans. Then a dozen conversations replayed in his mind, assaulting him with voices and faces that became louder, more distorted, and increasingly cruel with each round. *You should have known there were problems—you're a coward. You thought people would appreciate your care for them when this church wanted nothing but bigger numbers and more success.*

His mind flitted to the hours and hours of communion with the senior pastor and reciprocal prayers for deep struggles. He recalled the airline flight to Honduras when both of them feared they would die. The birth of the senior pastor's third child. The picnic when George was honored for ten years of service. George's mind was on a toboggan run without a path or a finish. He careened out of control until exhaustion and fitful sleep overcame him.

Betrayal sends us reeling from the past to the future like a bouncing pinball—from terror to regret. Betrayal stalks and haunts. It turns the past into a long series of questions and doubts. Betrayal isolates. It takes us to the end of a long, lonely dirt road and unceremoniously dumps us without provisions or promise of help.

People who have been betrayed often experience nausea. It is as if they have lost their footing and suffer the roiling seasickness of a world that has lost its foundation. Not only does betrayal rip away the foundation of trust and confidence in others, but it also isolates us in a web of memories.

George's thoughts flitted from indications of the problem to scenes of past intimacy that came to mind like swirling specters. He couldn't stop his mind from reeling, and the more he dwelled on those moments of laughter and happiness with the senior pastor and elders, the more he hated them and himself.

The only way to stop the swirling nausea was to turn his mind off. He turned on the TV and aimlessly surfed the stations. He got up and filled a bowl with nuts, but he wasn't even hungry. His memory was on autopilot, rapidly retrieving forgotten events against his own will. He busied himself, but activity couldn't stifle the memories.

Why is memory so closely connected to betrayal? Memory is our map for living life. We may know the terrain from home to work so well that we don't even seem to need to turn the wheel of the car; it happens without thought or apparent choice. But what happens when a detour takes us out of familiar territory to a part of town that is both new and scary? We take out a map to find our way.

Memory usually serves quietly and unconsciously as it helps us navigate life's normal twists and turns. If we know the terrain well, we aren't even aware of memory reminding us to turn here or to avoid this street at a certain hour. We simply turn the wheel and go our way.

But when tragedy, disaster, or betrayal strikes, we start searching everywhere for a guiding map to circumvent the problem. We scan images and scenes of our past at computer-fast speed as we seek a frame of reference that will help us comprehend our situation and how we arrived there.

George looked for "exclusion memories," which might prove he was not wanted in the group. He searched through "failure memories," which might explain why he was let go.

The disruptive and abrasive surge of memory and emotion indicates our frantic effort to find solace and safety when our foundation has fallen out below us. But in most cases, the effort to find an explanation or a resolution by scanning the past only adds more chaos to a soul that already feels like it is disintegrating. Each memory of exclusion or failure is contradicted by memories of inclusion and success, intimacy and respect. In a true sense, we are spectators of our own past that pulses before us. Though memory was meant to provide us a map to move into the future, it instead haunts many people as they look into the terrifying unknown.

DOUBT AND THE DISSOLUTION OF IDENTITY

Who are we? We are the rivulets from many high-mountain springs that merge into a fuller stream rushing down into the tumult of a rushing river. We flow and ebb to the sea, muddied by an undercurrent of depravity, sparkling with an incandescent dignity. Who am I? I cannot be defined by a scientist or dissected by a critic; I am not simple.

But I am Tremper Longman III's best friend. I am Becky Allender's best friend, lover, and spouse. I am their father, his friend, her husband, her boss, his and her colleague, his enemy. I am the network of all my relationships present, past, and future. And my conscious grasp of who I am revolves around the stories of those relationships. We never define ourselves in abstract (I am a pastor, a homemaker, a student) without also associating those labels with myriad stories remembered and forgotten.

Our identities are suffused with narrative. I am a confederation of stories, relationships, and memories. The DNA of my self-identity is made up of the strands of my relationships with people who have been the artists of my self-awareness. I am in their stories too. When betrayal cuts the cord to others, it also severs us from our past. One woman who went through a divorce burned all the pictures that included her husband. She refused to tell any story if it involved being with her former husband. She rewrote the past by simply refusing to have one. As a result she had no solidity, no depth to her being. She had torched her soul along with her pictures.

Memory provides us with our guiding templates for living life. When the past loses its capacity to connect us to others and guide us into the future, then we also lose confidence in ourselves. In one sense, betrayal not only disrupts our memories, but it steals our sense of identity.

Doubt is an acid that eats away at our stories. As the questions about what happened and what we did wrong multiply, our stories dissolve and we lose the confidence that those stories once provided. Doubt paralyzes us and makes even the simple decisions of life seem herculean.

George said that the two weeks after being fired were like wandering in a fog. He needed to buy a new suit for an interview and sat for hours in a men's department unable to make even a simple decision about what style or color of suit to purchase. He lost his footing. Doubt is a form of double-think that paralyzes us with the myriad options, the potential harm of another bad choice, and the shame that waits if we are mistaken again.

Our First Response: What's Wrong with Me?

Doubt stops us in our tracks and then spins us in a dizzying haze. George sank into the couch next to his wife. His face was etched with pain; his skin looked sallow and his flesh sagged. He had lost his spirit. He said, "I just don't know what I did wrong. I don't know what I could have done to make them happy."

The initial cry of betrayal is, *What's wrong with me?* The energy behind most doubt is a frantic rush for explanation. Often the search leads to self-blame or contempt. The human soul can't bear bad news. Even more, it can't tolerate bad news that seems to have no reason, no meaning, no explanation. When the reason behind the loss of relationship is unclear, the route to reconciliation is equally evasive. In the absence of other explanations for the betrayal, personal failure presents itself. *I wasn't sensitive to her needs. I should have gone to his birthday party. I was too quick to condemn, too busy, too needy.*

We don't have to look far to find failure. Every relationship is mired in a wash of mutual failure. In the normal course of events those failures are ignored or forgiven. They often are the basis of a deeper relationship as the parties extend grace and resolve conflicts. But the betrayal that ends a relationship, whether substantive or slight (or both), collapses that bridge of mutual grace. Once the central passageway for commerce and care is shattered, doubt sets in.

The spiral of self-doubt often begins with real or presumed weaknesses, with the betrayed oscillating between self-contempt and other-centered contempt. We feel most hostile toward our perceived weakness to want, our foolishness to trust, and our desire to be restored to someone who has broken our heart. The cry changes from *What's wrong with me?* to *I'm a fool! Why didn't I see what was coming? Why did I let him take advantage of me?*

Our minds go back to a lengthy history of desiring relationship with others and feeling disappointed. One middle-aged woman I worked with who had been unceremoniously dumped by a friend said, "I felt like I was back on the playground when Nancy Swisher talked all the other fourth-grade girls into not playing with me. I ran away crying, fell, cut my leg, and ruined my dress. It was like that all over again. I'm so stupid."

Our greatest self-blame is directed against our hunger for relationship with the betrayer and eventually against our desire for relationship with anyone. Like the waves of an earthquake, it spreads in an increasing ring of destruction.

Reconsidering Events: Someone Will Pay!

No one remains stuck in his own self-contempt. Efforts to unearth an explanation for betrayal usually snap back to an equally harsh extreme: blaming the other. We magnify the betrayer's faults, list and recite his calumny. Before long we regain the self-righteous equilibrium that had dissolved when pain surfaced and our failures surrounded us with howls of condemnation.

It's like being caught in a swirling twister: We sense we've been betrayed. We fear we've failed and brought on ourselves the dissolution of the relationship. Yet we turn again and see the betrayer's sin. We fail to see where we have actually been part of the dissolution.

Are we ever to be blamed for someone's sin against us? Absolutely not. If I am sexually abused, or if my spouse has an affair that mars my dignity, I am not the betrayer. Although I may sin before I am betrayed, my sin is not the cause of the other's failure. When sinned against, however, my response will typically be a sinful one: When I'm betrayed, I eventually betray others.

I may have been sexually abused as a child; the results lived out over the decades will most likely involve further betrayal on my part of myself and others, especially God. Often, a female abuse victim hardens her heart to others and ignores their care while mocking her own dignity through acts of sabotage like promiscuity or involvement with destructive men. Again, betrayal begets betrayal.

When we lose the foundation of a trusted relationship, we have no one to trust but ourselves, and yet it is the self that feels most foolish and incapable of making safe and solid decisions. We are in a trap. We are cut off from others. We are cut off from ourselves. We hate our desire. We want relief from our pain. We want someone to care and comfort us, but we also want justice, vengeance. The dark desire to make our betrayer pay places us in the strange position of being both a victim and an abuser.

No victim remains solely a victim. It may sound like heaping more guilt on the betrayed, but seldom, no, *never* will we endure harm without making someone else pay. This is not to say the resulting harm is of equal weight to the original offense—rarely is it. But the presumption that a victim is good, innocent, and pure while the abuser is merely evil is not only too simplistic, but it denies the darkness we know exists in every human heart.

The victim of the betrayal often shuts down. After all, how are victims to live with their anger? What are they to do with the hurt? What are they to do with the feelings that the betrayer is scot-free, happy, and getting on with life, while the victims' world is shattered? What is to be done with the hard fact that the betrayed must often face their own sinful contribution to the original wound? It is too much, too incomprehensible. Therefore, many who suffer betrayal eventually become numb. The shock of betrayal often leads to a fitful, waking trance. Then, even if the remorseful friend, spouse, or child wants to reconcile, the bridge, now collapsed, is forever condemned to decay.

Numbing Out: Who Cares?

In the roller-coaster ride of betrayal most victims settle for numbness, the respite of shock that blunts our emotions and dulls our pain. In this state of suspended animation we hear without comprehending and move but don't choose. The numbness of betrayal causes as deep a conflict as any other part of the process.

Recently Becky and I sold our house to move to Seattle. We were interviewing the last of four Realtors and were about to sign with one when our phone rang. "Hi, this is Janet. I'm a friend of one of your neighbors, who told me your house is for sale. If you haven't signed with a Realtor, would you call me?" The Realtor we were interviewing rolled her eyes and recited the reasons why selling by owner is foolish. We didn't sign and instead called Janet, who visited our home within the hour and then returned with her husband that evening.

A week later they made an offer on our home. We accepted it. I was in awe. The sale was far higher than any Realtor had promised, even with their fee taken out. We were thrilled. It seemed like a great gift from God, and we were grateful.

The extra money from the sale enabled us to seriously consider purchasing the house in Seattle we had been looking at for four months. It was the perfect home for our family. We had looked at over a hundred homes and felt sure this was the best choice. But my wife and I agreed I needed to see it one last time before making the decision. I traveled to see the home and then told our Realtor to make an offer. Later that day I learned the bad news: Another offer had already come in. Less than thirty minutes after I saw the house for the last time, it was sold to another buyer. I was stunned, confused, and crestfallen.

Why didn't I make an offer the day before? I berated myself. *I was a fool. I waited too long and was too indecisive. It was Becky's fault. She wanted me to video the house so she could see it one more time. It was the Realtor's fault. No, it is God's fault. He certainly could have granted this one desire. He provided for us to sell our home, tempted us with desire, set us moving toward what seemed good, and then in a thirty-minute gap snatched away what we had dreamed about for months! He betrayed us!*

My Realtor said, "I am so sad, but maybe there is a reason. Maybe there is an even better house for you just around the corner." A good friend said the same: "I bet God has something in store for you that will thrill you even more." Their kind words—sincere and possibly true—only deepened my sense of anger. I wanted to scream and throw things at God. I hated myself. I felt betrayed by God.

The ride up and down the waves of confusion, loss, and perceived betrayal eventually sent me reeling to numbness. I didn't care. I didn't want to talk. When my wife asked me to pray, I did so dutifully. Becky prayed that we would both remember what God had done on our behalf to sell our house in such an unpredictable and gracious way. When she said that, I felt one part furious and three parts apathetic. *So what. He enables us to sell the home and then pulls the rug out from under us. So what if I remember? It only makes the current confusion harder to comprehend. Faith isn't worth the struggle. It is easier not to care.*

MULTIPLE LOSSES

A loss of faith comes when God no longer seems predictable and sure. It comes when our heart desperately longs for him to change the outcome of a situation and he chooses not to act according to our best sense of what is good. It is when our healthy, beautiful child dies under the wheels of our car. Or when our happy, secure marriage crumbles. Or when the deep, God-given desire to have children dies with an emergency hysterectomy. Our heart aches for good things, legitimate desires. And when God refuses to act to keep those desires alive, we find that our faith falters. Sometimes it dies. When faith withers, so does our capacity to remember his redemption with awe and gratitude.

The result of lost faith is a refusal to remember, and therefore a loss of confidence and energy to tackle the daily ups and downs of life. To remain numb, to give up desire, and to refuse to dream is to surrender one's soul to the status quo. It is to live an utterly immanent life that is not drawn to the allure of transcendence. It is to live as a robot and merely survive. In turn, a loss of faith often leads to a distant, rule-bound relationship with God that does not stray but also does not desire. Life without faith becomes anemic and predictable, never sufficiently stirring to compel us to risk for the future.

When we lose faith, we also feel powerless to change our future. To feel we have been merely a pawn in the past is to look to the future as no different than what we have already experienced. For that reason, a loss of faith always leads to a loss of hope. In the next chapter we will explore powerlessness and the loss of hope.

CHAPTER 5

POWERLESSNESS AND THE LOSS OF HOPE

T he plane dropped from the sky. We arrived with a thud that sent a hard, bone-rattling tremor through my body. It was the same death shudder I felt when the Realtor told us our dream house had been sold a half-hour before our offer was submitted. *Indeed,* I thought, *maybe there is something better ahead. But maybe there is something worse.*

The day after the deal on the house fell through, I flew off to do a seminar. Now, with the plane nearly embedded in the tarmac, I found myself half lamenting we survived the landing. I didn't feel suicidal. I didn't want to die; I simply did not want to live, or at least live with the ups and downs of daily disappointment, dashed hopes, and barely lit desires continuing to smolder in spite of the rain. The loss of the house was but one of many things that had gone to seed in the past several years. This precarious landing symbolized my newly awakened conviction that life is not predictable, except in its unpredictability.

I arrived at my hotel, and the desk clerk recognized my name. She said, "Your wife just called. She was so excited. She was so cute. She told me to tell you, 'The perfect house just came on the market.' She is going to meet you in Seattle on Sunday. You need to call her right away."

I walked to my room stunned. I felt fury, excitement, dread. I wanted to call. I wanted to go to sleep. Was the Realtor right? Was our dear friend correct when she said, "Something good is ahead"? Or was this just another pothole that would wrench my tire, reverberate through the undercarriage of my soul, and leave me out of alignment and swerving? I could not take another blow that left me feeling powerless to keep my dreams from disintegrating.

Each day something of life is snatched out of our hands. A friend went to her physician for a checkup and asked him to look at a small spot on her nose. Within a week she was in surgery and a sizable portion of her nose was removed to cut out the cancer. Another friend called to ask me to pray for her daughter who had been date-raped a few days before graduating from a Christian college.

The world compels us to make bricks with less and less straw. The cry of God's people is no less anguished than in the days of the Exodus. He doesn't seem to hear. He has left us stranded in a land of luxury where we are enslaved and forgotten. Or so it feels. Some days.

Betrayal and powerlessness are siblings from a sulfurous underworld. They work hand in hand to steal faith and hope, confidence and joy. We feel powerless not only when someone betrays us, but when someone fails to rescue us or redeem us in the midst of a situation we cannot alter on our own. Powerlessness is the agony of being caught in a trap from which we can't extricate ourselves. We are naked, impotent, helpless, and without the resources, power, or friends to make the kind of difference we desire.

To be powerless does not mean we can't make decisions or respond to situations; rather, to be powerless is to be unable to erase the damage and paint the good we so deeply desire. Many frustrating situations can be changed with time, money, or education. For example, I am not powerless to lose weight; my daily decision not to eat a cookie or take a second helping does, over time, make a difference. It is simply so slow and so apparently pointless that it requires enormous hope to make progress. What makes most dieters feel hopeless is the fact that they will always struggle with the three primary origins of powerlessness: the world (food at every church affair), the flesh (wanting to eat), and the devil (the constant temptation to find a better god than the God of the universe). Victory in an area only requires more vigilance, passion, and choice at the very next moment.

No, we aren't powerless to change, and yet we are powerless to escape the incessant struggle and the slow, slow progress of change. I am powerless to stop the relentless assaults of the world, the flesh, and the devil. And more often than not, I fail in resisting their power.

THE WORLD: PERSONAL ASSAULTS

Jordan was nine the first time he was sexually abused by his sixteen-year-old sister. Though no proof exists, she was likely the victim of her uncle Jack's predatory abuse. Jordan's mother was almost certainly abused by Jack when she was a child. The morass of abuse sucked in each family member as victim, abuser, or observer. No one escaped the family shame. Most of the family stayed away from the house as often as they could and left home early, never to return.

Jordan was the youngest of five siblings. His family ignored him. But compared to the abandonment and abuse, he felt more horror in going to school. He had a learning disability that was either ignored or undiagnosed, and he spent the bulk of every day feeling like the class dunce. His teacher treated him with barely hidden disdain. His classmates used him as a dumping ground for their own fears and inferiority. He ate alone. He played with younger kids on the playground. He hated school.

Jordan faced daily assault and abandonment as well as his teachers' and classmates' disdain. He had no more power to stop their harm than to tilt the angle of the earth. But he tried, desperately. He pled with his sister to stop. He begged his mother to hear the truth. He worked at recess and after class to master reading. He gave other kids gifts, told them fancy lies to bolster his flagging self-esteem, and let himself be used as an errand boy. Nothing worked. All through school he was the nerd who just didn't fit in.

Jordan spent most of his waking hours watching TV and reading comic books. Today he is a single man, satisfied with few friends and an adequate but not demanding job. When life is like a bully, the natural, tragic response is to give it a wide berth, avoid being noticed, and do whatever is necessary to avoid more scrutiny.

Jordan's life involves more moments of powerlessness and pain than many, but no one is free to reenter Eden; we all live east of Eden. The angels guard the gate, and we are powerless to get past their flaming swords. East of Eden is a dry, barren desert compared to the rich, verdant valley we were meant to inhabit. We live in a world where floods, hurricanes, thieves, and bacteria break into our existence and we are helpless to stop them; we are powerless in their wake.

We're powerless even in matters as small as a broken appliance. The complexity of most "conveniences" daunts even the most gifted handyman. The expense of repair is nearly the cost of replacement. The time and frustration to get it boxed and sent to the company leaves most people in a quandary. It's easier to put it in a crawl space (planning to fix it later) and buy a new one. Over time the room where one stores old phones, stereos, luggage, and other paraphernalia testifies to our impotence to fix what is broken or discard what is useless. Powerlessness hangs in the air like humidity, sapping the body of vitality.

Illness, death, job loss—all come upon us like a thief in the night. Our efforts to keep ourselves safe are like locking the doors of our car: It keeps the honest person from the temptation, but no lock, alarm, or ignition block will keep the committed, competent thief from taking our car. We buy insurance. We have smoke detectors. We have our cholesterol checked.

But in vain do we gain the kind of mastery that allows us to direct life as we desire.

Not only does the world pose the threat of powerlessness, our bodies, too, constantly remind us that we do not even have the will to change our physical constitution or character.

THE FLESH: INTERNAL INEPTITUDE

Jane is thirty pounds overweight. All her life she has struggled with diets. She has succeeded and failed more often than the *New York Times* reviews diet books. She has given up. She gains a few pounds a year now and figures there are other, more important matters for her to address. One of those is her relationship with her husband.

He doesn't like her extra pounds but doesn't complain much. He simply drifts in and out of her life. She is furious and tends to explode a few times a month, throwing pots, slamming drawers, and then refusing him the right to sleep in their bed. The next day she feels ashamed but knows that if she apologizes he will nod, say nothing, and ignore her. It really doesn't matter what she does. Nothing changes.

Jane feels helpless to change her attitude or actions, and she struggles with an emptiness that will not go away. She has failed so many times to control her temper or her eating that it seems pointless to try again. When she picks up a book on anger or dieting, she feels an initial rush of hope, which dwindles quickly when she reads the same old material repackaged by another author.

Hope wanes to the degree our flesh is not molded to the design that God intends. It is not just our physical body that is hard to harness; it is what the Bible calls our flesh, or the principle of autonomous self-will. Our flesh wars against our spirit. We may want to love a friend who has hurt us, but when we see her, our face turns cold and our mouth fills with the taste of bitterness and anxiety. We pass by and speak in a tense and distant tone. We want to be kind—or at least a part of us urges us to be kind and long-suffering—but our countenance and tone reveal otherwise.

In the face of our commitment to get up early to study the Bible, the urgency to do so diminishes as the bedcovers provide a warm barrier between slumber and the demands of a new day. Guilt is not a great motivator at dawn. The alarm rings, and the hand naturally slaps it to gain another fifteen minutes of relief. Procrastination. Good intentions stuck on the shoals of reality.

Paul spoke of his own battle with the flesh:

> For what I do is not the good I want to do; no, the evil I do not want to do—this I keep on doing. Now if I do what I do not want to do, it is no longer I who do it, but it is sin living in me that does it.
>
> So I find this law at work: When I want to do good, evil is right there with me. For in my inner being I delight in God's law; but I see another law at work in the members of my body, waging war against the law of my mind and making me a prisoner of the law of sin at work within my members. What a wretched man I am! Who will rescue me from this body of death? (Romans 7:19-24)

Paul feels the war in his inner being between intention and practice. He is often the loser who fails to achieve what he knows is good. He calls himself wretched. He cries out for someone to rescue him because he is truly powerless in his own flesh to rectify the course of his life.

We all want to change, but change requires a herculean effort that seldom brings the immediate benefits needed to reinforce the initial cost and disruption change entails. The formula for change seems to be: high cost today—no gain for a long, long time; high gain in the distant future—*if* one perseveres daily in hope.

But the mounting remains of failures loom large against the horizon of hope. I failed with this diet. I failed in this relationship. I failed in this commitment. I failed in this project. I've failed enough! I don't care to fail again. I will only set forth to change myself when I absolutely must or when the prospect of success is nearly sure.

What this means for many of us is a life of endless repetition and a good but routine existence. Sometimes we feel like we're just surviving, merely getting through one day to the next. Working, raising kids, cleaning house, cutting lawns. The exhaustion of this life is heard in the phrase, "Been there, done that." Weariness. Dailiness.

Pointless repetition creates a reasoned and well-manicured suburbia, but it does not lend itself well to a life that stretches out for eternity. We are to yearn for God, to pant for his coming. We are to shape our present in light of the eternity we anticipate. By merely surviving, we live for a now that is not permeated by the leaven of heaven. But by reaching out to eternity is to live with an unquenchable hope, refusing to resign to being as we are in the world as it is.

THE DEVIL: SUPERNATURAL SNARE

The world is a maw open wide, waiting for us to slip. Our flesh sings a siren song, calling us to loosen the bonds of wisdom and abandon ourselves to debt, food, alcohol, TV, noise, busyness, or any other form of numbness. As if that were not enough, we have a personal, diabolic enemy committed to destroying us.

Evil works to delude and destroy. It wants dominion. Satan, as the ruler of this world's kingdom, seeks all of us as servants, whether as intentional slaves of darkness or unwitting sycophants. He seduces us with promised relief but then sets desire aflame, consuming any hope of satisfaction. He offers us power, then snares us in a web of helplessness. He works to subvert all truth, goodness, and beauty.

The world provides the cliff, and our flesh demands the right to stand on the edge. It is the devil who gives the push that sends us tumbling down to our death. Can we avoid the cliff or always stand back from the edge? Perhaps for a time, but not forever. Life is full of precipices, and the journey often requires us to walk near the edge. We are powerless to escape living in a fallen world, where our sinful flesh and the enemy of our souls work to destroy us.

How evil works is beyond our comprehension. Does it have the power to whisper new thoughts in our ear? Or does it take our thoughts and manipulate them by altering our circumstances? Does evil intensify our dark desires and simply give us the nudge we're already naturally inclined to follow? Or all of the above? It is my experience that evil operates on all three levels and more. But its goal is the same: Offer glory, then give nothing but heartache, impotence, and shame. Its primary tactic is to set up a Catch-22.

A Catch-22 is a diabolic bind in which we are damned if we go left and truly damned if we go right. It is a nonoption option that steals our reason and hope. A person recently told me of a tragic Catch-22 she faced as a young adolescent. Martha was the first in her family to dream of going to college. She wanted to be an artist. Her art teacher made it clear, however, that if she wanted his letter of recommendation she would have to pose nude for him. She was frightened and furious and had no one to turn to for help. It seemed like an innocent albeit lecherous demand. So she posed for him. He later used those pictures as blackmail to force her into a sexual relationship.

A man told me about a recent business trip with his boss. At the hotel, the boss departed with a woman who was clearly his mistress. The boss made it clear that this young man's advancement in the firm required an oath of silence. He agreed and then felt like a conspirator.

A Catch-22 often seems innocuous and a mere nuisance, but over time it can slowly entrap and snare a person's soul. At a later point the only way to break the bondage is to give up everything that the comfort of the web provided. Evil knows we would rather delude ourselves, deny the truth, and eventually justify even harmful behavior as our only choice. In the end, we will have lost our character, relationships, and soul. It is, in fact, nothing less than a grand conspiracy set into the very sinews of the earth to leave us without full power and control.

The conspiracy is actually set into motion not by the world, the flesh, and the devil; it is set into motion by God. God pronounced a curse (or a consequence) on humanity as a result of Adam and Eve's rebellion. The curse leaves us all powerless to one degree or another. A woman will be powerless in the experience of birthing a new being and in the agony of loneliness that eventually attends all relationships. A man will be powerless in the experience of tending the garden and in the futility of a world that will not easily succumb to his touch. But it is the world, the flesh, and the devil that use the impotency and barrenness inherent in the curse to snare humankind into an even deeper helplessness than that intended by God.

God's desire is to use our powerlessness to send us fleeing back to him. Evil wants it to send us reeling to rely on ourselves with even greater intensity. We unwittingly follow evil's plan when we attempt to escape our powerlessness through martyrdom, rebellion, or disengagement.

STYLES OF RELATING TO POWERLESSNESS

How do we handle being powerless? Most of us do one simple thing: We hoard power. We work hard to escape the sense of being resourceless. Rather than being broken by circumstances, we strive to extricate ourselves from the helplessness associated with being caught in the world, stuck with our flesh, and constantly barraged by evil. For a time this works, but the season will come when our best efforts to keep helplessness at bay will fail. The season may come through great tragedy or profound loss like death or divorce. Or it may be the proverbial straw that breaks our backs—like the car not starting after a rash of broken household appliances.

Most of us would prefer to keep at least the illusion of control in the midst of such onslaughts, so we develop coping styles that enable us to regain a measure of power. This is portrayed by Toni Morrison with extraordinary impact in her brilliant work *The Bluest Eye*. She wrote this book in the early stages of the Black Is Beautiful revolution in the midsixties, but its relevance is still fresh and disturbing. Morrison portrays the horror of self-hatred when a person's skin color, hair texture, and facial structure do not fit the vision of beauty as defined by the dominant culture. To feel ugly is to feel not only isolated, but barren and impotent. To be beautiful is to have access to opportunities and relationships not available to those who stand outside the blessing of the gods.

Morrison describes three characters: Mrs. Breedlove, her son Sammy, and her daughter Pecola. They are not only black but stained by ugliness that makes them unacceptable even in the African-American world. They depict three behavioral styles associated with powerlessness: martyrdom, belligerence, and disengagement. Morrison writes:

> You looked at them and wondered why they were so ugly; you looked closely and could not find the source. Then you realized that it came from conviction, their conviction. It was as though some mysterious all-knowing master had given each one a cloak of ugliness to wear, and they had each accepted it without question. The master had said, "You are ugly people." They had looked about themselves and saw nothing to contradict the statement; saw, in fact, support for it leaning at them from every billboard, every movie, every glance. "Yes," they had said. "You

are right." and they took the ugliness in their hands, threw it as a mantle over them, and went about the world with it. Dealing with it each according to his way. Mrs. Breedlove handled hers as an actor does a prop: for the articulation of character, for support of a role she frequently imagined was hers—martyrdom. Sammy used his as a weapon to cause others pain. He adjusted his behavior to it, chose his companions on the basis of it: people who could be fascinated, even intimidated by it. And Pecola. She hid behind hers. Concealed, veiled, eclipsed—peeping out from behind the shroud very seldom, and then only to yearn for the return of her mask.[1]

Martyrdom

Mrs. Breedlove wears her ugliness not as a mark of Cain, but as a badge of honor. Her husband is an abusive drunk. Her son is cruel and her daughter strange. But she bears her suffering with an omnipresent heaviness, a sigh of suffering so deep and profound that others can only turn their eyes in fear that they, too, will be taken on as one of her burdens.

Martyrdom, or self-righteous suffering, sighs and finds satisfaction in its helplessness. No one can, no one could help. No one cares. No one understands, and so I will bear this suffering with no complaint, which means with no desire. The self-righteous martyr suffers alone, publicly.

George, the pastor who was unceremoniously dumped, tried to handle his sense of powerlessness by becoming more "spiritual." Friends offered financial and emotional support, but he turned them away, saying, "God will provide." He slumped into depression, but in the presence of others he put on a happy face, salted his struggle with spiritual platitudes, and tried to see the good in what had happened.

His wife wept. He watched her with barely hidden irritation. He would read a passage of Scripture to her and then retreat into busyness. If she tried to help him organize his files or begin the process of looking for work, he would become stiff and irritated, and patronize her by telling her to go rest since she was so upset.

The effect of this kind of public and disconnected suffering is to make others feel guilty and powerless themselves. The martyr gains the upper hand through a stance of silence, service, and suffering. Silence is a chasm that an observer can't bridge with words or empathy. Service obligates the recipient without ever asking directly for reciprocity—the debt continues to grow disproportionately. Suffering becomes a torturous, underlying hum implicating the witness for being uncaring, thoughtless, and inhuman for not rectifying the martyr's pain.

The self-righteous martyr is in fact inhuman, demeaning, and demanding, twisting reality to make his victim look abusive or at least apathetic. George eventually led his wife to become nagging and fearful. She wanted to help, but his repeated dismissals of her made her feel excluded and frantic. She turned on him, and he withdrew into even more meaningless activity. Most martyrs do provoke others eventually to abuse them. Ironically, all rage turned against a martyr only serves to further his powerless power.

Belligerence

Mrs. Breedlove's son, Sammy, chose another route: belligerence. Sammy walked with a swagger and a chip on his shoulder that invited trouble. He provoked fights and seemed immune to pain, social restraint, or conscience. Sammy disturbed people with his disregard for life, limb, or liberty.

Belligerence is the swaggering threat of violence. It is cocky and sure and is not concerned about addressing injustice; rather, it seeks to create chaos. Violence can be used to change the structure of power to redress injustice. The American Revolution is an example of violence for the sake of justice. Most violence, however, is not justice based; it is an effort to restore pride and a sense of personal power through vengeance. Violence that stems from belligerence demeans and tears down in order to make someone pay. It is a Samson-like suicidal gesture that pulls down the pillars—not to escape, but to destroy those who have blinded us and made us feel helpless.

When George's wife or others tried to enter the fortress he had built around himself, he growled and bit the hand that tried to draw him out. After he verbally assaulted his wife, he would spiral into a funk of self-accusations and mean-spirited vilification of his failures. Over time his family kept their distance from him. When he walked into the room, his kids would leave. They didn't want to hear the eventual remarks about how they had to tighten their belts and cut back on unnecessary luxuries. They knew that in a matter of minutes Dad would begin yelling.

Belligerence creates chaos by mocking the goals we are unable to achieve. After losing his job, George felt incapable of providing for his family and their future. He saw college tuition, house repairs, and the litany of braces, lessons, and clothing bills that lay ahead of him like boulders in his path. He felt overwhelmed and he blamed anyone who came near him. He found bitter fault with the church, the elders, and the pastor. He began to mock faith and ridicule the truisms that once provided a buffer for his powerlessness.

Misery loves company. George wanted others to be trapped in the mire he could not escape. He began to thwart and frustrate others. The belligerent person feels powerless to change his world, so he tries to drag others into his impoverished and hopeless state. If unable to do so, he chooses the next best thing: withdrawing altogether.

Disengagement

Pecola suffers untold harm—she is mocked, beaten, raped. She is an object of scorn because she is an ugly black girl. She is in the lowest caste of her culture: unattractive, female, very dark. She has no resources nor a strong arm of help, no basis for redemption. She bears the internal innocence of Abel but the external mark of Cain. She must wander, an alien and a stranger, always in danger of being used as a dumping ground for hatred of anyone or anything that is different than the norm.

She hides. She strains not to be seen and to keep on the mask prescribed by her world. When she operates from a place of desire and is enticed into relationship by schoolmates, it always ends with her being abused and blamed and made to feel foolish. She escapes into a world of fantasy. Pecola dreams of having blue eyes. Blue eyes, blond hair, white skin bring nourishment and safety. Blue eyes give life, power, and joy. Anything less must be hidden.

The disengaged in our world do not use their powerlessness to make others feel powerless, as martyrs do, nor do they pull down the towers of power, as the belligerent; instead, the disengaged flee this world and fantasize about an annulment of their condition. The fantasy of winning the lottery, of inheriting something of surprising value, of receiving a check in the mail from an unknown patron wings many of us above our common lot of suffering. The romance novel, the soap opera, and the sports game serve as an escape that takes away the consciousness of our plight through a vicarious attachment to the dreams and lives of others.

To be powerless is to feel a constant agony of desire. To want is to feel one's deprived condition even more acutely. A single woman in her early forties told me that she doesn't feel single from Monday through Friday. She is able to keep so busy and engaged in her work that by the time she arrives home after eating out with friends, she craves the silence and distraction of TV or a quick cruise on the Internet. But when late afternoon on Friday arrives, she feels the weight of her loneliness and the helplessness to do anything about her condition. Often, she has a few drinks and goes to a movie with friends. The movie closes off her ache and she attaches her desires to the characters on the screen. She is not borderline.

She is not disconnected from reality. But the movies play in her mind as equally real and more compelling than her own story. She slips in and out of the stories on the screen and fritters away her weekend, longing to get back to the busyness of work.

Each style of managing powerlessness is a flight from hope. Powerlessness, like poverty, steals the passion to remember or dream. Albert Camus describes the soullessness that comes from poverty and powerlessness. He writes:

> But the heart wears out with sorrow and labor, it forgets sooner under the weight of fatigue. Remembrance of things past is for the rich. For the poor it only marks the faint traces on the path to death. And besides, in order to bear up well one must not remember too much, but rather stick close to the passing day, hour by hour.[2]

Those who get stuck in the experience of betrayal and powerlessness are locked into the present, doomed to run in the ruts that have been marked for them. For many, each day is but a repetition of the past and the inevitable fate of whatever the future may hold. No transformation. No change. No hope. The goal of evil is to destroy our future by stealing our hope.

Is this the end of the story? Of course not. But too often followers of Christ merely affirm, "heaven is ahead," "we are more than conquerors," or "we are new creatures in Christ" in order to escape a profound awareness of their true situation. One believer said to me, "I'm never powerless because I can do all things through Christ." Really. Can you raise your dead father from the grave? Can you pluck the pancreatic cancer out of your wife? Can you turn your child's heart to God? Can you stop the hands of time, your aging, the ravages of broken relationships, and a culture careening out of control?

Still many will say, "But we have the Holy Spirit and he empowers us!" Indeed, we do. But we have the Spirit to open our eyes, free our senses, and enable us to suffer as Christ. To suffer is to embrace our situation without flight, fantasy, or control. The Spirit empowers us to embrace and revolutionize our powerlessness.

It is not wrong to admit that our choices change little in this world; there is so much over which we can exert little if any influence. That doesn't mean our choices are meaningless; they matter and last into eternity because each of our individual lives is a thread of a great tapestry that in its corporate beauty is glorious. But we can't always see the future, nor how one seemingly small and insignificant choice ripples across countless lives.

I may not effect great change in my church or country, but my life can bring joy or sorrow to God. It is in the midst of our powerlessness that we occasionally see the wild work of God. Theologian Frederick Buechner wrote, "We are never more alive to life than when it hurts—more aware both of our own powerlessness to save ourselves and of at least the possibility of a power beyond ourselves to save us and heal us if we can only open ourselves to it."[3]

Just as faith is necessary to forming a solid, confident sense of identity, hope is crucial for the capacity to anticipate and shape the future for good. Our imagination grows in the soil of hope. To imagine what does not yet exist—to see into the future—is necessary for planning a vacation, investigating neurochemistry, writing a book, or even cooking a meal. Hope requires a sense of sacred discontent, innocent anticipation, and playful risk.

SACRED DISCONTENT

Until we become discontent with the rigors of trying to escape our powerlessness we will live locked into the present status quo. If we are fully at home in our situation, then we will not ponder a better tomorrow.

Discontent is the mother of invention. Discontent is holy when it compels us to dream of redemption.

Tamara White, the founder of the Prodigal House, a safe place for homeless teens in Denver, was drawn to the urban landscape because her church invited suburban kids like herself to interact with the poor in soup kitchens and recreational outings. But then she'd leave those she served to return to her safe world. She felt haunted and drawn to the squalor and hopelessness because the gospel offered such a radical alternative to a life of drugs, sex, and violence.

Tamara felt discontent with her suburban roots. She was grateful for her heritage, but she couldn't stand being a drop-in minister. She needed to be on the street, living in the milieu of those she loved. She not only wanted to see the poor redeemed, but she saw herself in the poor and longed for her heart to be redeemed through and with them.

Sacred discontent is not mere dissatisfaction that turns the heart to complain and disengage. It is a holy hunger to enter a heart or situation so that we can offer incarnate love and know the same at the roots of our soul.

Take the wife who admits her marriage is a tiresome moral sham. As she hungers for more, facing her fears and demands, she will struggle with the log in her own eye but will also refuse to allow sameness to remain the pattern for the rest of her marriage. To admit discontent and hunger for redemption requires that we face our part in the problem and compels us to yearn and dream of more.

Conversely, a person without hope accepts her present circumstance as inevitable. It simply has to be endured. No wonder endurance is often the trademark of the self-righteous. They live in unendurable situations with no complaint, no demands. In fact, the self-righteous live with no acknowledged, confessed desire. In the story of the prodigal son, the older brother attacked the father for not offering *him* a fatted calf for a party with his friends. "'My son,' the father said, 'you are always with me, and everything

I have is yours'" (Luke 15:31). By implication, the older son never asked; he preferred to slave in the back fields asking for nothing and owing no one anything.

The martyr in each of us refuses holy discontent. We would prefer to retreat in furious, uncompromising silence rather than face our need for someone to rescue us or at least join us in our helplessness.

Tamara White began the Prodigal ministry by simply hanging out on a street and offering food and conversation to homeless kids. For weeks on end, they tested her, took her money and time, and then ignored her. Finally, two kids sat down to ask her what she wanted. She avoided sounding too religious or weird but talked about how long she'd lived without a true, spiritual home. She intrigued the hard-core street kids with her strange savvy and sweet innocence. She began with a desire and a prayer. All good grows out of a desire to see the future shaped from the refuse of the present.

INNOCENT ANTICIPATION

Our imagination, our desire, cannot be set free when it is in the bondage of cynicism and dark despair. Hopelessness produces a refusal to see the potential of a new, bright, and good day; the agony of waiting is too severe when anticipation gives way to disappointment day after day. A child waits with innocent, eager anticipation. The moment is going to come soon. A child peers out the window on tiptoe: Dad will be home any minute.

Belligerence and contempt mock hope. Waiting stirs the belligerent to a violence that demands we get what we want now. Watch the faces of those waiting in line for a long time. The faces move from detachment to boredom and then to irritation. If the line doesn't move, you see people cluster in a community of complaint. If held up longer, those in charge will be pelted with contempt. The growing belligerence steals our innocence and robs us of anticipation.

In contrast, biblical hope leads one to wait with eager patience. After her initial contact with the two children, Tamara was eventually introduced to more. But it took months of relaxed waiting for the homeless kids to check her out and watch her reactions to their antics. If she had demanded quick response to her care, they would have written her off as a do-gooder. Instead, her patience mirrored their aimless wandering, but she lived with keen purpose that came from hope; therefore, she confused them and intrigued them with her sweet, passionate willingness to wait.

In the same way, a wife who enters her own holy discontent begins to dream not only of what her marriage could become, but what she is to be even if her husband does not change. It is difficult to dream in regard to our character. An angry and stiff woman can easily blame her fear on her husband or simply tolerate the way she is, even while she knows something softer and kinder wells up within her occasionally. To continue to dream when failure and disappointment cloud the sun is the radical gift of hope.

PLAYFUL RISK

Discontent moves us. Anticipation sets us dreaming. But without action, we are dreamers who will eventually stray into fantasy. To act for the sake of the future is to risk our present for a vague unknown. It is to stretch ourselves outside the parameters of safety that often serve as our fortress and prison.

It is easier to disengage. It is simpler to come home from work, eat dinner, watch the news and a few shows, read a little before bed, and slip away in the warm arms of slumber. At times, it is easy to fill our time with busyness that allows us to detach from holy discontent and the struggle of hope.

Disengagement is a flight from risk. It is a refusal to suffer any more losses. We would prefer to hunker down, dull our desire, and drift into distractions that take away our holy hunger for more. For many of us, the meaning of our lives will not be found until we risk moving out of our realm of safety.

Do we all need to start an inner-city ministry? Of course not, but we are called to playfully risk our lives on behalf of others wherever we are planted. The wife who has lived in a distant, lonely marriage can do more than merely survive. She can face her disdain toward her sexuality and ask God to lead her to new and ravishing freedom. She can confess her hatred of conflict and ask God to equip her to love boldly. There are an abundance of risks inherent every day in every relationship that, over a lifetime, draw a person to the allure of heaven.

Discontent took Tamara into the urban scene and intensified her burden for street kids. Her childlike anticipation enabled her to wait and not demand that change occur on her time schedule. Eventually, the two kids she initially befriended asked her to lead a Bible study. She empowered them to set the rules for when they met, how they would deal with disputes and conflict if others attended. She risked the whole enterprise by giving the ministry over to two kids who were on the run, using drugs, and in trouble.

Risks often appear foolish or even stupid. But hope makes us playful, free, and inventive. Hope is not naive desire but a calculated risk that declares, whatever the loss, it is better than remaining where we are.

GOD'S INVITATIONS

After I unpacked my clothes, I called my wife to find out about the new dream house that had just come on the market. I felt house-cynical after a day of feeling a manageable but low level of despair. I didn't want to feel excited and then crash again. My wife's voice was enthusiastic, full of awe and gratitude. I felt my disgust rise in response to her childlike passion.

Didn't she know it was just as likely going to be pulled out from under us or not meet the criteria we had established?

As she described the features of the home I felt hope rise. As my desire grew, I also felt the sickening sense of powerlessness that comes from looking across a chasm too wide to bridge on my own. The price was beyond our reach. Was it stupid to even look? Was I setting us up for feeling helpless again?

My wife made the decision for us. She had already secured an inexpensive flight to Seattle. First, I self-righteously chose to remain silent when she asked what I thought about the house. She said she could cancel the ticket for no charge. What did I want her to do? I said, "Whatever you think is best." I retreated to the martyr's silence.

She pressed, and I became belligerent and sarcastic. I didn't want to hope again. I told her if she wanted to ruin the next few days of my life while I taught on marriage and the bliss of marital joy, then I was game. She kindly and gently rebuked my efforts to derail hope. I relented. I half-repented and acknowledged I was afraid to dream and desire that something good could be just around the corner.

Soon after hanging up I retreated to the beautiful scenes of figure skaters at the Winter Olympics gliding across my TV screen. Elvis Stojko lifted into the sky for a blazing triple Salchow, and I was lost in the wonder and the fantasy of turning in the sky like a top. I could feel the applause and the mouth-open wonder as I landed with ease and elegance. I was swept away in my fantasy of glory. It was easier to lose myself in the beauty of the skating than to dream about what God might be doing in our lives.

But when my thoughts returned to the house, I had to admit the possibility placed before us was another invitation by God to hope, to allow desire to be shaped into a good dream. This house might not be available or the best choice. It didn't matter. Hope required that I maintain holy desire, the strength to wait, and the willingness to engage.

Engagement is risky. As we anticipate and hope, we expose ourselves to the repeated possibility of failure and shame. The next chapter explores our natural response to risk: ambivalence. We want to engage; we hate that the stakes are so high. Every day faith and hope lead us to love, or betrayal and powerlessness drag us into ambivalence and shame. The path we choose will determine our level of fruitfulness and measure of joy.

CHAPTER 6

AMBIVALENCE AND THE LOSS OF LOVE

My wife was the first person I saw when I disembarked from the plane. Her face was light and her eyes danced when we embraced. Her enthusiasm was contagious, and I was excited to talk about the past several days and the house we were about to see. Our favorite Realtor met us, and we drove in the rain to the place we might call home.

I immediately fell in love with the house. We walked around and made our pilgrimage through each room. My excitement soared when I ascended the stairs above the garage and saw the spectacular view from the study where I would counsel and write. I loved the house. I loved my wife. I loved God. I could feel my heart slowly unwind and thaw. It was true: Something better had been given when our dream died. I just couldn't believe it.

The price was still well above our upper limit. It seemed ridiculous to offer a substantial amount under what was being asked, but we had no choice. I tempered my hope. I cautioned my wife against undue enthusiasm. By the end of the day we tendered our offer and waited. Becky returned to Denver. The next day passed in slow, fitful steps. The offer was to be accepted or countered by 6 P.M. the next day. The hour came and our offer was accepted with a few minor changes. I was ecstatic.

I called Becky. I told her our dream had come to fruition. Her voice was thin and slow.

"Great. Now what?" I asked. "What's wrong? Why aren't you excited?"

Becky wept. "I don't know. It is so different than any place we have ever lived. I don't know if I even like the style of the home. It seems like such a big decision, and I think I may want to live closer to town or in the suburbs."

My wife was caught in the web of ambivalence. She was excited; she was terrified. She wanted to get out of the deal; she wanted the house decision to be over.

Despite my excitement, I felt ambivalent as well. Becky's tears hurt me, and I felt small for being so angry. I wanted to be kind. *Should I try to convince her?* I wondered. *Start over? Accede to her fears? Acknowledge she may be right?*

Ambivalence is the emotional battle with two (or more) minds, wills, and desires. It is not being double-minded in the sense of being duplicitous or two-faced; rather, it is feeling two contrary energies moving us in opposite directions, being caught in the bind of opposing desires, feeling divided and torn.

I felt torn between wanting to be done with house hunting and wanting to make my wife happy by responding sensitively and wisely to her fears. I didn't want to call the Realtor and tell her we had decided to say no. I felt like a fool. I couldn't please my wife; I couldn't let the house go. I felt overwhelmed, and in my divided and desperate state I could feel the storm surge of shame.

We feel shame when we are stripped of control, and fear of even greater failure prevents us from making a choice. When we feel shame, we turn quickly to contempt in order to cover our nakedness with self-reproach and/or blaming others. The cycle through ambivalence, shame, and contempt can progress at the speed of light. In a matter of moments after my wife's remarks, I had turned against myself for being impulsive, selfish, and foolish. I was exhausted. I hung up the phone and sat looking at my watch. I had to go teach a counseling course on marriage and the family. It all seemed too ironic. I saw no reason to give; I felt like I had nothing to offer.

We experience ambivalence daily. We love our kids; we could easily ship them back to the manufacturer at times. We love our jobs; we dream of winning the lottery and sailing off to Bimini. We are honored to be nominated to the pastoral-search committee; we dread the long hours of thankless work. The natural response to ambivalence is to feel depleted and detached. We may blame our ambivalence on a lack of commitment or inner strength, but much of it simply is due to the era in which we live.

THE AGE OF AMBIVALENCE

Our era may be called the age of narcissism, or we can say we live in a post-modern, post-Christian culture. But it is more accurately called the time of tension, the long era between the cross and the coming of Christ. We live in the time one theologian calls the "already, but not yet." I would call it the age of ambivalence.

We have already been given the gift of the Holy Spirit after the death and resurrection of Christ. We have the firstfruits of the harvest. But the day of completion awaits another dawn. We wait for the final climax of the history of God—the Second Coming is not yet. Even the verb "save" is found in the Bible in three tenses: the past tense (we have been saved), the present tense (we are being saved), and the future tense (we will be saved). Our bodies and souls live in the tension between having been saved and waiting to be saved.

Tension is the key element of ambivalence. We want to go to the left, and we want to go to the right. Or we want to go to the left, and we know we ought to go to the right. We're caught on the horns of a dilemma; we feel stuck at the crossroads.

Many of us can't make a decision unless our ambivalence is resolved. Usually that requires a level of certainty that is impossible to achieve unless we deny the ambivalence. So we pray, asking God to give us such clarity that we don't feel torn. Or we chide ourselves for feeling torn until the guilt drowns out the ambivalence. In either case, we hate to make a decision when the other path remains a viable and compelling choice. It just doesn't seem fair.

It unnerves us to think we really could have married another person and have been equally or more happy. The same is true for our jobs, decisions with our kids—the whole spectrum of life. It is one of the great conundrums of human life, and particularly of living as a Christian. The Scriptures tell us to love, but then God doesn't provide specific directions for our specific situations. He tells us to have faith but doesn't tell us how to do so. The same is true with having hope: The Bible outlines few concrete steps to lift us up.

How can God call us to do something and then not tell us exactly what to do or how to achieve it? I suspect there are two reasons. First, faith, hope, and love are as intrinsic to our being as breath is to our body. Being faithful, hopeful, and loving is not a matter of working hard, but of savoring and desiring more of the small amounts of faith, hope, and love that are already within us. Second, God gives us the frightening freedom to find our own way after naming the path of following him. He points us toward the way and then lets us discover him through our missteps and our successes. Freedom deepens and does not ease ambivalence.

The fact that another house appeared a day after our dream house was lost can't necessarily be interpreted as God's will. The fact that the builder dropped his asking price to our range is wonderful but can't be viewed as proof God wanted us to buy the house. Nor can my wife's sudden seizure of fear be read as an indication that buying the house would not have been a good decision. Events we call good are not necessarily a sign of God's favor. Many rich pagans are happy but not in God's will. Many godly people walking God's path suffer untold harm. We simply can't determine his design for our lives merely according to what turns out well and what does not.

If none of those factors should be the basis of a decision, is making a reasonable choice merely a matter of weighing the pros and cons? Or does one simply make a decision based on whoever feels most strongly about it at the moment? The punctuation of ambivalence is a question mark. And if we live in the age of ambivalence with a God who seldom tells us outright what to do, then is it any wonder we feel caught in daily and profound tension?

Dogmatism: Doing the "Right" Thing

It is exhausting to be caught in the throes of ambivalence. To not know the "right" thing to do (or even to know it while being drawn to the alternative) is to feel drained and overwhelmed by indecision and ambiguity. One way out is to muster arrogant confidence, the certainty of dogmatic conviction: This is the *right* and *only* decision. To maintain this perspective is exhausting as well. Dogmatism requires a level of arrogance that is like carrying an extra thirty pounds in a pack. It can be done, but it slows the carrier's pace and hampers movement. One may have packed for every possible contingency known to man, but such preparation makes the journey a toilsome and joyless march.

The process of buying a new home in Seattle had consumed me for over a year. I had been in touch with Realtors, read the classified ads, surfed websites, and talked with scores of people to get a handle on the market. I had done my homework and through the process had come to many definitive, dogmatic decisions about where it was best to live. I craved certainty. As a result, I tried to force my family into a structure that cramped them and limited God. Arrogance that arises from a hatred of uncertainty invariably compels us to push others to be and do what makes us comfortable, rather than allowing them to join in the process. Ambivalence often creates a dogmatic, pushy heart that violates love.

We can't escape tension. We can't avoid freedom. We can't resolve it in arrogant, dogmatic certainty without harming ourselves and others. But we can avoid ambivalence by sidestepping options or complex decisions. Just as we can outrun betrayal by not investing our hearts in the lives of others, and just as we can escape powerlessness by not taking on significant risk, we can escape ambivalence to the degree we submit ourselves to the status quo. If we don't think or feel, then we don't have to enter the world of the "already and not yet."

The goal of evil is to induce us to forget the goodness of God, to dull our dreams, and to estrange us from those we love. Both daily and catastrophic experiences of ambivalence can give evil a foothold to accomplish this goal if we don't catch on to its devices.

DAILY AMBIVALENCE:
THE UPS AND DOWNS OF LIFE

Janet is a new mother. She is in her late thirties and has struggled with infertility for twelve years. It has been exhausting. Every month she hoped her dreams would wed with reality and her womb would fill. Each menses mocked her desire, and she settled in for another month of rising and falling hope.

After many years, she gave up the dream of bearing children and began to pursue adoption. The phone call came on an ordinary Tuesday. In the morning she was filling out loan applications at work; in the afternoon she was sitting in the middle of a spare bedroom, weeping with her husband, overwhelmed at the prospect of getting a little boy. The weeks passed quickly before they brought Matthew home. They were giddy and overjoyed. Life was good.

It was good until that first month ended with little sleep. Matthew was a sick boy. He had to be rushed several times to the emergency ward when he cried himself blue. He was jaundiced, colicky, perhaps suffering from fetal alcohol syndrome. The wear and tear of late nights, worry, and mounting health bills birthed Janet's growing battle with ambivalence. She wanted Matthew; she wanted her old life back.

She eventually voiced her struggles about being a mom to a friend, who was horrified. She told Janet she was ungrateful and selfish. It was the last time Janet admitted she was torn in two. She withdrew her heart from honest conversation and suffered her ambivalence alone. In time, she learned not to trust fellow Christians who always seemed to have either an answer for her pain or condemnation of her struggle. Evil successfully stripped Janet of the joy of healthy Christian fellowship.

James is an entrepreneur. He took a job as CEO of a company that was struggling to meet its production goals. After three years, he increased the company's financial bottom line fivefold and catapulted its product to national attention. The company was approached by a national firm for a friendly takeover. A year later the company was purchased, and James walked away with a personal gain of over five million dollars. The sale made the papers. Within a month, he was called by his pastor, a national youth ministry, and several missionaries from his church. They all wanted his money.

James was wanted. Who doesn't want to be desired, pursued, needed, and enjoyed? James had the gift of making money. He was blessed with a Midas touch and he wanted to give, but he felt pursued to the point of being hounded. Over time he came to hate his gifts. Others assumed that since he had so much money, he ought to give. If he didn't give, they expressed hurt and aspersion. If he did give, they assumed he ought to give more. Few were grateful; most felt a degree of entitlement.

James feels torn in two. On the one hand, he loves to give; on the other, he hates feeling used. He expressed his quandary to his pastor, who told him, "God loves a cheerful giver." James continues to give, but with less hands-on, face-to-face engagement. He set up a charitable foundation that is run by professionals, and his involvement is limited to making final decisions. The ambivalence he felt opened his heart to feeling shame and led to his withdrawal from relationship.

Some common life experiences can lead to ambivalence. Three in particular seem to pave the way: We are likely to feel ambivalent when we attain our dreams, when our gifts are used, and when we're called to suffer.

Blessings: The Fulfillment of Dreams

A friend once said, "Be careful about what you pray. God may actually give you what you ask." I thought his words odd until I thought back to most of the dreams that I have lived to achieve. The desire is often sweeter than the realization. We can work like slaves to achieve a dream, drawn on through sweat and heartache by the allure of fulfillment, only to feel a sad and inconsolable ache once the goal has been achieved. The journey is often more compelling than reaching the finish line.

We all know the letdown that comes when a project or commitment has been finished. The joy of completion is hardly ever commensurate with the labor to get there. Janet dreamt for years of having a baby. The adoption brought her the dream of her life, and within weeks she realized her hands were full of new struggles she could not have foreseen. When our fulfilled dreams fall short of our expectations, we feel ambivalent—we lose hope and in turn lose the energy to love.

Without really knowing it, Janet and all of us dream not for a child, a marriage partner, a better job, or a clean bill of health, but for heaven. Our daily dreams are but the material wishes of our immaterial soul. We want a new car, indeed, but the smell of a pristine interior and the shine of a waxed, spotless exterior is but the hunger for a beauty unspoiled and a glory yet revealed. Consequently, all our desires are sweeter than their fulfillment. Over time, we may come to feel ambivalent not only about fulfillment but about desire.

Ambivalence can lead to a jaded, cynical view of love. Love is work; it pays little and requires everything. I heard one father say of his children, "They are useless appendages. They take my work, my wealth, my time, my energy, and usually all I get back is lip."

Parenting has profound rewards, but not in the measure of what most consider obvious returns. I have a framed picture of mountains painted by my oldest daughter as a fourth grader. Most likely it will never have monetary value, but it is one of my most treasured possessions. My son told me recently, "I read three pages of *Cry of the Soul* [a book I had coauthored], and I think you're a good writer." My heart swelled.

Love bears fruit, but the dividends come by a slow, slow process, and the return is usually a small symbol—a few words that reward the heart in a way that seems incommensurate with the sacrifice made. Blessings, small or large, leave us hungering for more, poignantly aware that the "more" probably will not be forthcoming until heaven. Are we willing to keep loving when the gain is not immediately great—even if, when it is, we are left wanting more? We must face that even blessings can leave us feeling ambivalent.

Gifts: Glory Revealed

We can also feel ambivalent regarding the gifts and calling God has given us. I long to be gifted and used. I dread it. God has endowed people with talents, gifts, and special anointing to accomplish his design. God is the Creator, but he shares the creative process with us. It is his joy to share with us the pleasure of creating, whether it be making money, food, a poem, or a birdhouse. It is exhilarating to use the gifts God has given us to bless another person.

Our gifts bless others and, for a time, might make a difference. But there is a price to pay for being gifted. The gifts I have are used. When I'm used I love it and I hate it. Am I being used because my gifts work for your advantage or because you like me? How do I separate my being from what I do? Am I really gifted? Why did God not give me more gifts or the gifts I really wanted?

James battles with a hatred of his financial gifts and the money he has made. For years, James hid his abilities under a bushel basket by driving cheap cars, wearing faded jeans, and living in an inexpensive home. His frugality was not the pursuit of a simple lifestyle; it was an attempt to escape admitting to himself and others that he had the wherewithal to do as he wanted, whether to buy a nice car or fund a new ministry. Having money caused too much trouble, both in choosing not to give to a person or organization and in providing an explanation for his decision. On the other hand, he enjoyed the power and privileges to which his gifts entitled him in the organizations he supported. He was treated differently and he loved the attention.

Gifts, abilities, and past accomplishments are both a curse and a blessing. We love the attention; we hate being wanted solely for our gifts. We would feel lonely if we were not needed; we feel pressure when we are expected to provide for others. Many people wish they had a better voice, more money, or the gift of tongues or teaching, without realizing that every gift, ability, or talent demands something of us as we offer it for God's service. Blessings and gifts open the door to new levels of suffering. If we fail to embrace our gifts and their consequences, then our ambivalence will turn to hate, both for our gifts and for the people we are called to serve.

Suffering: Welcoming Trials as Friends

Few passages cause us more discomfort than the one that tells us to view our trials and tribulations as a blessing. Blessings are hard enough to greet and embrace, but they are certainly more welcome than suffering. James the apostle unflinchingly states: "Consider it pure joy, my brothers, whenever you face trials of many kinds, because you know that the testing of your faith develops perseverance. Perseverance must finish its work so that you may be mature and complete, not lacking anything" (James 1:2-4).

Consider it pure joy. Get real. I don't usually thank God the moment a new betrayal or moment of powerlessness careens into my life. At best, I may eventually see the fruit of the suffering and acknowledge that it brought me to a good place. But at the moment it knocks me over, I'm disposed to see suffering as painful and pain as unwanted.

At the same time, I have experienced enough moments of redemption during the long walk in the dark valley that I do not hate suffering as I once did. I want ease, but do I really? If I were to play a tennis opponent whom I could easily beat, I would be unchallenged. If I were able to read a book and understand each line and reliably predict its successive thoughts, I would put it down as dull.

If life is predictable, lacks complexity and ambiguity, and requires little of us, then we are bored. If life requires us to enter too deeply into the mystery and muck of life, then we feel overwhelmed. More often than not, we attempt to calculate the ideal point between boredom and chaos but have yet to find the safe or thrilling spot. We are destined to feel ambivalence when we recoil from suffering.

CATASTROPHIC AMBIVALENCE:
THE LEGACY OF ABUSE

We might escape some of our daily ambivalence through denial, guilt, or naive optimism. Denial attempts to escape the web of ambivalence by refusing to admit one feels torn in two. It is easier to assert: "I'm fine. I feel good. There is no problem." Guilt faces the internal division but blames one's own self for it; whereas ambivalence leaves us feeling helpless and needy, guilt promises resolution if one only does "it" right the next time. Naive optimism, on the other hand, feels the ambivalence, refuses to take responsibility for it, but still escapes the bind by assuming there will be a speedy and easy resolution to the internal division. These coping mechanisms aside, however, ambivalence broke into many of our lives and set its most severe trap in the web of shame.

Ambivalence comes from many different sources, but none more tragic or clear than through sexual harm. If there is one diabolical by-product of sexual abuse (and of course there are more), it is the feeling of being torn to pieces. The victim of abuse is drawn into relationship by the abuser. Over 91 percent of sexual abuse is perpetrated by someone the victim knew beforehand. In most cases, the perpetrator draws the victim into relationship by offering tenderness, care, and protection. The initial involvement often offers what was missing in the life of the victim: kindness and respect.

This stage is often followed by physical touch that seems appropriate. A hug, a hand on the shoulder, or a fatherly kiss on the cheek deepens intimacy and adds sensual pleasure to the relational joy. Enjoyable physical touch allows the perpetrator to progress further and further toward the eventual abuse. The hugs last longer and involve a level of physical touch that is inappropriate but not obviously abusive.

The child or adolescent may feel some discomfort as the perpetrator inches closer to abuse. When the abuse does occur, the memory of the uneasiness is often the basis of the victim's self-disgust: "I should have known better. I could have stopped what happened; therefore, it is my fault."

The deeper disgust and shame, however, is the pleasure the victim may have felt during the abuse. An abuser is perversely committed to sexually arousing the child. When a child experiences arousal, it seems to her that she is a participant, not a victim. Abusers also compel the child to arouse them. The mutuality of arousal is a subterfuge to share the responsibility and guilt. No lie could be more diabolical.

What is the goal of evil through the damage of sexual abuse? Evil works to destroy the pleasure of giving and receiving. The intimate dance of love involves offering a gift, receiving it in gratitude, offering praise, and receiving the praise with joy. Give and receive; respond and engage. If one side or the other closes down, then the dance can't go on. Ambivalence is at the core of the shame. A victim of sexual abuse may say, "I felt both arousal and power in the sexual contact with my abuser. I simultaneously felt sickened and repulsed by that pleasure and power." The horror of contradictory, simultaneous feelings links ambivalence and shame. The shame in giving to and receiving from an abuser stains the joy in sexually (or in any fashion) giving to or receiving from another. Evil strives to stain our joy in loving.

The dance of love brings delight to God and disgust to evil. No wonder evil works to destroy faith and hope in order to leave love naked and alone. No wonder evil poisons the hunger of the heart with shame and then tears the heart in two, one part enjoying the arousal and the abuser's pursuit, the other part afraid, hurt, angry, confused, ashamed, disgusted, and alone.

Evil's intention is to alienate and deplete us in order to strip us of love's joy. Because it is in and through love that we gain a glimpse of the heart of God, evil uses sexual, physical, and emotional abuse to destroy our hearts. It seeks to infuse us with shame. When shame rules any portion of our hearts, we are blocked from love and left to fend for ourselves, alone in the world.

AMBIVALENCE AND SHAME

James, the gifted entrepreneur, was sexually abused when he was seven. His older sister, twelve, paid him to touch her. He would have done so for nothing; he loved the power, intimacy, and arousal that flooded through him. Not long afterward she showed him some of their father's pornography. They mimicked the positions, but he felt small and scared when she touched him. He eventually began touching younger kids in the neighborhood and then he felt a measure of power. He was consumed by the thrill and terror of the sexual games.

The sexual touching in the neighborhood and with his sister eventually stopped, but the memories still haunt and titillate in a convoluted mixture of pleasure and shame. Mostly shame. It followed him in every relationship and every activity. At a young age, he became aware of the thrill of making money. It also had a titillation. The planning, preparation, long negotiations, and ups and downs of the process were almost erotic and infused with shame and power. He hated his gifts and felt shame every time he was successful, but for years he refused to see a connection between his past abuse and the arousal in business. James never admitted to anyone that business deals were titillating, nor did he talk about his hatred of his body and the memories of arousal that made him feel ugly. Ambivalence grows to the degree we are unaware of its driving source of shame.

Janet, the woman who wanted to be a mother and adopted a child, had no history of abuse. She came from a caring, non-Christian family. Her parents were proud of her academic and business accomplishments and yearned for her to have a child. Her family was a hard-working, blue-collar family. She was the first to go to college, the first to have a professional job.

When she had her child, her parents visited. They couldn't afford a hotel, and so they stayed with Janet and her husband. It was the first time Janet's family met her friends. Her parents were socially ill-equipped and awkward when they met Janet's neighbors and church friends. Their manners, grammar, and dress mortified Janet each time the two worlds collided.

Janet felt sick to her soul for caring about how others viewed her family. She hated how she distanced herself from her mother. She was excited to share her new baby, horrified that her family was uneducated, ashamed it mattered, impotent to escape the roller coaster of ambivalence. She sent her parents home early. When she needed their help, she felt too ashamed to ask her mom to return.

Shame is the silent killer of intimacy. Like carbon monoxide, it is usually undetectable and deadly. Shame comes when an accusation exposes our dark inner world to others. Shame makes us feel unlovable and unable to love.

Most of us make our inner world off-limits to even our most intimate companions or spouse, because to open our heart is to reveal the confusion, disgust, arousal, and shame within. Instead, we wear a guise of normalcy, a veneer of acceptability—a mask that keeps relationships in place but leaves the heart alone.

Shame shuts us down. It blocks us from receiving and giving and leaves the soul hungry but too ashamed to admit its condition. Shame impedes anyone from entering to offer the light of love. We acquiesce to its isolation. *Who could bear the brokenness and confusion of my inner world? Who would want the glory of my soul when it is so commingled with emptiness and sin?*

Distance. The only hope for survival is in keeping our distance. Separate. Far enough apart that custom and prescribed roles provide the dutiful structure for acceptable relationship. Men shouldn't look into the eyes of women. A man should open the door for a woman. Women shouldn't engage men in difficult, taxing conversations; instead, they should putter and serve and let men talk among themselves. What era? Perhaps the fifties, but in certain groups this is still the norm, or at least the desired standard.

Regardless of how outdated those rules sound, there are rules in every culture, from fundamentalism to avant-garde punk, that mediate the trauma of freedom, the ambiguity of choice, the ups and downs of ambivalence, and the potential of shame. As the number of rules increases, the possibility of being in a position where one doesn't know what to do decreases. Most people are more comfortable in a rule-driven culture where behavior is prescribed and uncertainty largely eliminated. The resulting loss of freedom is rewarded with a greater distance from the prospect of shame. Such striving to avoid ambivalence and shame is the motivating force that shapes the soul of a Pharisee and the culture of legalism.

SHAME AND CONTEMPT

Evil prefers extremes. If it can't produce a structureless, chaotic, consuming culture, then it will work to bring about the opposite: a contained, constrained, orderly world of law and predictability, devoid of mystery. Evil will prompt the prodigal to demand his inheritance and flee the father to live a licentious life, or it will entice the older brother to slave away, doing right, obeying the rules, and stoking a fire of resentment toward the father for not providing the opportunity to rest and frolic.

Law not only enables us to structure life to avoid shame, it also gives the faithful follower of rules higher ground to look down on those who are not as consistent or committed. This is law's appeal and power. When I succeed at keeping the rules, I can look at others with other-centered contempt; when I fail, I can violate myself with self-contempt. In either case, where there is shame there will be contempt. As smoke is to fire, contempt is to shame.

Contempt hardens the heart by causing us to view others or ourselves through a lens of hatred. The lens anesthetizes desire at the same time it negates disappointment. Contempt sneers at desire and sees it as foolish and futile. Cynicism and sarcasm mock the foibles of others in order to gain safety from involvement with frail humanity or an unpredictable God.

Self-righteousness is not the bastion only of the religious; it is the fortress of all who don't want to involve themselves in the roller-coaster ride of ambivalence that comes when they care for people who will fail them. "I am all I need; I am enough," is the presumption of self-righteousness. If I need someone or something, it is only temporary and need not obligate me to anyone. It is acceptable to be involved with others as long as no one wants much or is dependent on the other. Reciprocal. Equal. Safe.

A passionate connection to a person that ultimately leads to the sacrifice of one's own identity and safety is viewed by the self-righteous as senseless, sick, and codependent. Nevertheless, the movie *Titanic*, already the top-grossing film in the history of Hollywood, turns this idea on its head, capturing individuals' hunger and willingness to give life even at the cost of their own. Our age is one of cynicism and sarcasm, well-groomed contempt, self-commitment, and pragmatism. That the general public resonated with *Titanic's* message, however, is evidence that our passion to sacrifice may be more deeply embedded in our hearts than is our desire to escape ambivalence and shame.

Why? Because we are created in God's image. No matter what we do or where we hide, we can't escape our essential design. We long to be free of shame's restraints, immersed in the passion of giving and receiving. We long to live a sacrificial life that matters today and tomorrow. But we are exhausted and depleted. We lack faith. We are afraid of hope. If we are to love well, we must first grow in faith and hope. But how? It is the allure of redemption that compels us to embark on the healing path.

The Allure of Redemption

The redemption of our hearts begins at our first cry and ends with our last breath. It is the journey that God has called us to walk even when we did not know there is a God, a journey, or a redemption. As a frightened five-year-old unaware of the hand of God, I was dragged to kindergarten and promised the world if I merely remained for one day. Then, after my four-hour ordeal, I was treated to one of the largest pieces of chocolate cake ever cut for a child. It ought not be too surprising that I anticipate heaven will include at least ten thousand years of lying at the bottom of a ten-thousand-gallon vat of moist chocolate cake. I believe I will lie at the bottom of the vat and become one with the cake, not merely orally, but through every pore of my body. There will be no possibility of drowning, nor adding unsightly pounds due to unnecessary calories.

But today I'm twenty pounds overweight. Chocolate cake is a taste of ultimate redemption and a reminder of my present lack of self-control and self-indulgence. I'm not yet completely redeemed, even if I have more of a taste of redemption than I did five years ago. Redemption, full and glorious, is still a day away. Full redemption will be pleasure that inevitably leads to celebration in community, frolicking in searching out the depths of God's goodness. The "not yet" aches in anticipation, the "already" reminds me I am not the same as I was yesterday.

I am called to live in the present, choosing to love based on the memory of redemption past and redemption future. If I refuse to trust, I will not offer myself to others, nor will I receive care from others. If I lack hope, I will not dream for others, nor desire their involvement. Faith that is founded on the memory of God's intrusion into my story and hope which is freed in the imagination of God's promise to shape my story for good combine to enable me to open my heart and live for love today. Faith and hope are the foundation of love. Evil works to destroy the integrity of the heart through doubt, despair, and shame. It labors daily to provoke betrayal, powerlessness, and ambivalence.

Many Christians seek to escape the hard task of facing damage; they want change without an honest look at life. The result is not only an incomplete redemption, but worse, a shallow grasp of grace. It is grace, the inexplicable tenderness of God to receive us and gift us with his presence, that redeems our hearts. Oddly, God uses the damage provoked by evil to win us to himself and to his purposes.

He uses doubt to grow in us a new perspective about our past, a perspective that enables us to say: "You meant it for evil; God meant it for good." He uses despair to grow a new purpose for our future that calls us to say, "His mercies are new every morning." And he uses shame to grow a new passion to sacrifice that enables us to follow the one "who for the joy set before him endured the cross, scorning its shame, and sat down at the right hand of the throne of God." Doubt, despair, and shame can't be eliminated in a fallen world, but they can be used to transform our hearts as we journey toward the staggering joy of full redemption.

PART THREE

———

THE ALLURE
OF REDEMPTION

CHAPTER 7

THE WAGER OF FAITH

---

wo truths glare at one another: (1) You can't live without trusting
someone, and (2) You can't live without being betrayed. We live
by faith. We are compelled to live by faith when we drive our
cars, fly on a plane, buy a stock. Faith involves placing our well-being into
the hands of others who we hope are committed to do us good. As I go
through a green light, I trust the other drivers' implied promise to stop at
the red light. When I invest my money, I trust my consultant is well
informed, committed to my good, knows my capacity for risk, and makes
prudent decisions.

Imagine what it would be like to mistrust everyone and operate with
suspicion in every interaction. Buying groceries would take hours. Each
item would have to be noted on paper and compared to the receipt. Each
item would have to be checked to see if it was properly scanned.
Ridiculous. Far more, such mistrust would utterly impoverish life. But the
other option is to open ourselves to unexpected and utterly certain
betrayal. Every day we make a wager of faith when we buy groceries or
cross the street.

The ultimate wager we make each day boils down to God. Is there a
God? And is God good? The author of Hebrews wrote, "And without faith
it is impossible to please God, because anyone who comes to him must
believe that he exists and that he rewards those who earnestly seek him"

(11:6). God provides enough clues to assure us of his existence and enough stories of redemption to reveal that he is good, but we can't see enough to say with incontrovertible scientific proof that God *is* or is *good*. Why? Because "Faith is being sure of what we hope for and certain of what we do not see" (11:1). God has rigged the universe so that faith requires trust— even if that trust is in oneself.

God has rigged every life with sufficient moments of splendor and delight to know he exists. How can I say that? Because creation—the stars, centipedes, and Philadelphia cheese steaks—testifies daily of his existence (Romans 1). Further, an internal gyroscope called "conscience" makes us aware every day of our own failures and the failures of others toward us. We are tuned to the channel of relationships, and we intuitively know good from bad, kindness from cruelty, delight from disdain, love from hate (Romans 2). Our past may blind us or distort what we consider good or bad, but our conscience continues to warn, chide, and rejoice in truthful loving.

When we gaze at the stars, we are struck dumb by the order, complexity, enormity, and beauty of the world. It is brazen to deny the weight of order and creative force that implies a Creator. But mere belief in God is no more life changing than belief in leprechauns or the Loch Ness monster. Such belief is intriguing but not relevant to how we invest our lives. Biblical faith requires more than an assent to God's existence. We can believe in God and still question or ignore his character. He exists, yes, but can he be trusted to be good and just, to reveal himself to us as we seek him?

My faith in God's character grows to the degree I remember God. Faith is trust in the goodness of God. I grow as I recall and recollect the stories of God in the Bible, in the lives of others, and in my own life. To recall is to name, with sufficient detail to be moved by God's presence, the life scenes or events in which he showed up as Rescuer. The external world and our internal gyroscope are never so clear that we have absolute assurance that a personal God is at work redeeming us. Instead, we have a gallery of pictures—a wall of remembrance that holds the faces of the actors in our lives who spoke their part in the play of our redemption.

Naming does not merely provide a caption for a picture; it allows the narrative of an event to be played out in our mind. Recall writes the play not so much as it merely happened but as we see it—recording the external and internal moments of what occurred; adding motivation, emotion, and suspense to the scene.

Recall (the naming of events) takes us to recollection (the ordering of events). Recollection is like arranging photos in an album. Rather than merely sticking pictures randomly in an album, we give meaning to each one by ordering them according to time, event, or person. We form a collection. A collection has a dominant theme that, in its separate parts, tells a story. Faith grows as we name the moments in which God appeared and rescued us and then gains a sense of the meaning of those moments for the rest of our lives. Memory is the key to faith.

The dilemma is that as I remember the moments where God has redeemed me, I am also left with the many moments he has chosen, apparently, to abandon me or—even more painful to admit—betray me. Many will say, "God never abandons and certainly never betrays." True. But then why are those sentiments a consistent complaint of the faithful who follow God (see Psalm 13, 39, 44, 88)? When we remember, we also suffer and groan (Psalm 77). We recall and recollect moments of horror that were not (apparently) redeemed and moments of glory that (apparently) ended prematurely.

We suffer when we remember. And as we suffer, we doubt. It is doubt that sends us on a search to comprehend God. And it is that search that leads us not so much to God as much as it brings God to find us. Do we find God? Indeed, but only because he finds us first. And it is in the wonder of being found that we enter a place of rest and stability that gives us not only faith, but a sense of our identity and calling.

God is telling a story. His story. He is intimately involved in the passing minutes of every one of my days and every one of yours. He also orchestrates and tells our stories. He is both author and narrator. Faith increases to the degree we are aware of, caught up in, enthralled by, and participating in his and our story.

REMEMBERING GOD'S STORIES

Nearly 70 percent of the Bible is written in narrative form. God is a story-teller who weaves his presence into every story in the Bible, even into stories where the name of God or the actions of God are not even mentioned, as in the book of Esther. He tells many kinds of stories, some in the form of history, others with a rich poetic style. Some would get at least a PG-13 (if not R) rating if shown at a local theater.

How does God tell a story? With drama. He tells stories that excite, confuse, entice, disrupt, and change the human heart. Drama involves a beginning, with setting, characters, and a search or problem to be solved, then a middle, with a plot that has tension, risk, and resolution, and then an ending that closes the story. As Don Hudson has written, every redemptive story has a beginning in innocence, moments of tragedy that bring a rise in tension and imagination, and a resolution that instills confidence and invigorates hope.[1]

The stories God weaves and tells are ones that take us to the very edge of our seat. Consider the Exodus, a foundational story about the consciousness and articulation of the identity of God's people. It is the core story, essential for understanding the historical books, prophets, and wisdom literature. The story takes many twists and turns, from Moses' encounter with the burning bush to his refusal to speak, God's appointment of Aaron, the plagues, the death of the firstborn, Passover, the departure from Egypt, and then Pharaoh's pursuit to seek revenge. In a classic scene Pharaoh's army is about to attack God's people:

> As Pharaoh approached, the Israelites looked up, and there were the Egyptians, marching after them. They were terrified and cried out to the LORD. They said to Moses, "Was it because there were no graves in Egypt that you brought us to the desert to die? What have you done to us by bringing us out of Egypt? Didn't we say to you in Egypt, 'Leave us alone; let us serve the Egyptians'? It would have been better for us to serve the Egyptians than to die in the desert!" Moses answered the people, "Do not be afraid. Stand firm and you will see the deliverance the LORD will bring you today. The Egyptians you see today you will never see again. The LORD will fight for you; you need only to be still." (Exodus 14:10-14)

The people of God, fickle and afraid, mock Moses and therefore doubt God. God has allowed the horses of Pharaoh to be so close the Israelites can see the breath from their nostrils. He brings the story to a narrative climax full of drama, uncertainty, danger, and death. Why? He could have avoided all the drama. He could easily have had his people pass into the Promised Land with little fanfare and intrigue; instead, the story blazes with breathtaking suspense, irony, and humor. Humor? Indeed, even God gets tired of Moses praying and responds, "Why are you crying out to me? Tell the Israelites to move on." In Exodus 14:15 he virtually says, "Enough religion. Now do something."

Why such drama? Drama rouses our interest as observers; it brings our senses, passions, and soul to their peak of attention—especially when it is our drama. We are made alive, thrown out of the predictable, safe ruts of daily existence. In a tragic and wonderful sense, it is suspense and drama that brings out the reality of what is in our hearts. The people of God are pushed against the Red Sea, and when their backs are against the wall, they turn against God. Drama reveals. It exposes us and allows the work of God to proceed in our lives.

We love drama; we are drawn to tragedy—until it becomes part of our story. Then we don't like to live drama's roller-coaster ride, nor do we like to recall past losses, betrayals, and heartache, because they shake our desire for stability. As a therapist, I have been asked thousands of times, "Why remember? Why return to times that were so painful when I can think about happy thoughts and not feel bad?" The answer is simple and often not compelling to the person in pain: because our past, especially our pain, holds the key to our future and to the joy set before us. Our past is a treasure map that, read well, can lead us to vast abundance.

Sorrow cannot steal our faith or even cause it to be lost; betrayal and loss steal our faith only when we refuse to remember, tell our stories, listen even as we tell them, and explore the meaning that God has woven into every one. If we want to grow in faith we must be open to listening to our own stories, perhaps familiar or forgotten, where we have not mined the rich deposit of God's presence. With better eyes and ears we will sense how God has worked to redeem even our most tragic experiences.

In *The Prince of Tides*, author Pat Conroy tells the story of a family riddled with abuse and decadence. In one horrific scene, the family is assaulted by a number of escaped criminals who rape the mother and two of the children. When the oldest brother returns home and hears the commotion, he peers in the window and sees the debacle. Helpless to stop the assault against his family, he approaches the cage where the family keeps a barely trained tiger, and he lets the tiger free in the house.

The younger brother, Tom, who is being raped, later says: "When those men picked our home to wreck havoc, they chose wrong." The tiger, familiar with the family, bypassed them and ripped the strangers to pieces. Those criminals chose wrong. And that story, sodden with horror, brought Tom and his family hope that redemption, odd and unpredictable, might come again.

It is our personal stories that not only bring us comfort and confidence, but confuse and overwhelm us as well. We are in the midst of a story war.

THE STORY OF WAR

One story can change our life. One story remembered can resurrect our future. In every heart there is a war to determine the central story or stories that will shape our perspective of life. Each of us asks the existential question, *Is God really telling a good story, and is my life one of his great stories?* How we answer will determine whether we are on the path toward healing or toward destruction.

There are two central stories that have shaped my own view and experience of life. The first involves an older man's invitation to relationship. He enjoyed me, listened to me, and shared hours of hiking where he introduced me to glistening leaves and flowers and told me the Latin names of trees. I was enthralled and proud that this mentor had so clearly chosen me over countless other Boy Scouts.

Then the hour came when his slow, sensitive care drew me to a car far from our campsite, and he asked me to touch him sexually. I ran. I remember feeling fear, confusion, and intrigue. I also felt fury. Not at him. At myself. It would be over now if only I had touched him. I knew intuitively the rejection of his request would bring our relationship to an end. It did.

In many ways this event served as a pair of glasses that colored my view of every other relationship. One is either a predator or a pawn. At best, one can escape either horrible option by remaining disengaged and distant. At worst, it is inevitable that the cycle of betrayal-hurt-anger-vengeance-betraying will go on ad nauseam. This early story influenced my disdain toward authority and instilled a deep suspicion toward mentors or anyone who offered me care. I remained suspicious of and hostile toward most relationships.

A second story involves a divine setup to relationship. I met my wife, Becky, in high school. She was beautiful, kind, and mysterious. I was terrified to ask her out, but I talked with her often in the hallway. Years after high school I ran into her over spring break in Florida, far from our Midwestern roots. We spent the day together and went to a party that night. She invited me to call her at her hotel the next day.

Time passed and I didn't call. Several days later I was at the airport and discovered I had accidentally picked up a friend's one-way ticket to Florida. I was in a huge jam. The attendant had taken my bags, in which I had foolishly hidden my wallet, and checked them onto the plane. When the ticket agent realized I had a void ticket he wouldn't get the bag off the plane. I was broke and stranded.

For some reason, I remembered Becky and knew she was likely driving back home that day with three other friends. It was 5 A.M. In a haze I frantically tried to recall the name of her hotel. The Beach something or other. I could not remember, so I tore open a phone book and found a full page of Beach something-or-other motels. I got change for the three dollars in my pocket and began calling. "Is a Becky Gilbert registered?" Repeatedly, the answer was no. After countless calls, I began asking, "Are there four girls from Ohio?" I was met with silence or mockery. Then I began asking, "Do you see four girls or a white Toyota?" Each call was met with irritation or indifference.

After spending nearly all my money I heard another hotel clerk say, "No Becky Gilbert. Girls? How do I know where they are from? No, I'm not going out in the parking lot to look for a white Toyota." I was a second from hanging up when I heard him say, "Wow. Hold on. There is a white Toyota with four girls leaving the lot right now." He ran out and asked if Becky was in the car. She answered the phone and I told her my plight. I rode back to Ohio with Becky and on the way fell madly in love with her. We parted ways in Ohio and did not see each other again for nearly five years, but the time allowed many other stories to converge that brought us both into relationship with God and then with each other.

I can't recall that story without shuddering. It was so close. Any of hundreds of factors might have intervened to keep us from driving home together that weekend. Any of a thousand factors could have kept us from meeting years later. Maybe we would have met at another time; maybe we wouldn't have. That drive home shaped my future by bringing me face to face with a woman, my wife, who has brought change to every area of my life and helped shape my heart, education, career, calling, family, and eternity. Without that moment, I simply would not be me; I would be so "other," so impossible to conceive, that I can claim that without that moment "I" would not exist.

It is harder to admit that the moment with my childhood abuser was equally life- and eternity-shaping. As tragic and contrary as that event was to the revealed will of God, I can peer back over the span of thirty years since it occurred and say, "When he chose my house, he chose wrong." In many ways, my abuser set the course not only for my heartache and struggles, but also for my redemption and calling. I do not thank him for abusing me (that would be obscene), but it was through the harm he caused that God eventually brought onto the stage of my story the characters, plot, and meaning of my life.

Every person alive has legions of stories of heartache and shame, loneliness and betrayal. But every human being also has at least one story of redemption that is full of surprise and delight. We all have at least one experience with a kind, affirming person who believed in us. Perhaps there are many who would say, "Not me." But look more closely. The story may not be richly personal or involve a long and enduring relationship, but we have all known a teacher who liked us, or a janitor who smiled when we walked by his work station. Even those fleeting moments are humanity mirroring the delight of God. And in those moments of delight, when someone's face brightened because of us, we tasted a morsel of redemption.

It is in that one story (and likely many more) that we can't deny or forget that God wooed us to the desert to redeem us. The process is not easy or mechanical, but the healing path of remembering our stories points toward God's inconceivable, slow-moving, strange plan of redemption. Betrayal strips us of story, connection, and intimacy. Memory serves to return us to at least one story of rescue.

But memory also brings to the surface other events of heartache and loss. *Why?* is the cry of the human soul. *Why did he allow that harm? Why did he not save me here?* Remembering our stories does not usually lead immediately to growth in faith. More often than not, when we remember even our most precious moments of peace, the peace is disrupted by memories that lead us back into doubt.

THE DISRUPTION OF SHALOM

A man I counseled said, "When I think about my past, I'm sad and confused. When I ignore my past, I'm happy. It seems quite simple: I need to forget my past and just look forward."

Simple? No. In fact, this view is quite silly. That's because we can only look forward and imagine the future from the standpoint of what we already know and have already learned. Perspective is built on cumulative memory. Without memory, there is no future—as in the tragedy of Alzheimer's disease. But my client's words were accurate: "When I remember, I'm sad and confused."

We strive for order, coherence, and wholeness in our lives. We want certainty. We long for shalom. Shalom is a peace that not only recalls all the pieces of one's life but sees how the parts fit together in a unified and glorious whole. Shalom involves rest and gratitude; it provides a momentary balance and harmony where all things seem right. We know few moments of this peace, but it is not unfamiliar to us. We can recall lying next to the heat vent as a child, pressing our cold feet against the grate and feeling cozy and warm. I used to love falling asleep in the backseat as we drove home from my grandmother's house. To this day, to be lulled to sleep in a moving car is a taste of innocence and shalom for me.

Disruption of shalom is the soil God uses to grow us to become the people we are meant to be. When we are disrupted by illness or death, the goal of spiritual maturity is seldom at the forefront of our thinking nor much comfort in our pain. But God knows that joy—real, succulent pleasure—is being like him. And we will not move to become like him and know the sweet joy he desires for us if we are comfortable where we are. When our peace is shattered, the resulting doubt and confusion send us on a deeply personal search that can transform us and lead us to abundant joy.

A client I worked with was a splendid man. He was gracious, kind, willing to sacrifice his time, money, and energy. He was well-liked and universally respected. He was a nice guy. He was a good father and a faithful spouse. But his wife was lonely and felt crazy for feeling angry at her "perfect" husband. In fact, he approached life with condescending, patronizing spiritual platitudes and a refined distance that she could never bridge. When she hurt deeply he would comfort her with barely hidden disdain.

For many years she suffered his mastery of life until she could bear it no longer. She left him. Of course, the Christian community offered him solace and condemned her betrayal. His view of himself was neither assaulted nor shaken. If anything, he was even more the good boy who suffered greatly for righteousness.

But in the months after his wife's departure, his solid and sure identity began to show signs of crumbling. His spiritual smugness was not as florid as in the past; he actually asked people to pray for *him*—not just their marriage or her heart. He began to question God and himself. He doubted God and pleaded, "How could you allow this to happen?" His searching, somewhat self-righteous questions set him up for a life-changing moment.

A pastor who had worked with him for years in various ministries came to him and asked for time to pray for him. He readily agreed. The pastor simply said, "I know your wife is wrong for leaving you. But if I were her, I'd have left you a long time ago. She is wrong, but your self-righteousness and spiritual superiority make her sin look like the pristine, driven snow. Let me pray for the disdain in your heart."

My client was stunned. He did not hear a word the pastor prayed; he was reeling with the word: disdain. He felt so betrayed, confused, hurt. Nothing could be further from the truth! He was a good man who had loved his difficult and demanding wife.

That night he fell into sobs that wracked him for hours. He recalled how often he had felt distance and disdain toward his absorbing and childish mother. Memory upon memory of her absorption and his disdainful defense against her pounded against his stilted heart. He found himself fighting to retain the image of himself as a nice man rather than admitting himself to be self-righteous and disdainful. It was a war of stories.

Finally, he heard God whisper, "Are you as afraid of being absorbed by me as you were terrified of being absorbed by your mom?" He confessed to God that he was. His confusion began to lift as he recognized how he had used disdain against his wife and every other human being—except for Mr. Jameson, his debate coach. He had loved his coach. He had suffered to make him proud, and no matter how well or how poorly he performed in a debate, Mr. Jameson always seemed thrilled to be with him.

Faces flashed on the screen of his memory. His mother. His wife. His coach. His coworkers, friends, and church family. Suddenly he clearly saw that he had never been a man like Mr. Jameson to anyone, especially to his wife. His heart felt oddly free in facing his dark, self-righteous cruelty and his deep hunger to love and be loved like he was once before.

Must all stories of redemption have such a dramatic script? Indeed, they must. But every story may not appear dramatic to those who hear it. I recall the moment when my middle daughter, Amanda, calmly pointed out that I had a large bald spot. I laughed and said, "No, I don't." I soon got a mirror and looked at the back of my head. I gasped. A large, white skull peered back at me, and in an instant I had a glimpse of my midage decline. Over the next few weeks God sent a series of moments my way that helped me see I could not do what I used to do, nor match up on the tennis court to younger players. When someone said to me, "You need to think about playing with people your age," I nearly dropped my jaw. Mortality, limits, and decay are hard to face. Once faced, they need to be embraced time and time again. This slow process, hardly dramatic to others, is intensely compelling to us.

All these stories disrupt our shalom and send us reeling into confusion and doubt. When the disruption compels us to search, we eventually find ourselves in a corner where we are forced to turn and stand face to face with God.

When will we encounter God? We can't predict. How will it change us when we do? We can't explain. But we remember moments when the search led us not to find, but to be found. We all know odd moments of epiphany that shake us to our bones with his presence and his words for us. And those moments lead us not only to trust him (a little bit more), but they serve as the foundation for our growing sense of who we are and who we are meant to become. Memories serve to form our identity.

THE REMEMBERED SELF

Who am I? I cannot know myself, nor can others know me, without speech and actions. I am my lived and told stories. Researchers in memory have discovered that we remember the past not as a picture or even as a video-tape that records the sequence of events that occurred, but rather as a story invested with meaning, interpretation, bias, and continuity. Often the parts we do not remember or the transitions from one portion of an event to another are gaps we fill in by inference, deduction, and imagination. It is not that we make up the past; instead, we encode and retrieve scenes with the aid of a narrative structure. If the scenes we remember do not make sense, we will link the elements we do recall with bridges that provide continuity and meaning.

We organize the stories of our lives into schemas that summarize the data as a unified whole. In many ways our memories are like images that flash on a screen, connected but not smooth and orderly. It is only when we tell our story or write our memories in a journal that they attain a systematization or story order. Once the story is told, we can begin to see the schema or theme that holds the memory together.

A schema is an organizing category that uses a word, a picture, or a sign to synthesize complex elements into a coherent whole. For example, if someone asked, "How was the movie *Titanic*?" The response might be, "It's a tragic love story with enough action to keep men involved." The schema is "love story with danger and violence."

We use schemas to summarize complex political views ("moderate"), religious persuasion ("high church"), and economic data ("old money"). So if we say, "He is a moderate, attends a high church, and comes from old money," we could somewhat reasonably assume the person does not drive a Volkswagen bug, listen to Jerry Garcia, nor sport shoulder-length hair. Schemas allow us to summarize, predict, and make judgments about our world.

We remember an individual event or story by employing a schema to encode, store, and retrieve the memory at a later time. Imagine that your memories are stored in bins marked with summary schemas and then sorted out on the basis of their intensity, vividness, repetitiveness, connection with other memories, and relationship to enduring concerns and unresolved conflicts. You may find that one memory (or several) in the bin symbolizes others that are not retrieved. For example, you likely have a few memories of elementary-school shame, but you don't recall the majority of events that made you feel awkward and small. It's as if one memory serves as a schema for the other memories.

We are wired to take in experience and hold it up to the light of what we know while allowing what we know to be changed by new data. We do that by creating "summary structures" that work from the global to the particular, and then reshape the global from new particulars. For example, we might learn from a racist father that all Jewish people are stingy. But then we meet a gracious, giving Jewish man who forces us to rethink—that is, rename and then recollect—the data in a new schema.

We each develop a schema, or theme, that crystallizes our many varied and asymmetrical parts into a unified whole. We are unable to function without organizing masses of data into summary themes. When I try to describe my wife to a stranger I often say, "I have never known anyone more kind and equally more sneaky and wild." The words *kind, sneaky,* and *wild* are theme words. If my hearer asked about sneaky and wild, I would say, "Let me tell you about our second day of marriage when she hid in a closet and scared me out of my senses, and I fell into a plant and then the bed."

Themes order stories. Stories give rise to themes. Who am I? It depends on which story, and therefore which theme, is most true: the story of my abuse (betrayal, suspicion, anger) or the story of my redemption in meeting Becky (redemption, surprise, joy). I can be harsh, acerbic, suspicious, and distant—in which case, I am little more than my past abuse. I can also be gentle, kind, whimsical, and wild—and then I am the story of how God introduced me to my wife.

Of course, I am the product of all my stories, but I can consciously embrace the stories I know to be most uniquely me. I was damaged by abuse. I was redeemed by my wife. I was harmed by many events, and I was won by God through only a few. Which have the greatest power? It is worth noting that few books, movies, TV shows, or oral stories end in disaster, chaos, and meaninglessness. Why? Because redemption touches us more deeply than tragedy. But without tragedy there could be no redemption.

God is at work redeeming me. He weaves my personal stories around specific themes and characters in order to shape my identity to reveal his unique being. I was abused, and I know the beginning of my redeemed story. My story changes daily, and the telling of old and familiar stories often takes on new depth and meaning.

Not only do my stories change, but so does my guiding schema. My schema changes as God disrupts my life. And God disrupts my life every time shalom is shaken. But it is not only disruption that shapes my new schema—it is also the moments of closure and resolution. Even though our stories are ongoing, occasionally we get to see the end of a chapter. When the chapter ends well and our heart is at rest with shalom, then we are compelled to make the wager that God not only exists, but he is good.

THE WAGER OF FAITH

Most days I don't see the drama of God's story in my own. I get up. I go to work. I come home. I watch the news. I eat dinner. I read, talk with my kids and wife, watch a video, and go to bed. Most of us don't live on-the-edge, dramatic lives. But there are moments when I turn a corner and

God is waiting for me. Truly. I can't say for sure it is God, because then I would have perfect sight, but I sense the mystery of the ages playing out in my small life. I know there are divine encounters, strange appointments with a person, a book, or an event that change my day, my life, forever.

How could I know that in one counseling session, like thousands before it, a woman would ask me out of the blue, "What do you know about sexual abuse?" The question came in 1986. I was a professional therapist who had worked with people for eight years. I knew little to nothing about sexual abuse, but I didn't want to appear stupid to my client. I also didn't want to lie. Thankfully I told the truth. "I know little to nothing." She looked at me and said, "I know. If you are willing to work with me, I will teach you everything I know about it." Like no other moment in my career, that one marked the beginning of a healing path that has taken me through barren deserts and deep valleys to the face of God.

Go figure. Who? What? When? Where? How? Why does God make himself shine in certain ordinary or tragic moments and not in others? I don't know. All I know is that God intrudes into my daily story in extraordinary ways.

The ancient Greeks knew two kinds of time: *chronos* and *chairos*. Chronos is clock time—the grind of daily routine. Chairos is a moment of glory—an epiphany when God shows up and begins a new epoch, a new life. It was a chairos moment when I dialed the number that would reach Becky before she began her drive back to Ohio; the same is true of the moment my Scout leader asked me to touch him. God is not revealed only in the good and happy moments but in any moment that transforms our souls, that defines and fortifies our life schema or crushes and reconfigures it.

The wager of faith is that God is telling his story through mine—that he exists and he is good. He told two core stories, the Exodus and the

Cross; all other human stories will mirror to some degree the drama of his rescue and redemption. The wager is played out each time I recall (that is, name my memories) and recollect (order them by discovering their meaning).

Few people have a list of the scenes that have shaped their lives. Fewer still have written out the scenes in narrative fashion. And even fewer have even asked the question, "What are the themes of my stories?" It is not enough to ask, "What is God trying to teach me?"; far more, we must ask, "What does God want me to become?" We get a glimpse of the answer only by considering the themes of our stories.

To discover our themes, we must listen to the core stories of our life. We must listen in the same way we embrace a friend: with open arms, waiting, anticipating, holding, and then letting go. It is not something done in a day; it is a lifelong process. But in calling forth our core stories, we must also participate in the ordering of them. Themes don't smack us in the face when we look for them; instead, we must actively arrange, rearrange, and create the order that makes the most sense at any given point in our lives.

My client who faced his defensive flight from his absorptive mother embraced the core theme of his life: self-righteous disdain. Was this truly the man he was meant to be? He knew the answer was no because of his love for Mr. Jameson. My client entered the story war and recalled scenes with his mother and Mr. Jameson. His mother severed his confidence by her demanding emptiness. Mr. Jameson, on the other hand, offered him delight and kindness and invited him to be human. The war challenges us to choose which story we cling to as the deepest schema, the most central story of our life.

This war-torn man won the battle of stories: He heard and answered the call of Mr. Jameson and turned from the priggish self-righteousness that had kept his mother at a distance. As a result, not only did his wife reenter relationship with him, but he became one of the few voices in his rigid church to speak of the horror of self-righteousness.

The wager of faith is simple: Which stories will win my heart? My client's memories of events involving his mother outnumbered those involving Mr. Jameson by the thousands. But which face would he decide was more like God's? Which story would claim his heart? The wager is won only when even the smallest story of redemption means more to us than the greatest betrayal and loss.

But how is one to believe, to have or live with faith when there are few such stories in one's life? How is one to grow in faith when the stories of loss and betrayal not only outweigh in number, but drastically outweigh in intensity, the stories of redemption?

SEED FAITH

The stories of betrayal and redemption compete in me for my soul. I believe, and I don't believe. I am both a man of faith and unfaith. I trust in the God revealed in the Bible, and I still doubt at times that he exists and that he is good. How am I to grow when my faith seems so small?

Jesus shocked his disciples when he told them how much faith is needed to deal with terrible harm:

> Jesus said to his disciples: "Things that cause people to sin are bound to come, but woe to that person through whom they come. It would be better for him to be thrown into the sea with a millstone tied around his neck than for him to cause one of these little ones to sin. So watch yourselves.
>
> "If your brother sins, rebuke him, and if he repents, forgive him. If he sins against you seven times in a day, and seven times comes back to you and says, 'I repent,' forgive him."

The apostles said to the Lord, "Increase our faith!"

He replied, "If you have faith as small as a mustard seed, you can say to this mulberry tree, 'Be uprooted and planted in the sea,' and it will obey you. (Luke 17:1-6)

There are times when I think the Lord gloried in disturbing his disciples. This passage distresses me every time I read it. It startles me with the ferocity of his condemnation of betrayers, saying that death is better than harming the innocent. Equally striking is his rapid turn to forgive, once there is repentance, the one he just condemned to death. Even if the harm occurs again and again.

The severity of his condemnation and the equally severe depths of forgiveness boggle, infuriate the soul. He can't be serious! Could he possibly be saying I am to forgive the abuser if he repents and then repeats the harm again and then repents?

There is no stronger statement about betrayal in the Bible. If you take advantage of a little one and violate him in any way that breaks his trust, then it is better to throw yourself into the deepest part of the sea with a weight around your neck that takes you quickly to your death. Unless of course, you repent. Then a sin equal to the first might occur: unforgiveness. The original betrayal is worthy of death; the second sin—unforgiveness— is a betrayal of the gospel. Jesus links both sides of the coin—the betrayer and the betrayed—and says, "Each must come to grips with his greatest need: The betrayer is to repent, and the betrayed is to forgive. And not just once but again and again and again."

His disciples wince and ask for more faith; Jesus' response is (almost) to mock them and then glory in the power of even the smallest, teeniest amount of faith. The mustard seed was the smallest seed known in the time of Christ, but it grows into a huge tree. Jesus essentially says, "You could recreate the earth with the teeniest morsel of faith. And instead of seeing a human being, a sinner worthy of death, drowned in the sea, you could plant a tree from nothing and actually grow its roots in the same sea." Either drown yourself or uproot trees that will grow in water.

Jesus appears crazy; of course, he is brilliant. Forgive? Insane. Forgive again and again? Absurd and ridiculous. But wouldn't it be fun to invert the world? By a speck of faith uproot trees and plant them in the sea and grow fruit with a bobbing miracle of redemption. We long for the world to be reordered and changed. Without always acknowledging it, we truly long to be restored to those who have betrayed us and to those we have betrayed. It is the siren call of shalom.

"But I doubt," you say. "I'm hurt. I'm angry and I don't like the way my story is being told. I want relief and I want peace and joy; instead, Jesus calls me to cancel the debt of the one who deserves to die and then garden in the ocean?"

Jesus breaks down our schema of life, our view of right and wrong, justice and peace. He inverts reality as we see it to recreate the world as it was meant to be if sin were not blinding our eyes. And with a story he calls us to hunger for what our souls know they desire: Peace. Joy. Redemption. Our faith is small, our anger enormous, our memory dull, but the story rings true and clear, and we can't escape the story of the Cross.

What then is faith? It is the childlike wonder in a story so good it can't be true, but deep down to our toes we know if it is not true then we don't exist.

My story involves betrayal and loss. I want my abusers to drown. Instead, I find the story has taken me, like Scrooge in *A Christmas Carol*, on a journey that reveals the emptiness, futility, and harm of my own betrayal. Suddenly I am the one who is meant to drown. Instead, One throws himself into the sea of sin on my behalf and I am pardoned, freed from any penalty. And where there was a drowning man moments ago, there rises a tree of fruit from a seed that was inconsequential.

The story is better than *Rambo*. It is better than *Rocky*. *Hoosiers*. *The Color Purple*. *Titanic*. It is a story of such suspense, drama, irony, complexity, and simplicity that all I can do is marvel, *I have a part*. My part is to forgive on the basis of knowing I am forgiven—to bless betrayal as that which first prompts my flight from God and then reveals he is faithful, loyal, and true.

CHAPTER 8

THE DREAM OF HOPE

T

he door to their daughter's hospital room clicked shut behind them as John and Maria followed the doctor into the hallway. The physician looked straight at Maria and said, "Your daughter is not improving. Her white-cell count has dropped, and she is not responding to the treatment. I'm not optimistic about her outcome."

John's mind raced at the word "outcome." The doctor meant Jennifer was going to die. Leukemia was her killer. The physician did not suggest any other treatment options, nor did he offer even a hint of hope. He said nothing more than that he would be in touch if anything changed. As he turned and walked toward another patient's room, his day was just beginning. Life for Maria and John seemed like it was coming to an end.

Their daughter died five weeks later. As summer faded away, Maria watched other kids in the neighborhood prepare for the first day of school with new lunch boxes, backpacks filled with empty folders, unmarked pads of paper, and nervous excitement. Maria looked out her living-room window and hid behind the curtains. Her face was stained with tears and her hands gripped the cloth with vengeance.

As each child bounded by her house, she felt her heart break. Her daughter should be racing down the stairs, late as she always was except in death, and running with her friends to the first day of school. Maria watched the street empty as the bus filled with life, drove away, and left her with only memories and broken dreams.

Maria told me she had never felt so impotent and empty. She wanted to grab one of Jenny's dresses and a pair of her shoes and drive them to school. She knew the urge was bizarre and irrational, but she felt like she was betraying her daughter by not taking her clothes to school. She imagined what she would do once she got there with a dress and shoes, and she saw herself fall down in the middle of the school, pleading with God to bring her daughter back to her.

She knew nothing would bring her daughter back. Her strong urge to drive to school died inside her, but so did all desire in general. It was the first time Maria truly realized her daughter was dead. It was the first time she knew that nothing, including the public humiliation of herself and God, would bring her daughter back. It was the day all her desire, all her dreams died.

Maria suffered with depression for months. She lost a vision for her future because she had no hope that life could offer purpose or joy any longer. Maria was caught in a vortex of powerlessness and despair.

A MADDENING CALL

Most of our days are spent in familiar and often pleasant routine. Years may pass with normal ups and downs, gains and losses, but life can change irrevocably in a moment. Most days we don't feel powerless, but when a stormy moment blows in and rips the roof off our souls, we stand naked and impotent to change the course of the winds. We are powerless to keep tragedy at bay.

When the storms come, we typically respond to them by raging against the gale or turning away from the loss, resigned and despondent. Most choose the latter option, because once we relinquish desire the loss does not seem so severe. But resignation is always a betrayal, not only of desire but also of hope.

Hope is the quiet, sometimes incessant call to dream for the future. The present moment is not enough to satisfy our souls completely; no matter how good or bad, the now leaves us hungering for more. And our insatiable quest for more is the root system of biblical hope. Hope cannot be killed, not ever, but it can be drugged numb and sleepy. Even then it will still function, but in a more material and simplistic manner akin to wishing to win the lottery or anticipating the purchase of a new car.

Biblical hope is substantial faith regarding the future. Hope looks at the shattered remnants of the soul hit by the storm and envisions not merely rebuilding, but rebuilding a life that has even more purpose and meaning than existed before the loss. Hope is the dream of shalom, the anticipation of joy that courses through us and prompts us to rise and rebuild, to envision and risk for what is not yet. Hope takes the experience of loss and powerlessness and uses it as the raw material for writing a new and unexpected story.

When we lose hope, we stop remembering and telling stories that arouse our desire and anticipation. Our thoughts become narrow, focused on loss rather than on what will one day be sure and true.

As Maria's depression deepened, she wisely chose to see a physician who prescribed antidepressant medication. The drugs helped, but the deepest change occurred when Maria and John began to tell stories about their daughter. Jenny was precocious and wise beyond her years; many stories about her brought both tears and laughter. But for the first three months after her death, John and Maria did not tell those stories, and they seemed to be forgotten. But as they began to remember and tell the stories, they wept together rather than apart. As they wept they also began slowly to laugh. And as they laughed they felt an odd relief and surprise: They felt hope. They did not falsely hope their loss could be filled or removed; they knew it would be a wound for the rest of their lives. Instead, they began to hope that, in some way, God would bring them moments of peace and joy that would never be erased in this life, in spite of their sorrow.

God confuses us as he allows harm and heartache to enter our lives. But oddly, in the midst of loss, he also confirms his love in a way that is both mysterious and maddening. Maddening! God disturbs us and then woos us and wins us.

Why must the healing path involve such suffering? Nothing can fully explain God's intent or make suffering seem good, but we are left with an odd connection between loss and comfort in Jesus' words: "Blessed are those who mourn, for they will be comforted" (Matthew 5:4). The juxtaposition is so striking as to render the statement either insane or truer than true. Blessed means happy, full of joy, overflowing with bounty. His words are pleasantly poetic until leukemia kills your daughter or your son is run over by your car. Then this promise becomes either a sweet, anemic truism or a surging, life-changing truth.

Paul describes the suffering of life in the terms "light and momentary," compared to the weight of glory that awaits our homecoming. He says,

> Therefore we do not lose heart. Though outwardly we are wasting away, yet inwardly we are being renewed day by day. For our light and momentary troubles are achieving for us an eternal glory that far outweighs them all. So we fix our eyes not on what is seen, but on what is unseen. For what is seen is temporary, but what is unseen is eternal. (2 Corinthians 4:16-18)

Sometimes when I read Paul's words I'd like to hit him. My suffering, though minor compared to John and Maria's, seems anything but light and momentary. How did Paul achieve that perspective? How did he come to so anticipate heaven that all else paled in significance?

There are two aspects of growing hope: to see with the eyes of faith that which is not now but will one day be, and that which is now and will one day be even better. Only the lenses of faith can put suffering into perspective. When faith enables us to remember how God has redeemed portions of our past, our anticipation of when and how he will redeem us in the future increases. Faith is the foundation for hope; hope is the wind in the sails that takes faith forward into the future.

HOPE: A MEMORY OF THE FUTURE

Faith and hope are inseparably linked. Faith is hope regarding our past; hope is faith regarding our future. Gabriel Marcel defined hope as "a memory of the future." In his elegantly simple and profoundly surprising phrase he links our future with our past; faith with hope. The writer of the book of Hebrews does the same: "Now faith is being sure of what we hope for and certain of what we do not see" (11:1). If I have faith, then I will hope; if I do not have faith, then I am not likely to anticipate the future with joy.

Hope is not to be understood as a mere wish. If I say, "I hope the weather is good for the wedding tomorrow," I have used the word hope to mean desire or wish. Biblical hope, unlike a wish, is solid and sure; if Christ came the first time, then I can be equally sure he will return again.

Does that mean our hope is only for heaven? Indeed, it does and it doesn't. We can say as believers that since Jesus came, he will come again. The promise of his coming and our resurrection in the future is the surfeit, or superabundance, that flows into our uncertain present. The far future infuses hope into our near future. The far future (which may come tomorrow or in ten thousand years) is certain: He will come and all things will be redeemed beyond our wildest imagination. The far future spills over into the near future—not with the promise that the wedding day will be dry or our daughter will be healed, but with the promise that rain and death can't steal the purpose God has stamped into our being. Confidence in the far future is the safety net that allows us to play on the high wire of the present and near future.

Even though it infuses the present, biblical hope is essentially unseen. It is beyond the horizon of all empirical and felt experience. Instead, it is based on the promise of One who has shown himself to be a faithful witness. The Word of God is our faithful witness of what will come. What is our hope centered upon? On the Day of the Lord.

HOPE IN HIS COMING

In the Old Testament the Day of the Lord was the beginning of radical, total, cosmic change. The Day of the Lord was divided into two parts: destruction of all that is of darkness (Isaiah 13:9; 27:1; Jeremiah 46:10; Ezekiel 30:3; Joel 2:31) and restoration, reconciliation, and blessing for all who are of the light (Isaiah 28:5; 60:19; Zechariah 9:16). The prophet Isaiah gives the day dramatic flavor:

> On this mountain the LORD Almighty will prepare
> > a feast of rich food for all peoples,
> a banquet of aged wine—
> > the best of meats and the finest of wines.
> On this mountain he will destroy
> > the shroud that enfolds all peoples,
> the sheet that covers all nations;
> > he will swallow up death forever.
> The Sovereign LORD will wipe away the tears
> > from all faces;

he will remove the disgrace of his people
>   from all the earth.
>   The LORD has spoken.

In that day they will say,

"Surely this is our God;
>   we trusted in him, and he saved us.
This is the LORD, we trusted in him;
>   let us rejoice and be glad in his salvation."

The hand of the LORD will rest on this mountain;
>   but Moab will be trampled under him
>   as straw is trampled down in the manure.
They will spread out their hands in it,
>   as a swimmer spreads out his hands to swim.
God will bring down their pride
>   despite the cleverness of their hands.
He will bring down your high fortified walls
>   and lay them low;
he will bring them down to the ground,
>   to the very dust. (Isaiah 25:6-12)

Hope in the far future is tied to our hunger in the present. Food, sex, and violence are the doorways of the present that lead us to anticipating the Day of the Lord. It is our insatiable hunger for *more* that increases our desire for the Day of the Lord. It may seem scandalous (God usually is) to tie the far future (or heaven) to food, sex, and violence, but it was God's idea. The Day of the Lord is depicted in Scripture as a cosmic wedding feast that brings the bride together with the bridegroom to eat and drink and anticipate the first night of sexual union. It is also a day of destruction that puts the face of evil into muck, drowns it, and then rips it to shreds with the wheels of victorious chariots. In simple terms, it is the end of every good movie, book, and story. The villain is paid back; justice reigns. The divided are brought back together; mercy shines bright and glorious.

Our desire to see what is not now materialize later increases our hunger for that day. Take the time I talked with my father after he returned from a chemotherapy treatment. He was weak and frail. He had a portable phone and was talking to me as he walked to the upstairs bathroom. He said he was feeling ill and may need to hang up quickly. When he got to the doorway he stumbled, and I heard him crash to the floor. The phone fell out of his hands and slid out of his reach. He began vomiting. For the next twenty minutes I listened helplessly as he purged the poison out of his system.

I was powerless. I could do nothing. At first I wanted to hang up so I did not have to hear his retching nor feel my rage and battle with my urge to withdraw. Instead, I stayed on the phone and prayed for him and dreamt of the day when I would be able to put my foot on the neck of evil and make the evil one pay for my father's agony.

It is suffering that draws forth rage and a desire for someone to pay for the harm. And someone *will* pay—it will be Satan himself, and we will have our moment to put our boot on the neck of evil and twist and shout for joy. If we are not angry, not full of holy fury for the harm evil does, then biblical hope will seem distant and tepid. Only as we face the scope of what is not meant to be, which will one day change, are we drawn to hope for the day.

Hope also grows when we experience the best of what this life has to offer and end up hungry still. When we get a taste of what will one day be by enjoying an hors d'oeuvre of the banquet ahead, we crave more.

Few earthly hors d'oeuvres are as stimulating as food and sex. Eating and sex are the most intense sensual experiences God has ordained. And he uses our experience of both to whet a desire for the "more" that will be enjoyed only on the wedding night with our Lord. No wonder evil works so hard to taint and shame sex and appetite. No wonder it tempts us to overindulge and sin in those areas and then uses both natural consequences and shame to kill our hunger for more.

Think of the finest meal you've ever eaten. Recall the most pleasurable sexual moment with your beloved. Then realize that your memory offers but a glimmer of the glory that awaits you. Hope grows only to the degree that the pleasures of this world serve as a window to the glory of the next.

The Day of the Lord will bring a harvest of fruit in the desert, trees will clap, and fruit will be too big to carry. The wolf and lamb will feed together, and the lion will lose its appetite for meat and will eat straw (Isaiah 65:25). There will be a change in the creation order in that the sun, moon, and stars will disappear because the glory of the Lord will be the only light necessary (Isaiah 60:19). It will be a wild, holy, wonderful day.

And we are to dream it now. It is a surprise package wrapped under the tree, and it is the big, wondrous gift of Christmas. And no one is stopping us from picking it up, shaking it, and holding it in our lap. We can't open it, but it is intended to increase our anticipation to a point of passion.

REMEMBERING REDEMPTION

How are we to dream something that we have never seen and which is beyond our sight in this life? We dream from memory. We know from pain what we most deeply desire. We know what it is like to be divided from another through betrayal. We know what it is like to be powerless to stop the harm inflicted by someone more powerful. And we long for reconciliation and revenge—for a day of peace when the divided will be restored and the wicked will be destroyed.

In our first year of marriage, I once became so upset about something that I shattered a china vase given to us as a wedding present. The gift was of incalculable worth to my wife. I felt terrible shame after my outburst, apologized, but I knew the vase was ruined. Becky swept the pieces up, and I fled to my books.

Weeks later I scrounged enough money to buy a vase that was similar but not identical. Becky received the gift and said it was not necessary to replace what could be mended. I had no idea what she meant, but she asked me to take the vase back. I did.

Several weeks later the vase I had shattered stood on our rickety kitchen table. Becky had taken the vase and painstakingly glued the pieces back together. It was no longer pristine, but it bore the intersecting spider lines of fissures healed. My wife beamed; I felt an odd shame that was full of sorrow and gratitude. Before I'd felt small and ugly for ruining one of my wife's treasures, but when I saw the restored vase, I felt as if she had given me a bittersweet draft of grace. She had not only forgiven me, but she had given us a new treasure that was both broken and whole, ruined and redeemed. Every time I look at the broken-but-healed vase I feel a surge of hope; it is for us both an icon of redemption.

Sin and its effects cannot be eradicated, but redemption can bring an even greater strength to a relationship or a heart than existed before. The scars of sin and death can't be erased, but they can become the weather-beaten marks of character that bring depth and intrigue to what would have been merely a beautiful but ordinary vase. God's passion is to weave glory out of the broken shards of past sexual abuse, an affair, financial disaster, a divorce, death, or any other experience of powerlessness or sin.

Maria and John, prior to their daughter's death, were sincere and committed Christians. They had grown up in good families, attended college, met each other through a Christian ministry, and married after graduating. They attended church and were involved in teaching Sunday school. They were conservative in faith, lifestyle, and politics. They had little time to do much other than work, play with their kids, go to church, and go out on a date occasionally. Their lives revolved around their home and church until their daughter died.

For a few months after Jenny's death the church family was supportive and provided food, prayer, and daily encouragement. A few closer friends wept with Maria, and a number of men tried to express their sorrow to John. But after a few months, they expressed a subtle expectation that John and Maria's grief should be over and their needs few. The phone no longer rang, and other tragedies took their supporters' time and effort. Maria and John were not embittered nor surprised. But at the point the church turned to other matters, their grief and needs grew exponentially.

It was at that point that Maria saw the physician who prescribed anti-depressants. She also suggested that Maria might want to join a group of parents who had gone through the loss of a child. Maria was sufficiently depressed to take the medication, but attending a group with grieving parents sounded atrocious. She didn't even suggest the idea to John.

Weeks later while they were watching a news program, a facilitator for an AIDS group talked about how the prospect of death makes ill people alien to the community of well people. Only in a group could the isolation and despair be broken. Maria wept uncontrollably after the facilitator finished. John was clueless but held her until she could talk. She poured out her fear of joining a group for grieving parents and yet her need to do so.

John and Maria went to the group, suspicious and terrified. After they had been involved for five months, one of the facilitators asked them if they would work with another leader as co-leaders of a new group. They were nervous, but their lives had been so touched by the group's gift of care and honesty that they could not refuse.

Prior to joining the group, Maria had rarely talked with non-Christians about her faith. She always felt uncomfortable associating with people who did not share her religious views. She knew she should share her faith, but it seemed too daunting. In the group, she had shared her confusion about God and his plan; she wept with others who had no faith and still hated God, if he even existed. John and Maria began to see that tragedy is impartial; it visits those who despise Christ as well as those who are covered in his righteousness. But everyone needs to talk, to rage, to weep with others who are unafraid of the depths of loss.

In an odd way, John and Maria began to taste new hope to be truly human—to feel, to doubt, to struggle, to seek, ask, and knock without having to have an immediate answer or much of an answer at all. They felt alive, raw, and full of sorrow, life, death, and hope in ways they had never known before. They began to see a change in their character and experience freedom to talk to others about their most cherished convictions in a winsome and compassionate way.

Hope focuses not on circumstances, but on Christ's coming and the redemption of our character. If my hope is centered on getting a new job or being healed from an illness, then I have given my heart to what is tangible and material. My heart will never become any bigger than that in which or in whom I hope. But when my hope is centered on the coming redemption, I begin to take on his glory. As I become more and more molded by the far future, the now becomes both more bitter and sweet. Bitter in that it is not enough; sweet in its foretaste of what lies ahead.

There is an ancient language in us, a memory from Eden that resounds in us as we recall our past and read about the promises of our future. Hope is leaning into the unknown, risking our lives for a future that is promised in the Word and tasted in a few hors d'oeuvres from our story. We are meant to sensualize heaven, not spiritualize it with images that bore us to tears.

To remember the future is to see tomorrow through the eyes of yesterday. What was yesterday? The loss of a job, victimization, bottomless grief, pointless sacrifice that brought little good? Was it deep struggle, an intense drama and terror that eventually brought us to our knees and to the face of God? Everything hinges on the past. We will project the past into every new moment and either repeat our past themes of victimization or marvel at the work of God in redeeming us in spite of our questions and doubt.

What divides the two paths—the healing path from the path of victimization? The answer is simple: desire. C. S. Lewis said it is aspiration that changes the heart. Mere desire. Desire that settles not for an approximation of what our heart longs for, but presses on to imagine the ultimate and total fulfillment that will drench us in joy.

To remember the future is to dream—to imagine redemption won in the wake of innocence lost. It is to surrender to our insatiable impulse to see the broken pieces of our past cemented together into a stronger whole than existed before our innocence was shattered. To remember the future is to recall and recollect the Exodus drama that took us to the edge of despair only for the waters to part.

We move into the future not with a map, a plan, or a clear structure, but with the whisper of a story that reminds us we will again see the goodness of God in the land of the living. The whisper is the voice of God's Spirit reminding us of the cross and our individual moments of exodus. The whisper is also our own voice that mimics the Spirit by calling our memories to the stage and seeing the themes of redemption time and time again in our lives. God reminds us, we replay the stories, and then we move into the future with the confidence that God is good.

GROWING HOPE

How does hope grow? It grows in the soil of daily faithfulness as we live for something bigger than ourselves. Hope is a muscle that must be nourished and exercised daily to grow through the normal nutrients of knowing and doing God's will. I wish hope progressed naturally and easily just as our body develops from infancy to adulthood. Instead, hope grows through encounters that require us to risk, struggle, surrender, and wait.

Risk

Hope is solid and sure, but only for the final outcome. It grows only to the degree we lean into the unknown and risk the present for the sake of the future. The risk of hope is seeing what can't be seen. It is seeing the future from the redemption of the past and then setting out toward what God has called us to become and to do.

I know a young man who exemplifies this process. Once an engineer with a good-paying job and a newly built home, a book about God's calling prompted him to ask God to free him from the hold money had on his life. During that period the opportunity arose to lead a youth camp in Olympia, Washington. He loved Christian camps because as a young boy he had come to Christ at a summer camp. He and his wife leaned into the future and risked all they had, leaving it all to follow this dream that God had infused in their hearts.

All went well until they tried to sell their home. It took seven doubt- and despair-filled months. Had they made a godly decision? Had they run ahead of God's plan? The battle with God's silence brought them to their knees. They refused to sweep away their doubts and fears; they equally refused to stop hoping. Their despair was filled with hope; their hope struggled daily with despair. At a point well into the battle, in desperate prayer, they turned over their house, their lives, and their future to him, and within a day the house sold.

So is that the key? Surrender to God and he will sell your house in a day? What if, instead, he lets the house burn to the ground and sends you into abject poverty? He has done all of the above and more. Surrender is not a magic key that opens the treasure chests of our material world;

instead, surrender to hope sets us on the healing path of risk. We must risk our money to make more. We must risk difficult conversations to grow intimacy. We must so hunger for a different tomorrow that we risk losing today to gain it.

The writer of Hebrews says,

> All these people were still living by faith when they died. They did not receive the things promised; they only saw them and welcomed them from a distance. And they admitted that they were aliens and strangers on earth. People who say such things show that they are looking for a country of their own. If they had been thinking of the country they had left, they would have had opportunity to return. Instead, they were longing for a better country—a heavenly one. Therefore God is not ashamed to be called their God, for he has prepared a city for them. (11:13-16)

The couple above wished their new life would provide more family opportunities and a better quality of life, but deep inside they turned away from the known and comfortable to step into the unseen and new. Hope propels us to start the journey, but hope will only grow if we determine to leave family, friends, and farms. We can't grow in hope if we are committed to comfort. We must set out for a city we can't see with no promise of how our journey will progress or end on this earthly plain.

Hope grows as risk invites us to struggle with God. But hope grows only if we accept the invitation. Many people refuse to struggle and just write God off. What determines a person's response to risk? Oddly, if one is satisfied, risk is unlikely; therefore, God rigs the world to compel us to risk when we would naturally shy away from it. There is no greater picture of the struggle of hope than the story of Job.

Struggle

The ground opened and swallowed Job's health, wealth, reputation, and family. In a divine interplay between God and Satan, a wager was made about the righteousness of Job. Satan taunts God with the wager that Job will break covenant and curse him when Job's blessings are gone. Job doesn't curse God, but he does struggle with God's silence. He moves from quiet trust in God's goodness and sovereignty to an outright demand to bring his complaint directly to God's face. And yet he hopes. He hopes in bold protest and demands, even at the risk of his eternity, that God will speak. He says to his noisy counselors,

> Keep silent and let me speak;
>> then let come to me what may.
> Why do I put myself in jeopardy
>> and take my life in my hands?
> Though he slay me, yet will I hope in him;
>> I will surely defend my ways to his face. (Job 13:13-15)

Hope is not docile, anemic patience that serenely waits with hands folded and eyes closed. Instead, hope cries to God in despair and protest. Job knocks on God's door until he answers. Hope cries out for God to turn from his silence and speak. Jacques Ellul describes the struggle involved in hope. He writes,

> Hope comes alive only in the dreary silence of God, in our loneliness before a closed heaven, in our abandonment. God is silent, so it's man who is going to speak. But he is not going to speak in God's place, nor in order to decorate the silence, nor in taking his own word for a Word from God. Man is going to express his hope that God's silence is neither basic nor

final, nor a cancellation of what we had laid hold of as a Word from God. This word has now ceased, but its object, content, and reflection are still in our memories, and we accept it because the witnesses who received it and transmitted it were worthy of trust.[1]

Hope is not an absence of sorrow but a refusal to allow powerlessness to silence our cry or to shake our confidence in God. Instead, we are to call on God to be God—to protest his silence and anticipate the day when he speaks. And we are to risk despair by asking God to show us himself. How much easier it is to presume he will not show himself and learn to live with his absence. How much easier it is to listen for good words that speak of him but do not comfort us with his presence or lead us forward with his promise. If we don't miss his presence or doubt his promise, then how can we hope? Gabriel Marcel writes,

> By a paradox which need surprise only the very superficial thinker, the less life is experienced as a captivity the less the soul will be able to see the shining of the veiled, mysterious light, which we feel sure without any analysis, illumines the very centre of hope's dwelling place.... The truth is that there can strictly speaking be no hope except when the temptation to despair exists.[2]

Life is a captivity littered with disappointment and partially satisfied yearning: captivity to a body that does not work as we wish; captivity to a heart that longs for freedom to truly love, to worship from the depths of our being and does not; captivity to the particulars of our culture, race, socioeconomic history, and era, when we would rather be radical, world-conscious Christians. In every arena of life, I long to burst free of the constraints of my flesh, soul, and world. I can't. But to the degree I know the sorrow and despair of being held captive, the more I look toward the bright dawn—the veiled, mysterious light that breaks into the world suddenly, swiftly, and with life-changing results.

When will I see his breaking in again? When will I see his handiwork in my marriage, my relationships with my children and friends, and even more so, my enemies? I have seen him redeem my soul. Introduce me to my wife. Set me on the course of a calling, a career, and a job. I am fortunate to recall many stories that inflame hope. But each of us needs only one remembered story to propel us to hope for more. The questioning, yearning heart that cries out to God and refuses to let desire die knows what it is to be a captive of hope. A captive is one who suffers in hope, who hopes against hope (Romans 4:18), but in spite of it all, he cannot refuse to risk all for what is ahead.

Surrender

Job eventually got his audience with God. He got a whole lot more than he expected. He believed God would come to his senses and see that Job did not deserve to suffer. Instead, God confronted him with a maelstrom of questions that brought Job to a point of silence. After encountering the holy, righteous God he said,

> I know that you can do all things;
>> no plan of yours can be thwarted.
> [You asked,] "Who is this that obscures my counsel without
>> knowledge?"
>> Surely I spoke of things I did not understand,
>> things too wonderful for me to know.
>
> [You said,] "Listen now, and I will speak;
>> I will question you,

and you shall answer me."
My ears had heard of you
    but now my eyes have seen you.
Therefore I despise myself
    and repent in dust and ashes. (Job 42:2-6)

Surrender is turning over all that we are to God's mercy. It is laying down our arms and confessing that his power and glory outnumber our puny weapons. Even more, surrender confesses that our deepest desire is not to succeed in business, to marry, to have kids, to be well or simply happy; instead, our deepest hunger is *to see him*. Surrender goes even further: It despises anything and everything in us and outside of us that compromises our passion to be caught up in his glory and love.

Surrender frees us to admit our powerlessness, our emptiness, and our hunger for glory. And it frees us to enter our frustrating, boring, and despairing moments with imagination. We each live in the midst of what "is." Hope compels us to look beyond what "is" to what "will one day be," and that is the Day of the Lord.

It is in imagining the "will be" that we often fail to linger. Most of the time we face what is and either resign to it or work to change it to "what could be." But focusing too soon on "could be" makes us critical and merely pragmatic rather than able to exercise our capacity to dream wild dreams. It is the "will be" that softens our judgment, deepens our childlike anticipation, and in turn enables us to shape the "could be" with greater creativity.

I remember one of those is/will be/could be moments when I sat at a banquet where I was to speak. The food was rubbery and the mood solemn and dull. It was work, somewhat pointless, that required enormous energy because I sensed in my spirit no joy, no gratitude, no privilege in being part of their fund-raiser. I later learned the dark mood resulted from the resignation of several board members, which had followed a poorly handled issue among the staff.

It is always a risk to speak at a fund-raising dinner when you don't know the people or the organization well. I had agreed to do it as a favor to a good friend who knew a board member. But sensing the dark and angry mood at the dinner, it seemed like my choice to speak was foolish. My mood grew more foul, and my hope disappeared in the darkness. I began to struggle. I resented being away from my family to attend an event for which no one, including the sponsoring host, had much energy. The nearly empty church basement, poor food, exhausted faces, and my growing irritation all melted together to create a dreary mood.

I can't explain how my struggle turned to surrender. I suppose it began when I recalled my wife saying, "I will pray for you tonight." I recollected the many, many times my wife's prayer life had brought remarkable change to my heart and circumstances. Her face—sweet memory—haunted me. I surrendered to God's grand plan by surrendering to the kind eyes of my wife. I heard her say, "Don't be such a twit. Enjoy yourself and see what God does through you."

As I chewed my infrangible chicken, I began to imagine what this group would be like, what I would be like, if we were having hors d'oeuvres before entering the King's banquet hall. What would that tired, irritated-looking man be like if he were petting a lion that was munching on straw? What would the mood in this church be like if the cups were flowing over with wine? Soon the irony of "what is" compared to "what will be" tickled me. I felt a lightness return that was neither cynical nor supercilious. I pictured the couple in their eighties having a child, like Sarah and Abraham. I dreamt I was speaking with the wind of the Spirit pulsing through my body as it passes through a wind chime.

The evening was strange but neither pointless nor without passion, at least for me. I preached my heart out and talked about the inconceivable glory that compels us all to constantly stretch our being, in fact throw our being to God in hope. I may have preached to an audience of one, but that night I heard, I smelled, I tasted heaven. I was at my best that night because I did not see anyone in the flesh; I saw them in the light of what we will all one day be. Seeing only "what is" is earthly; seeing what "will be" without denying "what is" is heavenly. This eternal perspective is gained only by imagining the strange, unruly, wild party of God.

As we surrender our imaginations to a future glory, we are not recasting the present in terms of how we want the world to be (that is illusion), nor are we reordering our lives to add new elements and delete the ones we don't want (that is delusion). Instead, surrender is holding reality firm in the grip of unflinching honesty while also seeing every moment in the light of the invisible, eternal, and redeemed. It is the visionary gift of the interior decorator who can come into a dilapidated room and see new form, color, and structure. She sees reality and she sees potential—simultaneously. The eyes of hope see the shining, residual glory in every sinner and the greater glory of what will one day be revealed through their existence.

Hope pushes back the effects of the fall—it plants flowers in a weed-strewn vacant field. It labors for a lifetime to set up another scientist to discover the cure to Lou Gehrig's disease. Hope preaches in a small, rural outpost in a sparse state, dreaming that someday a child who hears the rhythms of the water and the cadence of the words will write *A River Runs Through It.* Hope suffers but refuses to anesthetize the pain; it dreams and refuses to give in to the visible and the dull. Hope is the wager of the talents we have been given through faith (Galatians 5:5).

Wait

Hope waits but does not sit. To wait is not to sit idly by, whittling our life away until something happens. That is killing time, distracting ourselves to death. Hope strains with eager anticipation to see what may be coming on the horizon. Hope does not pacify; it does not make us docile and mediocre. Instead, it draws us to greater risk and perseverance.

I know a man who has been beaten down countless times in life. He has failed in several businesses and then was let go from another job. Whatever the reasons for his failure—the marketplace, downsizing, a difficult boss—he gave up. He took a position in the federal government that rewards meticulous, slow, and underachieving performance. The work allows him to crawl into a hollow existence of endless, pointless paper-pushing that has no apparent value to anyone.

He is married to a woman who gave up on the marriage after her husband gave up on life. She ached for him and wanted him to succeed. She was proud that he had risked time and energy to follow his dreams. She was still proud of him when he went to work for a large corporation. But over time she saw his spark and enjoyment of life dwindle. Despair slowly spread its net over the couple. Within a few years they gave up touching each other, reading together, and talking. They joined the mass of humanity that has surrendered to the flashing images of sitcom humor and crime-show tragedy.

They exist, barely. They repeat the same routines and replay the same theme of pointlessness in their relationships. Failure in business doesn't have to become the theme of one's life. But it has in theirs. They raised two kids who couldn't wait to escape the dreary, dull routine of their parents' lives. The couple gave up on intimacy and learned to settle for scraps from the table of life. They did not protest; they did not despair. Instead, they died a deeper death and gave up desire.

As painful as their lives are, they justify their existence on the basis of heaven: All things will one day be good, so why strive, struggle, protest, and despair now? They are the epitome of the phrase "so heavenly minded they are no earthly good." But biblical hope does not mean we resign ourselves to the future in light of the pointlessness and powerlessness of the present; it does not mean we repeat our patterns and themes until glory descends. Instead, hope invests the present with the teeming, brimming abundance that is our promise of glory not only in heaven but now.

If this couple truly had known the hope of the Day of the Lord, perhaps they would have read sex manuals and taken a Thai cooking course. Perhaps his job would have been miserable for a time, but he would have sought counsel, training, and a mentor to help him discover his gifts and then used them for the glory of God. Good sex and fine food are available to every couple who hungers for eternity. These, along with longing for the day of judgment, invest our present with a bright abundance that anticipates all that is yet to come.

The apostle Paul did not lose heart even when he groaned deeply, because he anticipated this soon-to-be-revealed glory. Paul dreamt of heaven, but he also put his hope on eventually making his way to Spain. Spain was the furthermost western spot known in that day: the ends of the earth. Paul longed to proclaim the gospel from Jerusalem, to Judea, and then to the outermost parts. Spain was the end. He longed to reach the end, not only of life but of his vision for his life.

God had other plans—Paul would eventually be beheaded in Rome—but nothing prevented the apostle from dreaming there might be a way to reach Spain even near the end of his life (Romans 15:24,28). The dauntless missionary writes:

> Not only so, but we ourselves, who have the firstfruits of the Spirit, groan inwardly as we wait eagerly for our adoption as sons, the redemption of our bodies. For in this hope we were saved. But hope that is seen is no hope at all. Who hopes for what he already has? But if we hope for what we do not yet have, we wait for it patiently. (Romans 8:23-25)

Hope prompts Paul to eager anticipation, his legs itching to run, as he waits for the moment when he can bolt with boyish joy to the presents hidden under the tree. Paul remembers, risks, struggles, surrenders, and then waits to see how God will craft the challenging moment into a new story that, remembered, will lead to even greater hope.

Hope frees us to live for God's purposes. Hope frees us to serve a greater good than our own happiness or comfort. It frees us to love and anticipate our future even if we are awaiting our execution.

Paul writes at the very end of his life these striking words:

> For I am already being poured out like a drink offering, and the time has come for my departure. I have fought the good fight, I have finished the race, I have kept the faith. Now there is in store for me the crown of righteousness, which the Lord, the righteous Judge, will award to me on that day—and not only to me, but also to all who have longed for his appearing. (2 Timothy 4:6-8)

We are hearing the words spoken right before he was beheaded. He will die as a drink offering—what a poignant and ironic term for one who is about to lose his head and spill his blood. But that is not of great concern. He has fought well and he has finished the race and he now awaits the victor's wreath placed on his head (again, such lovely irony). The wreath is not just for Paul, but for any who long for Christ's appearance. Hope makes us victors who succeed because we live for nothing more or less than his coming. Hope is not in a change of circumstances, but in the confidence that our character will change as we live for his coming.

Hope compels us to live for the future by pouring ourselves out as offerings to God in our relationships with others. The primary way we give God glory is through loving others. Evil intends for us to succumb to betrayal by giving up on relationships; it intends for us to resign to power-lessness by giving up on the future. Once we lose faith and hope, then we are more susceptible to ambivalence and shame. But just as God restores faith and hope, he redeems shame and births love. He calls us to dance with unbridled passion.

THE DANCE OF LOVE

One night Maria talked with a social group at church about the grief group she and John were participating in. She shared how it had restored their hope and sense of purpose even though they could find no answer for the loss of their daughter. Several women in her group were offended that this help had come through a "therapy group" in a secular environment instead of through prayer in the church.

Maria was incensed. She held her tongue but could barely constrain her fury. The church had no support group that allowed grieving people to struggle with God for as long as the healing process required.

John and Maria found their work in the unbelieving world too enjoyable to quit, but after weeks of conversation and prayer they felt God's call to live out their story in the church as well. They put a notice on the church bulletin board. Within two weeks they started meeting with three couples and two single women who wanted to talk about grief. The group took heat from many in the church and was barely endured by the church leadership.

Within three months, the church board sent a letter to John and Maria indicating their concerns about "the things being communicated in your therapy class that do not square with the Word of God." They asked John and Maria to meet with the board the following week to defend what they were doing. In reality, they were not running a class nor doing therapy. They had merely formed a support group for folks who had encountered significant loss.

The wife of a board member told Maria that someone had reported John as saying, "You can't grow unless you rage at God." Maria was exasperated. John had talked about owning up to one's anger, even anger toward God, but John had not used the word *rage,* nor had he implied that raging at God was a prerequisite to spiritual growth. He had merely pointed out that the psalmist frequently expressed anger toward God. John had been misquoted; far worse, the group now seemed to be the target of a theological witch hunt. Maria wanted out of the group and the church. She didn't want to fight nor to be hurt again.

Maria had been studying 1 Peter. One day her eyes ran across the phrase, "love one another deeply, from the heart" (1:22). She had already determined not to meet with the leaders and had closed her heart to their inquisition. But God began to woo her, reminding her of the many ways in which he had already guided her and protected her heart from becoming hard. Then he began to beckon her to dream, to imagine how their ministry to grieving people might touch a few hearts in the board meeting. Her heart battled with God. At one moment she surrendered and said, "Yes, I will go." Over the next hour she tried to talk herself out of attending the meeting, which might evoke the same nausea she felt when she met with her daughter's physicians.

The meeting could not have gone worse. The board claimed that John and Maria had been seduced by secular psychology. People who trust in the sovereignty of God put grief aside soon after the loss, they were told. They were criticized for inviting others to acknowledge their anger toward God rather than to confront anger for what it is: unfaithfulness and ingratitude.

John, a naturally quiet and gentle man, tried to explain what experience had taught him and Maria and how they felt called to offer to others what God had offered to them. One leader sniffed, "We are not interested in experience, only in the Word of God." The board decided to terminate the group and agreed to talk with the participants to inform them of the errors John and Maria had taught them.

The men who made this decision were committed, sincere Christians. Their decision was flawed and brutal, but their desire to honor God was not in question. Yet John and Maria left the church that night almost as devastated as when they drove away from the hospital after their daughter died. The church had, in essence, made their daughter's death seem even more empty and pointless.

Maria wept all the way home. John was silent. Once home, they each disappeared into their own worlds. After an hour, John found Maria folding laundry in the basement. Her tears moistened every dry shirt and towel. He held her and told her he would not give up a work that he believed was of God, nor would he become hard toward the people who had just broken their hearts. He confessed his hurt and anger, but he refused to turn his heart over to death or despair.

At the moment John chose to extend his soul and embrace God in the midst of his pain, he chose the healing path. As he refused to go numb and withdraw from Maria, he opened his heart not only to her, but to his own healing. He did not merely survive the blows of the meeting, he put his arms around the hurt and betrayal by approaching Maria and then inviting her to be with him and God in their pain.

John asked Maria to pray with him—for their wounds and for the people in the group who would be confused and heartbroken again. He said he also wanted to pray for each man who had been at the board meeting. As he prayed, Maria was too overwhelmed to join him, but she marveled at the depth of his tears and the anguish in his voice.

John had rarely chosen the healing path in the past—why now? Prior to their daughter's death, John was a fairly typical Christian man. He was moral, sincere, and somewhat detached from his family. He loved his kids but preferred to spend time alone. He read the Bible, but with little vigor or intrigue. He believed in the gospel, but for him, good news had more to do with a raise at work, his new sports car, and the progress of the White Sox.

Maria had been the one who wanted to attend a Bible study and find a ministry they could participate in together. She had always wanted John to be the spiritual head of their home, but she had not counted on God inviting him to sit at the head of the table in this way. She was so proud of him in this wrenching moment. So confused by what God seemed to allow. Furious that the path God had put them on seemed to be getting worse, not better. But ultimately, she could not forget God. She could not kill her passion for the people in her church. She was amazed that a small portion of her heart was gentle toward the men who had patronized and demeaned them. She struggled deeply, but she could not deny that someone held her heart in an embrace she could not escape and did not desire to flee.

Healing the heart is never a mechanical process, nor is it a mystical breakthrough that only a few ever achieve. It involves a gut-wrenching choice that feels terrifying and foolish—but inevitable when one's heart is gripped by God's grace. Maria knew that more losses, more terrible deaths were ahead, but her heart was captured in awe and gratitude, not only for her husband, but for the God who had allured them to the desert and won their hearts. She would not give herself over to shame and despair.

Love is the fruit of faith's memory and hope's desire. To remember God's Exodus goodness is to find a solid rock in the midst of swirling seas. To dream of God's coming redemption is to struggle and keep hope burning in the midst of unexplained suffering, in the absence of God's intervention. It is not possible to love others unless our hearts are growing in faith and hope. Faith and hope birth love as we live out our calling in anticipation of his coming.

REMEMBERED LOVE

We love only because we have been loved. God gives each of us the memory of at least one face that offered surprising kindness and inexplicable grace. The powerful weight of grace is so great that even an ounce of kindness challenges a ton of neglect and shame. It does not take away the damage nor neutralize its effect, but it does draw the heart to more. The haunting, comforting memory of being loved is the North Star that guides us forward on this odd journey.

My grandmother's face is a North Star. She was stricken with crippling rheumatoid arthritis when she was forty-five. I never knew firsthand of a day in her life that was free of pain. But she was a sprite—an impish, playful woman with dancing eyes and a passion that had drawn her to be a flapper in the twenties. She hated to have her picture taken, but she always lived with an elegance born of suffering well.

She loved me. I was named after her husband's favorite hunting dog. My grandfather was Oliver Wendell Holmes Bope. When my mother asked him which name of his to call their first grandchild, he bellowed, "Would you straddle a son with any of those names?" He then said in passing, "If you want to name him for me call him Dan, after the pointer that just won the Nationals." I was always grateful they had not given me the name of the dog's line: Comanche. It would have been too hard to explain.

She read to me; she explained my mother to me. She mediated between my father and me. She indulged, spoiled, and railed at me in the way only a weary, wide-eyed grandmother can. She loved me, and I loved her.

When great sin entered my life in my early teens, her face was the only one that flashed before me prior to my indulgence. Even though her eyes did not restrain me, they haunted me for a decade until my life was turned over to the God she worshiped.

My grandmother died in a nursing home. My parents and I sat with her when she was caught in a coma, unresponsive to us or the world. My parents wanted to take a brief break and went out for dinner. I stayed with her. I told her in my parents' absence how she had uniquely stood before me as the face of God. I told her soon she would see the face of God and hear from him the most glorious words a human being will ever hear: "Welcome, my good and faithful servant." I told her how her love was a growing fire in my heart that God had fueled and directed toward his purposes. I wept. I laid my hands on her shriveled shoulders and then put my hands on her face. Her breathing became more shallow and labored, and I heard a rattle that stirred her body like a small quake. I could feel her spirit leave, and her breathing quieted. She died.

It was a holy, agonizing moment. I don't know if she heard. I know she knew. But I longed for her to hear me shout her glory to the heavens; instead, the heavens welcomed her to a glory I cannot utter.

My wife has a gallery of pictures that I must pass through in order to make my way into the world every morning. It is my wall of witnesses. My children. My parents. My wife's parents. My grandmother. I glance at the faces before I go downstairs. Before I leave my house I look at one of the paintings my grandmother finished in the early years of her arthritis. The strokes are labored and the colors mute. It is a gift she gave me when I got married. It has been an image, a face, a reminder that I am loved and called to love and suffer well. It is my grandmother's face that not only reminds me but also draws me to a future day of love.

Love requires faith, but remembering puts us in a bind. After all, not all our memories of love are "North Stars" that guide us confidently into the future. The memories that sting most are those that remind us of love that led to shame. Shame is the exposure of our foolishness to have trusted that another person would be true and good toward us. If we give that person our heart and then are betrayed, we have nothing and are nothing. We are no one. We lose face. It is losing face that most deeply provokes shame. All of us have memories of romantic, filial, professional, and ministry relationships in which we have lost face.

The memories create a dilemma as to which story, which face, we will allow to define us. We can't answer the call to love unless we adore the faces of others. We can't love without potentially losing face ourselves. We can't love unless we remember the faces in our lives that have been our bridge to God. But in remembering we also recall faces that have scorned, used, and betrayed us.

We don't want to remember. But if we refuse to remember then we can't recall the surprising events that narrate God's wonderful, dramatic, maddening process of redeeming our lives. Love that is remembered draws us to a love that has not yet come—a dream woven with desire that draws us forward into the unseen realms of the healing journey.

DREAMT LOVE

A friend told me that he dreams several times a month of nailing the book he is writing to a huge, wooden church door. That dream is usually followed by one in which he is driving a Fiat on the hairpin turns of an Italian Alpine road. He approaches a tight turn and fails to slow down, plunging his car over the edge. As the car falls through the air, the manuscript flutters from the car seat into the thin, barren sky. He admits he goes from the grandiosity of a Luther-like experience to plunging to his death because he was not sufficiently cautious and wise. But after every dream he is humbled and energized to return to the labor of writing.

Dreams in all their forms—from the night's unconscious play, to daydreams we would be too embarrassed to tell, to plans we sketch out on yellow pads in a brainstorming meeting—are the raw material that gives shape to our desires. It is desire that creates our future. And it is desire that draws us to love—not only other human beings, but God himself.

Emmanuel Levinas, a brilliant Jewish ethicist, stated:

> In Descartes the idea of the infinite remains a theoretical idea, a contemplation, a knowledge. For my part I think that the relation to the Infinite is not a knowledge, but a Desire. I have tried to describe the difference between Desire and need by the fact that Desire cannot be satisfied; and Desire in some way nourishes itself on its own hungers and is augmented by its satisfaction.[1]

Desire, not just "truth" or information, draws me into the future. I believe Jesus will return; I believe at death I will fly to his face. The future is described in various apocalyptic dreams and visions that, although they give me a glimpse of what will occur and how the end of time will come, satisfy few of my questions about heaven. The information does, however, fuel desire for the day to come. And come soon. Desire, in turn, fuels our hearts to lean into the future and shape it for the sake of the face of love.

We are all given faces of love—a relative, a teacher, a neighbor, a coach, a big brother, a boss, or a mentor. Those faces, whether they were in our lives for a day or decades, serve as a window through which we peer into the glory of God. Even so, our nagging doubts do not entirely go away: Maybe the dream is all a nice fable, a good story, but not true. Perhaps investing for the sake of love is an insane wager that rarely returns sufficient dividends. Maybe we'll even be left holding the bag, naked and exposed. Nothing exposes our utter powerlessness and potential for betrayal like loving someone. Nothing causes us greater ambivalence than love.

Faith is our ballast, the ground of confidence that enables us to withstand sorrow and loss. Hope is the wind that drives us forward to risk for redemption. Faith and hope take us to the greatest comfort and most radical danger of our lives: love. Love calls us to open our ambivalent hearts, wait in desire, embrace others for a time, and then free them to follow the calling of God in their own lives.

OPEN HEARTS: READY TO ENGAGE

John and Maria's experience in the grief group couldn't have been more surprising or unnerving. They were well-loved by unbelievers and through their care came to love God more deeply than ever before. To be loved by anyone awakens in us a hunger for more. And the hunger for more, if it stirs the deepest urge of our life (to know and be known by God), turns us not only toward more human love but also toward the transcendent.

The healing path always leads us back into the human fray to be betrayed and to savor both human and divine love. Love enabled John and Maria to respond to God's call to offer their church what they had learned in their grief group. As a result their losses mounted. They discovered afresh the love of God through unbelievers and then got hammered when they offered love to the believing community. It seemed unfair and mixed up.

Their temptation to shut the door to God's people was fueled by hurt, exhaustion, and self-righteousness. But whenever we make our hearts available to God, he works his way in and draws us tenderly to his open arms. It is like being in the presence of rich, sincere laughter—we are drawn to laugh with those who laugh. God's pursuit of us wins us with his kindness and then draws us not only into his laughter but also into his tears.

There is a door to every heart. And every experience in life is either invited in or turned away. It is impossible to describe the door or say it is a mere metaphor. We take in or we turn away. We hear the knock, or we ignore the noise and turn our attention more deliberately to other stimuli.

The decision to hear a knock and open the door is a moral stance that determines how much we are willing to change and grow.

What determines whether we hear the knock or let it fade into the background noise of our lives? The older I get the more the question baffles me. A seventy-year-old woman I met at a sexual-abuse seminar began our conversation by saying, "Where were you fifty years ago? I have struggled with the damage of sexual abuse. Until now I never understood that I have run from intimacy for fear of facing the arousal that came during the abuse." I heard her kind compliment; I also heard the anguish of nearly five decades lost to the flight from love.

But then she stunned me. She said, "I can't explain why God wants me to look back over fifty years of broken marriages, kids who don't like me, and the regrets of giving my life to a career instead of relationships. But I do know this: I'm glad it is now and not never, now rather than waking up in heaven and realizing I squandered my entire life." Her tears streaked her wrinkled and lovely face.

Deserts can be restored with rain; faces redeemed with tears. But why then? Why not earlier? For whatever reason, this elderly woman's heart became available to God when it did; stepping onto the healing path was for her both choice and mystery.

We work out our salvation in fear and trembling, knowing God wills and works as he chooses. He meets our desire with his presence—disruptive and strange as it is—and then dances with us only as wildly as we wish. Many times, we simply don't want to dance with him, even if we say we do.

At many moments in life I do not make myself available to dance. I recently drove to the airport, listened to music without listening, and focused on the road without seeing. I parked and caught a van to the terminal. I stared ahead. I stood in long lines for over an hour, and less than fifteen minutes after sitting down I couldn't remember a single conversation or thought I had during that time. I was in the airport trance that many frequent flyers enter to escape the tedium and loneliness of travel. I don't feel undue moral culpability for being in that dissociative state, but I'm troubled to think how often I enter an evening meal with my family, or watch the evening news, or read a book in the same frame of mind. Am I awake? Is my heart open to hear the people who have a claim on my heart?

Gabriel Marcel said that availability is a "receptiveness to the abundance of the world."[2] The world is fragrant with the glory of God, often hidden and frequently intertwined with the strange and unexpected. The abundance is present, nevertheless, in the twinkling of nearly every moment. "It is the ability to abandon oneself to whatever one encounters…to transform mere circumstances into 'occasions' or indeed into opportune situations. It is to contribute to the shaping of one's fate by impressing one's own distinctive mark upon it."[3]

"Response-ability," then, is my capacity to hear the call of abundance (or the lack thereof) and pledge myself to the good of others in that moment. I am responsible to receive the call and respond with who I am and what I can offer to further glory. Commitment is a pledge, an oath to the welfare of the other. I made that oath to my wife when I received her and gave myself to her as her husband. I pledged myself to my children. I will do all I can to advance their lives to become the people they are meant to be.

But what am I to do about the woman sitting across from me in the terminal who has a two-year-old and a newborn baby? Her baby just lost a sock, and apparently she has not noticed. She looks harried and in great need of help. I'm on a tight deadline and can't afford the time to talk. The sock beckons. Her face calls me. She has not even noticed me, but she is part of the abundance of the world, and I am part of that abundance too.

I recall moments in which chance conversations have led to the introduction of God to a near-total stranger. Other conversations have provided me with the language and cadence of a character that was precisely what I needed to finish a writing project. Other times a stranger has reminded me that I left my coat on a chair, and the kindness in his eyes haunts me for hours, giving me greater passion to offer the eyes of God to others. I don't know where any moment will lead. I only know one thing: Openness to the abundance of the world invites us to swim in the mystery of God's ongoing story.

The call does more than invite; it compels. It complicates. If I had not seen the sock fall off the baby's foot, I would not be in a position to hear the call nor look directly at the mother's face. I would not remember the many "chance encounters" that seemingly went nowhere, nor others that were clearly inscribed with God's presence.

By faith in God's love of story, I put my computer down, walked over, picked the sock up, and handed it to her. She was grateful and remarked how harried she felt without her husband. It was her first time to fly with the kids. The flight personnel said boarding would occur in a few minutes. She began gathering up her children and bags. I asked, "May I carry something for you?" Initial investment led to furthering my commitment.

I helped her and her kids onto the plane, got them seated, and then went to my seat. The flight attendant, who had noticed my kindness, said, "Well, you will get a star in your crown someday." I looked at her and said, "Do you believe in a God who rewards?" She looked at me dumbfounded. She said, "I used to. Do you?" The conversation was brief but sweet and lovely. I'm so grateful for the drop of a sock.

Love begins when we ask, seek, and knock. It grows as we commit ourselves to respond to the signs of abundance with an open heart. But shame warns: "Don't be a fool. Don't get involved. Don't risk, you will only be sorry." And shame is often superficially correct. Desire, when allowed to grow, will inevitably meet disappointment. Love that gives will inevitably get us in trouble. But shame is ultimately a lie. It says we are nothing, no one; being awake and involved will never pay off. The truth is, however, that when we love we discover that one set of kind eyes can boldly face the harsh eyes of a hostile crowd. One kind word can out-maneuver a hoard of hatred. The promise of abundance mocks the illusion of shame's power.

Jesus said, "Ask and it will be given to you; seek and you will find; knock and the door will be opened to you. For everyone who asks receives; he who seeks finds; and to him who knocks, the door will be opened" (Matthew 7:7-8).

The promise of Jesus is profligate. It is a prodigal pledge that any asking, seeking, or knocking that opens us to God will be met with the teeming presence of God. Again, his is not a presence we can control nor persuade to show up when we want it, as we want it. But it is presence nonetheless that sings through desire and disappointment with a lilt we can't deny. And what God pours into our open hearts he desires us to pass on to others with gentle, lavish patience.

HEARTS THAT WAIT:
LAVISH PATIENCE AND PRAYER

Love is sustained by hope. Love is exhausting. We don't often see the rewards in this life. My wife told me that my thirteen-year-old daughter, Amanda, gave her one of the highest compliments of her life. As they were driving home from a tennis match, Amanda said, "You are the coolest mom I know." Becky thanked her and asked what prompted that remark. She said, "All my friends think you are the kindest and most wonderful mom they know. I feel so lucky to be your daughter."

My wife was stunned. I felt thrilled for her, and yet my first question after she told me—"Did she say anything about her father?"—revealed that I felt desperate for encouragement too. A compliment from one of our kids can nourish us for weeks. Hope enables us to give and receive while waiting for the fruits of love to grow.

The second dimension of love is lavish patience that continues to give and receive even when the seeds of love have not popped above ground. In one of the most foundational and lyrical descriptions of love in all the Bible, Paul tells us, "Love is patient, love is kind. It does not envy, it does not boast, it is not proud. It is not rude, it is not self-seeking, it is not easily angered, it keeps no record of wrongs. Love does not delight in evil but rejoices with the truth. It always protects, always trusts, always hopes, always perseveres" (1 Corinthians 13:4-7).

Paul begins this section with "patience" and ends it with "perseverance." All that is in between resonates with the idea of reticence as opposed to brash, forceful demand. Love is not pushy, nor does it require an immediate response. Love filled with hope "involves the relinquishment of the desire to push impatiently ahead; for it depends on a sequence of events that proceeds independently of our actions."[4] Love waits.

Waiting is often thought of as inactivity or passivity. Nothing could be further from the truth. Waiting is a bold surrender to desire. I could get a free cup of coffee in the hotel lobby, but it is probably brewed from cheap beans and has been sitting in the urn for hours. Or I could wait thirty minutes until I get to the airport and get a cup of Starbucks' freshly brewed coffee. The decision is simple: I don't just want caffeine, I want caffeine with flavor, aroma, and full-orbed pleasure. Waiting requires the discipline to set aside short-term pleasure or quick satisfaction for a greater fulfillment. Waiting is sustained by the anticipation of fullness; therefore, it is sustained by dreaming.

A believing heart dreams through prayer. Waiting does not mean sitting. It means kneeling, submitting, and humbling myself not only to the expanse of dreams desired, but to the acknowledgment that I can't make the dream appear. Dreams that involve the depths of what my soul desires are utterly outside the realm of my control. I desperately want my children to love God and live their lives to make the glory of the gospel known with passion and creativity. Can I make that happen? Of course not. There is much I can do to teach, model, and live the gospel before my children, but their choice to live for God is not my decision, nor can I guarantee that anything I do will lead to that end.

When it matters most, I am most helpless. Yet when it matters most, I am most susceptible to looking for a way around my powerlessness. It is like waiting to be seated at a fine restaurant that does not take reservations. You've been told it will be twenty minutes, the universal euphemism for an hour. A half-hour passes and the crowd has not thinned; the waiting area is bustling with people. A gentleman in an expensive tailored suit, sunglasses, and a dark tan approaches the maître d'. They speak in the sonorous tones of Italian, and within moments, his party is whisked to a table that has likely been sitting idle in expectation of his arrival.

Panache. Chutzpah. Some have it, most don't. Some people seem more able than others to make their dreams happen. This is true as long as the dreams are material, but when the desire has to do with desires of the heart—love, forgiveness, reconciliation, healing—then we are on a level playing field where boldness is merely the courage to desire without relenting. Bold prayer bombards heaven relentlessly with the cries of our soul.

Jesus, after teaching his disciples how to pray, then compared God to an irritated neighbor who doesn't want to answer the door after he has gone to bed. Jesus says,

> Suppose one of you has a friend, and he goes to him at midnight and says, "Friend, lend me three loaves of bread, because a friend of mine on a journey has come to me, and I have nothing to set before him."
>
> Then the one inside answers, "Don't bother me. The door

is already locked, and my children are with me in bed. I can't get up and give you anything." I tell you, though he will not get up and give him the bread because he is his friend, yet because of the man's boldness he will get up and give him as much as he needs. (Luke 11:5-8)

This is another passage in which we're tempted not to take Jesus seriously. In the ancient Near East hospitality was a deep, abiding value that ruled relations. If a guest arrived and you were unprepared to receive him, it was considered more than a faux pas; it was a scarlet blemish, a blood-red shame. It could ruin the name and reputation of the family. All those who heard this story would understand the extent of the emergency implied in the situation. But the comparison of God to a reluctant neighbor had to be both disturbing and comical. God sometimes seems like an early-to-bed, finicky neighbor. If you knock, you'd better knock hard. And when he bellows down to quit disturbing him, then keep knocking. The racket alone will get him up.

Jesus invites familiarity and urgency. Far more, he invites desperate, bold prayer. Many pray with a perfunctory, soulless recitation of magic words, sincerely said but robotically offered. It is not dissimilar from flight attendants who read the information required by the FAA in order for a flight to take off. It's good information that most people ignore, including the one reading/praying it.

Bold, naked prayer leaves us between God's promise and absence, between a divine rock and a hard place. On the one hand is the sure promise of his love, on the other is his silence or apparent inactivity. The waiting continues. I cry out: Redeem me. Change me. Heal me. The tears flow and my heart beats fast in anticipation of the dream fulfilled. I open my eyes and the room has not changed, the clouds have not parted, and my soul often feels more empty and alone than it did before I prayed.

Hope in love feels so foolish and reckless. When we consider the wager of love, shame nearly always mocks, "You are a fool. You've risked everything for nothing. Protect yourself. Wouldn't your time be better spent mapping out a plan and working toward the unreachable goal? Or even better, wouldn't it be easier to numb the desire and distract yourself with something that doesn't leave you feeling more hungry and farther from the dream?" No. Hope has penetrated my soul and seized me. My arms are open and outstretched, moving toward the dreams I welcome from afar.

Love is the most profound risk of life. We open our hearts and then refuse to harden our hearts or trivialize our desire for full, glorious redemption. We wait without time limits. We anticipate that God will arise and our shame will be averted when he hands us our three loaves of bread.

John and Maria stretched out their hands in prayer. Maria could not pray, but she allowed her heart to admire her husband. Her tongue was silent, but her heart stretched out to God as John spoke on their behalf. John wept prayer. He did more than believe; he cried out in desperation, despair, and anticipation. His despair was infiltrated by hope; his hope was salted with the tears of destitution.

When we are naked in our desire without despising our desperation, shame no longer holds its power to steal our face. Tears wet our face and soften the soil for fruit to grow. Shame prefers rocky, barren soil where nothing can take root and flourish. Tears of desperation, offered to God as a confession that no one and nothing can satisfy us but him, protect us from evil's assault of shame. Tears bring comfort. Comfort draws us to receive from others and from God and, in turn, calls us to give.

The cycle of love—giving and receiving—gains momentum as prayer draws us to hate deadness more than shame. Hope draws us with anticipation, desperation, confidence, and uncertainty to remain ready and supple for the dance of love to begin.

HEARTS THAT EMBRACE: THE DANCE OF PASSION

Love is an embrace; a touch of skin on skin, a breath of fragrance that stirs us to surrender to the jouissance of God. Joy. Joy is not a strong-enough word in our day because it is so often separated from sensuality. Jouissance is joy celebrated in sensuous touch, smell, sound, sight, and taste. It is a worship that brings body and soul into a unity, a shalom that we rarely experience.

Such fleeting tastes of joy are incredibly sweet. As I walked down to the kitchen this morning to get a cup of coffee, I saw my son bounce off our trampoline in a less-than-graceful stumble. My daughter Amanda ran to him and threw her arms around him. I heard her say, "You are incredible. What a jump. What a landing!"

How did Amanda know to affirm her brother's somewhat shattered male ego rather than inquire about his physical pain? Andrew was slightly wounded, but his sister's response gave him a sufficient lift to rise and return to the mad toy.

I stared at my children. I wanted to run to them and grab them in my arms. The moment lasted only a second. Their next interaction was a fight as to whose turn it was to jump. But in that glimpse of kindness, care, and wisdom I breathed in the fragrance and abundance of God.

God's touch begins as he waits for us, sees us, and runs toward us, just as the prodigal's father did. God looks for us. Daily. He scans the horizon and refuses to lose hope. He remembers his love for us and strains to see whether today is the day we return to him.

Nothing is more incomprehensible than God spending his time waiting for us. God so humbles himself for the prospect of reconciliation. He runs. A father in the prodigal's day would never run to a son who had shamed him by taking his inheritance and spending it on licentious living. He would wait until the son came to him and abased himself, then he would sentence him to taking the role of a servant until his debt was repaid. Instead, this father runs to his boy.

It was customary for men of that time to wear long, flowing robes. A man would need to hike up his robe and tie it to the side in order to be mobile. In King James English it was "girding up your loins." It was appropriate for a man to show his legs in public on only one occasion—in battle. In running to his son, the prodigal's father further shamed himself by likely showing his legs in public.

In tears, he embraced his son. He didn't wait to hear what his son said, nor did he offer rebuke or instruction. His joy was complete simply knowing his son was alive and in his arms. Love is an expression of the delight we find in the face of the other. One cannot love "dutifully." A person who loves merely because it is a choice or decision has denuded love of delight. Love becomes service that obligates rather than frees.

The father's eyes were full of wet, liberating exultation. The son repents. He'd practiced his litany of confession before he arrived, probably a thousand times before he saw the white robe running toward him. Who knows what expression he wore as his father clung to him and wept the convulsive tears of relieved joy? I suspect he was awkward and afraid. He knew what he deserved. And when grace comes at first, we all wonder how long it will last before tenderness turns to rage.

The son draws a breath, drops his arms to his side, and steps away from his father: The confession must begin. His well-rehearsed words come out stiffly with an effort at humble self-respect. The father doesn't interrupt. He waits until his son's fragile soul has finished. I suspect the father looked one more time into his son's eyes before turning away. This is the boy's core fear. He hopes he can earn his place back into the family, but if his father refuses to see him or turns from him, he will be a wanderer and an alien the remainder of his life. He stares at his father's back. ·

Suddenly the father shouts, "Quick!" The son must be befuddled.

What is happening? Is the father calling for servants to throw him off the property? The son can't believe his ears: "Robe, ring, shoes, calf, celebrate. My son who was dead is now alive!" It is party time. Love doesn't keep a record of wrongs; instead, that which divided us is burned in the fire that browns the meat of celebration.

And oh, what a party! Excellent food, drink, music, dancing, and stories. Glorious stories of rescue, redemption, and reconciliation. It is not equivalent to a potluck. It is not a gathering where we eat casseroles, drink from Styrofoam cups, and break cheap plastic forks on overcooked mystery meat. God is at the center of the ring, his hands on the shoulders of his friends, dancing in jubilation.

Close your eyes. Imagine God dancing with you. The music sweeping around your head, the food and drink lightening your feet, the sounds of friends singing with the band. It is a graduation day. The honor has nothing to do with an accomplishment or a good performance; it has to do with nothing other than being hungry, naked, and alone, and then coming home. It is the most extraordinary party of life.

Get real, you might be thinking. *Nice story, but love is a tad more mundane in most people's lives.* Always? No. There are moments. I love coming home from a trip and driving into my driveway. My dog, Maggie, a rambunctious, slightly daffy Australian Terrier, sees my car as I approach the house and she goes crazy. She runs in tight circles, moving toward the car in cyclical progression. Usually she blows a tire somewhere in the process, falls, and quickly picks herself up in wild excitement. It may be for some a grotesque parallel, but every time I see her passion I think of my prodigal father. If I look into the eyes of my wife and children, I don't see that same exuberance but I see delight, joy. I may want my wife and kids to run tight circles in the front yard when I come home, but a smile in the eyes of my wife, a warm hug from Andrew, a squeal from Amanda, and a teenage nod from Anna is about all the glory my soul can bear.

Love is joining God, waiting and looking for the prodigal to return. It is running every time someone we've waited for returns, holding them in a jubilant embrace. And then it is shouting: "Quick, quick, quick!" Love is knowing our God feels the same and more toward us.

Hearts That Let Go: The Freedom of Love

Every good party must come to an end. The music fades and the plates of food are empty. It is time to clean up. The gala is over. Never entirely, but the cruelty of clock time is that all earthly glory must fade in deference to the great glory that will one day come and never depart. All love on this earth must be held with open hands.

I recall my first daughter's birth. She was born close to death after eighteen hours of horrendous labor and an emergency C-section. As soon as the umbilical cord was unwrapped from her small neck and her breathing stabilized, they brought me to the surgery room. I stood outside and watched green forms rush back and forth in the frantic labor of creation.

Moments later they brought a wide-eyed, dark-haired, intense baby girl out of the room. The nurse looked at me; I was a wreck. Tears were streaming down my exhausted, unshaven face. She stopped and said, "Do you want to carry her down to the nursery?" She handed me my daughter and I cradled her. I will never, never forget that walk of thirty yards. It is indelibly imprinted on my soul. As I carried her slowly to her first earthly bed I saw a vision of me walking her down the aisle at her wedding. I felt an abrupt shift, a deepening sorrow, an excruciating mixture of joy and loss. *She is going to leave us someday.*

I walked into her room a few minutes ago. She is eighteen. In several months she will leave for college. I look at her sleeping form under the covers, and I could wail. I'm so proud of her, so angry at her I could choke her.

She is leaving and the loss seems insufferable. I pull myself together by rec-ollecting the mystery of emptying love. Paul wrote,

> Your attitude should be the same as that of Christ Jesus:
>
> Who, being in very nature God,
> > did not consider equality with God something to be
> > > grasped,
> but made himself nothing,
> > taking the very nature of a servant,
> > being made in human likeness.
> And being found in appearance as a man,
> > he humbled himself
> > and became obedient to death—even death on a cross!
> > > (Philippians 2:5-8)

He emptied himself and made himself nothing. Love pours itself out, becoming obedient to death, even death on a cross. Love lets go of its inalienable rights; it leaves others free to respond to or reject it.

Love does not grasp and hold on to others, compelling them to live for us. We care for, provide for, instruct, and rear our children. And then they leave. The same model applies in mentoring relationships. Each person we encounter is a being we are meant to bless and serve. Each person is meant in some way to bless and serve us, or the lack of mutuality will strip the relationship of truth and depth. The intertwining of hearts nourishes and grows courage to walk further on the long healing journey.

And then our paths separate due to death or any other transition that breaks the continuity of our day-to-day care. It is naive to think that a rela-tionship will continue as it was when a move occurs or a schedule changes. The ever-present reality of change prevents many of us from investing deeply and wildly in others: *You are going to leave. And the loss of your presence seems far greater than the joy of joining you on the path.* In the end we'll be left alone with shame, whose ugly voice will remind us: "See, I told you it was going to end and you'd be sorry you gave so much. More moderation, more self-control, more savvy rather than sentimentality would have saved you this pain."

For nearly a decade Becky and I have skied annually with our dear friends, the Dupees. When our vacation week of conversation, food, and frolicking is finished, we return home with heavy hearts. We hate to see them leave. The moment of separation when I drop them off at the airport is one of the loneliest points of the year. But I wouldn't try to circumvent the loss because I also recall the moment they arrive and the joy—utter joy—of seeing their faces. Such joy is not possible without loss—at least on this side of the veil. I wouldn't trade those moments of sorrow and joy for all the perks, privileges, and power found in this soiled, tired world.

As we experience it, all human love deepens our sense of wonder that God has suffered his love so patiently and with so little reward. My daughter is leaving us to go to school. The Father, at some point, bid his Son good-bye to become flesh. My children will suffer, and I will be helpless to stop it. The Father allowed the Son to be tested without direct intervention and only allowed an angel to provide sustenance at the end of the forty days. We allow our children to make mistakes and suffer when they sin. The Father bore the agony of being separated from his Son as he became sin on our behalf.

Yet God's reward is ours too. It is for "the joy set before him," the Day of the Lord, that Christ endured and scorned the shame of the cross. It is for jouissance that we open our hearts to, wait for, hold, weep with, party with, and then release others to take our love and walk the healing path to God—at their own pace, in their own time, even with digressions and twists and turns far from the path of life.

It is for joy we love. John the apostle summed up the reason to love in these simple words: "I have no greater joy than to hear that my children are walking in the truth" (3 John 4).

HEARTS THAT ENGAGE: THE GREAT DISCOVERY

Redemption makes us careless. Care less. Not entirely, but closer and closer to the psalmist's cry: "Whom have I in heaven but you? And earth has nothing I desire besides you. My flesh and my heart may fail, but God is the strength of my heart and my portion forever" (Psalm 73:25-26). The more redemption matters, the less hold the powers of the earth have over us. The less fear and shame can constrain us and shape how we speak, live, and die, the more gratitude and awe mold us to become like Jesus Christ.

The great discovery of the healing journey is that in getting a glimpse of God we see our past, future, and present from the perch of an eternal now. God is above time. He is not constrained by clock time. He is ever present. That means the abuse I suffered as a child is "now" for him. The day of my departure from this earth is "now." All is now. And all reflects the mysterious goodness of God, even the agony of the cross. My birth, abuse, redemption, and death are all held in his kindness. He holds time in his hand the way a man holds his son's hand as they cross the street. He leads and lets me walk in the safety of his presence.

If all is now for God, then I can live out my clock time with expectancy and joyous anticipation. What will he do today? What will I comprehend by the end of the day that I do not know as I rise from bed? Will today be the day of my departure? Will I be called to suffer in ways that try my soul beyond any measure I have known before? Will it be a nice day, sumptuous and robust like a piece of divine chocolate cake? Joy is not an absence of struggle or sorrow, but the taste of the presence of God as he surprises us with his gracious love, whatever our circumstances.

The day beckons me to story—others, my own—to dream, and to the privilege of suffering for the sake of redemption. I open my arms to the day.

Before the day is more than a few minutes old I must make decisions that will affect the remainder of my day and my future. Decisions I made months ago shape today. Previously made commitments will interact with newly arisen circumstances that I could not have comprehended when I pledged myself to be available. How could I know that I must speak at a conference even though I am depleted and overwhelmed by other commitments? How could I know that I would have to cancel an appointment to see my daughter play in a regional tennis tournament? Decisions. Commitments. Directions taken. On what basis shall I make the daily choices that inevitably shape my life and the lives of others? How do I choose between one good and another equally good opportunity?

Faith, hope, and love invite us to become the people we are meant to be. But being *moves*. Being *does*. Who we are ought to move us to do that which is most consistent with our calling. And what is that? We usually succumb to the exigencies of the day. Today is trash day: I take out the trash. Today is the first day of the month: I need to pay bills. As necessary as it is to be shaped by the external demands placed upon our lives, it is not enough. It is unbecoming to do only what is required; instead, we must live out the deepest purposes of our lives.

It takes a lifetime to discover exactly how our past shapes our future so we can live wholeheartedly and passionately in the present, but we can begin. We can seize the present with greater insight and vision.

The healing path takes us beyond self-discovery to God-discovery. This change, by definition, plunges us into new relationships with new goals: to live out the qualities of faith, hope, and love in service to God—and through him, to others. Here is the point along the path where we begin to experience one of the most profound characteristics of the abundant life: changed relationships.

The final section of this book offers a vision for how the power of redemption takes hold in our daily interactions with others as the force of evil is broken in our lives. Chapter 10 points toward what it means to live a radical life shaped by our unique calling. Chapter 11 considers how that calling shapes our conversations with others and what it means to invite them to life. Chapter 12 summons us to live out faith, hope, and love in the community of other sojourners.

PART FOUR

EMBRACING
REDEMPTIVE
RELATIONSHIPS

CHAPTER 10

LIVING A RADICAL LIFE

M y ten-year-old son Andrew and I sat on our porch as a spring day was coming to an end. As darkness surrounded us and the heavens began to glow, he looked at me and said: "Am I here for some reason?" It was a moment that nearly took my breath away. I spoke slowly and quietly so as not to disturb his deep questioning with the flap of words. "Yes, son. You are the only you this world will know, and something about your life is meant to make something about God known in a way no one else can do." The wind, cool and gentle, brought us the smell of mountain pine trees; we sat on the porch in silence and waited for God to make his purpose known.

Faith, hope, and love free us (to a degree) from the regret of the past, the fear of the future, and the emptiness of the present. Our growth inevitably draws us to ask questions about our purpose and calling: Why am I here? What am I to become? What am I to do?

The healing path does not lead directly to healing, but to engagement. First, we are called by God into relationship with him. We are also called into service for him. To serve God is to bring our story to him and allow our life themes to make God's story known to others. Our common calling is to make known the glory of God even when we do the most basic things of life like eating and drinking (1 Corinthians 10:31). A radical life begins with the premise that I exist for God and for his purposes, not my own.

Living a radical life requires being fully human. The Latin word *humus*—soil, dirt—implies earthiness. As human beings we are common dirt enlivened by the breath of God (Genesis 2:7). We see, smell, taste, touch, and hear God in a creation that bears his intimate mark but can't contain the glory that awaits. God leaves sensual traces of himself everywhere: in fine chocolate and a great burger, in a Bach fugue and the wail of Jimi Hendrix, in the waft of barbecued ribs and the fresh breeze off the sea. A radical life grasps both the weariness of this soiled world and its capacity to transfix us with God's glory.

Listen to one who lived a radical life—the poet Gerard Manley Hopkins:

> The world is charged with the grandeur of God.
>> It will flame out, like shining from shook foil;
>> It gathers to a greatness, like the ooze of oil
> Crushed. Why do men then now not reck his rod?
> Generations have trod, have trod, have trod;
>> And all is seared with trade; bleared, smeared with toil;
>> And wears man's smudge and shares man's smell: the soil
> Is bare now, nor can foot feel, being shod.
> And for all this, nature is never spent;
>> There lives the dearest freshness deep down things;
> And though the last lights off the black West went
>> Oh, morning, at the brown brink eastward, springs—
> Because the Holy Ghost over the bent
>> World broods with warm breast and with ah! bright wings.

A radical life is one that knows the world is soiled and smeared in toil. Yet grandeur pulses through the ecosystem, freshness rises, and the Spirit sings if one merely has eyes and ears to hear. A radical life has eyes and ears for the deepest purposes of God.

Yet to live for his purposes is not to forsake the passions and burdens of our daily life; rather, we are to give them to him for his glory. The practice of giving up so-called secular interests in order to go to church, Bible studies, prayer meetings, choir practices, potlucks, and other social activities with other Christians has taken many believers out of the culture. Too often we withdraw from our neighborhoods to a Christian "ghetto."

Paul Schuler, the young pastor at Cross Sounds Church on Bainbridge Island, Washington, once invited his leadership team to join him on a Saturday morning for an outreach to the community. The men who had invited Paul to plant Cross Sounds Church were committed to evangelism, to discipleship, and to ministering to the community. It is hard to know what they were thinking they might do that morning: perhaps door-to-door cold-call evangelism or follow-up with church visitors. Certainly, they did not anticipate that on Saturday morning they would be involved in the first annual Humane Society–Cross Sounds Church Dog Wash.

Several adamantly opposed the idea. They would walk the streets for Christ and take the hostility that often comes with cold-call evangelism, but wash dogs? No way! Not one of those guys would wash a dog at home, nor consider washing a dog in public, but it was a stroke of genius to serve an affluent community of Washington State environmentalists and animal lovers by washing the paws of their pets.

All the money earned was donated to the Humane Society. The community newspaper thought it was a treat for a church to give its time to the community and publicized the event widely. This young and sojourning church chose not to wait until people came through its doors; instead, they took the church outdoors into the world where people live. The men who served the pets got wet, one dog ran away, and they discovered in a small but significant way what it means to leave the typical Christian ghetto to live for Christ in the village.[1]

Leaving the Ghetto for the Village

The church in America is not doing well. In a brilliant and troubling book, *The Death of the Church*, Mike Regele writes, "The combined impact of the Information Age, post-modern thought, globalization, and racial-ethnic pluralism that has seen the demise of the grand American story also has displaced the historic role the church has played in that story. As a result, we are seeing the marginalization of the institutional church."[2] His research indicates that baby boomers, even though they seem to be experiencing a rise in spiritual interest, are not returning to the church in large numbers. His research also suggests that the generation often called Gen-X finds little in the content, method, and form of the traditional church that speaks to its unique situation. Regele's survey found 17 percent of Americans indifferent to or disillusioned by the church, with the numbers growing every year.[3] Seven out of ten people surveyed were involved in some religious activity, but the largest growing segment of boomer participants were drawn to the New Age.

The trend in many churches is to circle the wagons, remain inwardly focused, and serve primarily the needs of those who are already attending church. Church consultant Ray Bowman has found that most churches spend less than 3 percent of their annual budget on intentional missions to their community.[4] And the community is not coming in droves to the church for answers, hope, or even as a part of a traditional ritual of good community involvement.

A number of megachurches are beacons of light in a rising darkness. Unquestionably, God is using many churches to invite tens of thousands to the gospel, but as a rule, even those with large numbers sit on the margins of culture, either oblivious to the church's descent or hopping mad about the decline of its prestige and power.

There is a shrill, chest-pounding demand among some that we must return to a "Christian America." The stridency and self-righteousness often associated with those views only seem to kindle a more intense "secular" response of disdain that insists Christianity return to the margins. The defensive world says, "Don't impose your views on me." The angry church clamors back, "You are not only imposing your godless philosophies on me through the public schools and the media, but you are taking my freedoms away." The result is an intractable debate that further serves to divide and distract the church from living the gospel.

What exactly are some Christians calling society to return to? No monolithic, singular Christian viewpoint has ever structured our society; pluralism has been the United States' foundation since its inception. And even if there once was a culture we associate with a more civilized, uniform, and predictable era, it is no more possible to restore that consensus than click our ruby heels and suddenly return to Kansas. Instead, our more important task is to engage culture by listening to its poets.

Paul provides an example for us in Acts 17, where his visit to Mars Hill and his interaction with those who shaped Athenian culture is recorded. He saw their efforts to name reality in the fact that they had built a statue for every god they knew. They had even erected one to an "unknown god" so they would miss no chance of blessing. Paul quoted their poets and, understanding their desire to cover their bases, offered them a name—that of Jesus—inviting them to meet the God they did not know.

Regele writes, "The context in which we develop the spiritual maturity of our congregations must be the transformation of our communities."[5] We will not reach the marketplace of merchandise, information, and ideas by changing the tempo and lyrics of our music, being conscious of not using spiritual jargon known only to insiders, and preaching more relevant and honest sermons. Better music, linguistic sensitivity, and honest sermons would help if the world came to our doors, but in most cases unbelievers see no need to pass through our portals. We must move into a world that will be intrigued with us only if we live surprising, compelling lives that offer more than can be found in other stories and communities. Our calling is to be in the world without living according to the elemental principles, the core assumptions, of a fallen order. We are to be in the world, to incarnate the gospel in the flesh of our stories and struggles.

What is my calling? What is my son's reason for living? It is to become more human, more unique, and ultimately, more like Jesus Christ.

MORE LIKE JESUS

What does it mean to be like Jesus? What is the point of asking the question: What would Jesus do? He was too unpredictable, he upended too many structures of expectation to be much of a model to know what to do in any given moment. All I can imagine is that he was a lot of fun to accompany to a wedding, not safe to go with to the temple, and a great benefit to have in the bow when a storm hit. He was playful, confusing, intense, enigmatic, and so human most would not recognize he was sinless.

Christians don't seem to grasp that the goal of redemption is to make us more human. Instead, we labor to be superhuman and lose what makes us most like Jesus—our humanity. Jesus was fully human and fully God. I will never, never be fully God, but by taking the healing path I can become more and more like Jesus by becoming more human. We are never more holy than when we become human like Jesus.

What exactly does it mean to be more human? To answer that question, we must look at Jesus. In his life and relationships we discover that being fully human involves living with greater intrigue, imagination, and incarnate care for others.

Intrigue

Human beings are material and immaterial, flesh and spirit, visible and invisible. Our being is a unity of two spheres: earth and heaven. We are not only created from two different spheres (visible and invisible), but we're mixed up because our dignity that comes from being made in the image of God has been infiltrated by depravity. Depravity is the passion to be as God and to rule life as if we were the central and sole being in the universe. Depravity is rooted in the heart; it darkens every relationship and has severed our relationship with God. "The heart is deceitful above all things and beyond cure. Who can understand it?" (Jeremiah 17:9).

The heart of every human being is an unexplored continent, dark and foreboding, beautiful and compelling. Proverbs 20:5 says, "The purposes of a man's heart are deep waters, but a man of understanding draws them out." So why aren't most of us more intrigued? When we have opportunities to enter into the hearts and stories of other people, why do we often pass them by?

Few people are intrigued by others. Few people follow up conversation with an invitation for others to tell their stories. We are rarely curious about each other's individual tastes, convictions, and interests, let alone the stories that provide the thematic structure to our lives.

In radical contrast, Jesus was deeply intrigued by human beings. When he encountered the woman at the well at the noon hour, the heat of the day, he asked her for water (John 4). What was so extraordinary is that she was a three-dimensional loser: a woman, a Samaritan, and an outcast. In Jesus' day, men never addressed women in public—they had little recognized worth except to their own family as one who served its needs. Samaritans were enemies of the Jewish people in that they had established a competing place of worship outside Jerusalem. The hour at which the woman arrived to get water indicated she might not have been welcome there either; the other women would draw water in the early morning. The Samaritan woman was an outcast, possibly a prostitute.

At every level, Jesus (if he were a respectable Jewish male) ought not to have spoken to her at all, let alone engaged her in a theological, sociological, personal conversation. But he did. He questioned, debated with, and provoked her; he listened to the words she both said and didn't say. He responded to her to the point that she became incensed with his lack of hate for her. She rebukes him and says, "You are a Jew and I am a Samaritan woman. How can you ask me for a drink?" (John 4:9). His pursuit of her shocked his disciples, penetrated her heart, and astonished a whole village.

Our calling is to be more in awe of, more willing to risk entry into the stories of others. But when we enter we are not human if we merely listen and ask questions; we must imagine and speak to the dream of glory. To be human is to see what can't be seen, to give ourselves to the future through the labor pains of creative struggle.

Imagining the Unseen

The old saw—creativity is 90 percent perspiration and 10 percent inspiration—is painfully true. Creativity arises every time a discontented heart dreams. Birthing the unseen and unformed legal brief, funding proposal, or dissertation or coming up with words to touch the heart of an angry, suspicious colleague invites us to posit there is a world beyond what we know. The work to vacuum and straighten up a room is a small taste of an order and beauty that will one day descend. The labor to find the right verb to express an idea, to revise over and over, proofread, and then struggle again over the same paragraph is not perfectionism (though it could be), but a longing to capture, even for a moment, a glimpse of the unseen God through beauty that is apprehended today.

"Once, having been asked by the Pharisees when the kingdom of God would come, Jesus replied, 'The kingdom of God does not come with your careful observation, nor will people say, "Here it is," or "There it is," because the kingdom of God is within you'" (Luke 17:20-21). Jesus saw what others had no imagination to see.

In Luke 17 he met ten lepers on the road. Lepers were the vile outcasts of their day. Their disease was crippling and contagious but not understood; it seemed safer to isolate lepers and keep the contagion at bay. No respectable or sane person would associate with lepers. But Jesus saw beyond their disease. He looked at the horror of the body but saw the far deeper reality: the heart.

Jesus healed all ten outcasts, but only one returned to thank him. Apparently, the one who returned was a Samaritan. The man knew true healing was not a matter of external change, but of a transformed heart. Gratitude for change goes only skin deep when superficial alteration is our prime concern. Of greater importance is the invisible world within each of us that needs God's deepest care and most powerful creative involvement.

"So we fix our eyes not on what is seen, but on what is unseen. For what is seen is temporary, but what is unseen is eternal" (2 Corinthians 4:18). Using our imagination to see the unseen gives up convention and the-way-it-has-always-been-done to see what has yet to be revealed. If the imagining is of God, it leads not merely to gratitude but to a passionate desire to draw out the glory of those in our care.

Incarnate Care

Intrigue takes us into the complex web of story and the deep purposes of the heart. Imagination moves us to glimpse what a human heart and life is meant to become. Incarnate care takes on the suffering of others to bear the cost (or a portion) of their plight. To care means to become "care less," not "care full," regarding ourselves. To be more human in the way Jesus calls us to be human is to be willing to live with a holy indifference toward our own plans as we give up our agenda to join the dreams of others.

Jesus seems to have really liked Samaritans. He told the story of a man who was beaten and left on the road to die. Two religious men with no "response-ability" walked by the pulp of a man. They were not available to him. They were not called by his wounded face; he was merely road kill in their blind eyes. But the Samaritan, a follower of a false religion, stopped, picked up the wounded man's naked body, and allowed the blood to stain his shirt. The Samaritan got dirty—he was human—for another.

Incarnate care is not concerned with whom we help or what has caused their disease. If we have resources to help, then brokenness calls us to action. Just think if Christians had been the first to enter the fray of blood and death in the early '80s when AIDS became a national epidemic. Instead, many in the evangelical community passed by in pharisaical indifference.

Incarnate love seeks out the lost and says little, then gets the best room and board money can buy and tends to the care of the wounded. Shouldn't that be the redeemed heart's response to the sexually and physically abused, the raped, the battered, the homeless, the neglected? Sadly, in the twentieth century the Good Samaritans usually are not Christians, but their pagan neighbors.

LOVING LIKE JESUS

The passion (from the Latin *passus*, meaning suffering) to enter the hearts of others binds us to their fate. Their gain is ours and so is their loss. Once linked like Siamese twins to the hearts of others, we will fight for them, against them, and alongside them for their glory. If they weep, we weep. If they rejoice, we celebrate with them. Even if we are not disposed to cry or to laugh, we can join their situation so deeply that their world is now our world.

And why do we do this? What call are we answering when we wrestle with others in the mud and glory of being human beings in God's image? The same call Jesus answered when he became human and gave his life on the cross. To follow Jesus is to disturb, draw, and direct others to the Father.

Disturbing

We are naturally self-satisfied. If our normal way to work is detoured and we are forced to take an alternate route, even if it adds only a few minutes to our travel, we often find ourselves disturbed and irritated. We don't want anyone messing with our predictable lives. Rituals structure space and time and give continuity to our lives; disrupted rituals cause us to feel groundless and lost.

Predictability—ordered time and space—is crucial for daily functioning, but it can quickly become more important than relationships. God will not bear being replaced by order, an institution, or the blessings he provides us. Hosea tells us what happens when a self-satisfied life becomes more important than God: "When I fed them, they were satisfied; when they were satisfied, they became proud; then they forgot me. So I will come upon them like a lion, like a leopard I will lurk by the path" (Hosea 13:6-7).

God disturbs us. And he calls us to disturb and disrupt one another. Otherwise, why are the wounds of a friend considered a sign of faithfulness (Proverbs 27:6)? Disruption stirs the pot of complacency and brings to the surface the burnt pieces that we would prefer to sink to the bottom.

Years ago two friends, Tremper and Larry, heard me share about a tough situation of conflict with another friend. I was feeling hurt. At one point Tremper said, "Look at Dan's eyes. When he gets angry his eyes begin to bulge." I was incensed at his callous remark. And I could feel my eyes widen and protrude even more. He was right. I had never noticed that my eyes bulge when I'm angry.

A year after that remark I was staying in a hotel that used plastic keys, the kind of plastic cards that open a door by sliding into an electronically sensitive slot. I hate those doors. Most people slide their card into the slot and watch the door respond with a flashing green light, welcoming them to their home away from home. When I do the same thing the door blinks at me with a red light that says, "No way, pal. This ain't your room." But it is my room. The light is wrong. Sometimes it takes me five minutes to get it to work. This time I worked for at least ten minutes, inserting slowly, quickly, alternating responses, praying, muttering, demanding the door open. It didn't.

Eventually I stormed down to the front desk. I was furious. As I approached the counter I could feel my glasses protruding from the pressure of my bulging eyes. Tremper's and Larry's faces came into focus. I heard the Spirit whisper to me, "So are you going to kill the kid for giving you a bad key?" I wanted to do so, but instead I was civil. I handed him the key with a smile and said, "I think there has been a mistake." He checked the key and said, "Oh, I'm so sorry. I gave you the wrong key." "Well, it's not a capital offense," I responded. "I have done much worse and been forgiven."

He looked deeply into my nonbulging eyes and asked, "Are you a Christian? My brother who is one of those born-again types said I'd run into people like him at this job." I nearly swallowed my eyes. In an instant, it became clear that the disruptive words of a friend had not only forestalled the harm I intended to inflict on another, but they gave me the grand privilege of talking about Jesus.

Speaking truth in love is simple and requires our very life and soul. More often than not it is merely saying to the emperor, "You are buck naked. Where are your clothes?" It is not difficult to see areas of failure in others, but it requires a kindness and a depth of participation that may cost us the relationship if we speak. The difficulty is rarely in knowing what to say, but in saying it with a heart that grieves for the other's pain and depravity and dreams for their freedom and glory.

Drawing

Disruption awakens the heart and points to the far horizon. A growing hope to be human and alive to God enables us to begin the journey. But no journey can be completed without provisions—we need food, water, good shoes, warm and dry clothing, and shelter. We need companionship—fellow travelers with whom we can walk for a portion of our travail. And we need the comfort of Christ to draw us onward.

When Jesus ascended to the right hand of the Father, he gave us an indwelling Comforter, the Holy Spirit. The Spirit reminds, tantalizes, and fills us with a hunger for what we will one day enjoy and become. And Jesus also gave us each other; we are all members of his body, and we are called to draw each other forward on the healing path through courage-giving care. We know the word as "encouragement," but often that word is merely a synonym for a nice compliment. Encouragement—the drawing forth of another's courage, strength, resolve, and passion—comes from offering him a glimpse of God's delight.

It is delight that has given me the courage to continue the healing journey. One specific moment of delight has been especially sustaining. When I went to seminary, I was out of the drug culture less than a year. My hair was still midback and my grasp of Christianity slim. I had given up illicit drugs, but I had not curtailed my drinking. My days were spent in classes and studying. Around 9 P.M. I would head off to the Glenside Pub to reward my diligence. I saw nothing inconsistent about my behavior since I had already given up a lot of my past indulgence. I would drink for several hours and then come back to my room in a dull fog. Often the morning hangover pinned me in bed until I had to rush to my first class.

I recall passing Dr. Ray Dillard as I exited the library early one morning. I was not feeling well nor looking exceptionally bright and polished. It was the morning we were to meet in a small prayer group with Dr. Dillard. He stopped me and said, "Dan, are you joining us this morning for prayer?" I glanced at him. I could not hold a direct look into his eyes. I said, "No sir. I'm not feeling well and I thought I'd go back to my room and lie down." Dr. Dillard looked at me and his eyes sparkled. His face was full of intense kindness as he said, "Apparently this is an illness that will taper with a few hours of sleep. Once your head clears why don't you come talk with me. I know something about your illness. I have suffered it in my life." He turned and was gone. I watched him walk to his office. His face was too bright to see, and I was grateful he put me in the cleft of a rock and showed me his back.

I met with him later in the day. He didn't condone or overlook my drinking problem, but his eyes were moist with tenderness, fierce with delight in what he imagined I could become, as he described events in his own life that had been ruined by alcohol. I not only felt awakened and disturbed but drawn by the light in his eyes as he spoke to me. In his face I began to comprehend how the Lion of Judah can also be our paschal lamb. The professor's face was like flint, hard and sure, but his eyes sparkled with tender care. He scared me. He drew me with his wild intensity and equally humble kindness. He loved me with holy delight.

A year later he read this passage to me, "The LORD your God is with you, he is mighty to save. He will take great delight in you, he will quiet you with his love, he will rejoice over you with singing" (Zephaniah 3:17). God, my mother, holds me in her arms like a newborn. She coos. She beams in delight and sings me to sleep with a lullaby of love. God graces us with his Word. I know God loves me because the B-I-B-L-E tells me so. And then he gives me faces and memories that draw me to see the Word in the flesh of my own stories. As I write I can hear Dr. Dillard's laugh. I feel his piercing eyes and I wonder: If he could look at me with such strength and tenderness, then what must it be like to look into the eyes of Jesus?

If I am to be like Jesus then I must have a rare face. How tragic when people hide their life marks through plastic surgery and cosmetic coverings. One only need recall the wizened, world-weary, impish face of Mother Teresa to get an image of the nature of delight. Let my hair flee and my face sag! Let my body decay and the creases of suffering show. It is not brush-stroked beauty that draws the heart; it is the rare presence of delight that captures us for the journey.

Directing

A radical life is committed to disturbing and drawing others to God. Further, a radical life is willing to be directed and also to direct others on the healing path, where they will grow in faith, hope, and love.

One of the most thrilling movements in the church is a return to spiritual direction, silence, and simplicity. One friend said of her church, "There is so little silence between the words that I drown in all the noise. I leave and need to go sit for hours to rest from all the frenetic activity of worship."

Noise. A radio is on in my daughter's room, my son is watching TV, and I write as I listen to Van Morrison. I'm more afraid of silence than I am of cacophony. Silence brings us face to face with our greatest fears and our deepest desires—most of us prefer noise and distractions to quiet centeredness.

Several years ago a dear friend invited me to a three-day silent retreat at a North Carolina beach home. I balked. I didn't have the time or the desire to be in the presence of five other people and somehow commune with God in silence. It seemed not only pointless, but frivolous. But my wife urged me to go. I went.

I found the silence not as frightening as I feared. I loved the people I joined. And the spiritual director, Fil, was a kind and frighteningly perceptive man who listened to my spiritual journey with sensitivity and silence. He hurt with me. He laughed with me. He embraced me as I left. My mind felt caught between the sweetness of silence and the rising storm in my heart that seemed only to subside when I walked. I walked and walked. I knew I was slowing down and running simultaneously.

The next day I fought the stillness that brought both tears and comfort. It felt too good to indulge and too strange to rest in. Sadly, I squandered the gift. I sank in fantasy, felt swarmed in worry, attacked by guilt, and devoured by emptiness.

My final day began with a meeting with Fil. I recall nothing of our time but one question: "Why are you so afraid to play with God?" Several of my stories had led him to that assessment and query, but I looked in his imploring eyes and felt a shudder that made me want to run out of the room either shrieking or dancing. I couldn't figure out what was gripping me.

When I left Fil, I walked first to the beach. "Play with God." Ridiculous. Pray, ponder, praise, produce for—yes. But play? I grew up fast and alone as an only child, and by an early age play had become mostly destructive and antisocial. How could I play with God? He is not present, real, or fun. It dawned on me painfully: I didn't like God. I loved him, but I didn't like him. He was more like an articulate professor I wanted to learn from and impress, but he wasn't a friend, and certainly not a playmate. But the Spirit urged me to play—not alone, but with the Trinity.

The rest of the day was too holy for me to describe. I will not try. Hours passed and thrilling transcendent moments intersected with the mundane passage of time. My great fear had been that if I availed myself to God, he would not show up. It became clear that my real fear was that *I* would not show up. When I did, he did in ways I relish as I think about the beach, the gulls, and the odd glory that he sets on fire in ordinary bushes in our path.

Directing is not telling, or at least not primarily. There are times I am to tell—"The affair you are involved in will kill your heart and break God's." But most of the time directing comes through asking questions that expose the state of the heart.

A dear friend told me of the revolution that occurred when another friend simply asked him over coffee, "What was the most God-honoring, thrilling moment of your life? And what has changed because of it?" The question took my friend to the memory of ministering in a state-run nursing home to older men and women, most of whom had been abandoned by children and other caretakers. Each visit brought him untold sorrow and gratitude for the simple care the elderly residents gave him. He usually left more encouraged than when he entered. But he had gotten busy and the several hours a week it took to visit were soon swallowed up by other activities. His friend's question began to direct him toward the deeper passions of his life.

When we are directed, we follow the brilliance of God, who reveals our nakedness, sometimes simply by asking which bush we are hiding behind. To be directed and exposed by God is to discover how he would have us live out our unique calling.

DISCOVERING YOUR UNIQUE CALLING

Every human being is meant to become more truly human, and thus more like Jesus. But we all do it so differently. Are we to be intrigued about exactly the same things? No. But we all are to be more intrigued by the human soul. We all are to dream and labor in imagination to anticipate the coming glory. About the same things? No. But we are to be equally committed to eliciting the glory of those with whom we are called into relationship. Are we to care for, disturb, draw, and direct every human being we meet? No. But we are to love those whom God has placed strategically in our path.

Our general calling is to be human and bring glory to God—to delight in good food and be in awe of the rumbling thunder, to glory in what both point us toward. But what is our unique calling? It is to use (and be used by) our stories to tell the story of God. He has given us our unique set of stories to make something known about himself, something that reveals his infinitely variegated being. We must follow the path of our personal redemption to understand the calling that we alone can answer.

We are each a character God has scripted into his divine play. You and I are being redeemed in a unique and utterly distinct fashion. There is only one way to the Father, through Jesus Christ, but neither my path nor yours has ever been trod, nor will it ever be again.

Why then do we compare our life walk to others'? And why do we so seldom stand back and marvel at what God has done in us and through us? Again, it is the same battle with faith, hope, and love. Do we believe that even the slightest kindness, the smallest sacrifice, reverberates through the heavens and brings a smile to God's face?

Listen to the writer of the letter to the Hebrews:

> Through Jesus, therefore, let us continually offer to God a sacrifice of praise—the fruit of lips that confess his name. And do not forget to do good and to share with others, for with such sacrifices God is pleased. (13:15-16)

God is pleased! He smiles whenever we give a cup of cold water to anyone in his name. Every time we say, "God, you are so good. Thank you!" and then offer a neighbor a smile, our kids a hug, or our boss a sincere "How are you?" we bring delight to the heart of God. He is not hard to please. Is it self-doubt that keeps us from believing our lives matter to him, or is it simply pride? Must we do big things, noticed by many, to ensure God's approval, or are we content with the quiet, faithful service that may be the means to redeeming our little corner of the world?

To respond to our individual calling is to live out the themes of our stories—themes that fill us with sorrow, anger, pleasure, and joy—for God's glory. God has crafted each of us with burdens we can't escape. A burden is something that breaks our heart, tightens our fists, and compels us to cry out *yes!* when redemption comes. Your burden might be to preach the Word faithfully in a culture that has lost the meaning of truth; it might be to hold the head of an AIDS victim as he sips from a cup; it might be to run a multimillion-dollar corporation in a way that not only makes money, but enhances the dignity of those who work in the firm. A burden may be concrete (AIDS), theoretical (rightly dividing the Word), cultural (racism, sexism, ageism, abuse), situational (Irish missions), or relational (caring for an aging parent).

A burden is a passion that typically arises from the mesh of our story. As a result, to neglect our burden is to lose our soul. Burdens grow, develop, and change, but the essence of every burden is to see luscious fruit, green plants, and flowers grow where there are broken, dry clods of earth, weeds and thistles running amok.

What are the themes of your story? Where does your heart break with sorrow for what is still unredeemed? What arouses your anger when you see evil score another victory? What brings a *yes!* to your soul when you give? God calls us from our core burdens to specific arenas of service and worship. God calls each of us to live as a unique human being in a particular world with specific people. And he equips us with gifts, talents, and skills to fulfill our radical calling of making him known.

A *gift* is a charisma, or spiritual disposition, that enables us to carry out tasks for building up the body of Christ—like the gifts of teaching or healing. A *talent* is a physical disposition or aesthetic ability to do something well—like the ability to sink a twenty-foot jump shot, manage money, or sing solo soprano in a choir. A *skill* is a learned procedure that most people can be taught to some degree—like playing the piano or giving a speech. Gifts are supernatural endowments; talents are physical proclivities that are not the norm; skills are learned techniques for accomplishing certain tasks.

Calling is often thought of as what we do—our occupation. There are times when a calling is also an occupation, but more often than not, calling is how we live out our burdens in conscious and committed use of ourselves for the glory of God. Calling is not an office, an occupation, or a career. A personal calling is not something that can be discovered simply by taking a spiritual-gift inventory or test. It is revealed only as we walk the healing path and identify our unique burdens and dreams, as we follow our hearts toward what causes us to weep, scream, and sing with delight.

Am I called to be a therapist? A writer? A teacher? No, I'm called to live out the gospel in whatever sphere I wish to enter that enables me to use my gifts, talents, and skills to bless others and glorify God. I suspect I will be remembered as bearing a unique calling in the area of sexual-abuse recovery. But my life is yet to be lived fully and my calling may get clearer as my journey progresses. No one has the right to say to another, "I know your calling; it is such and such." But we can listen and offer tentative and holy thoughts.

I listen with and for my children. As I sat on the porch with Andrew that night I thought of how funny and friendly he is. When he was four, he would hang out with all the contractors who were building houses on our street. The lunch van would pull in to feed the workers around 11:30. The woman who drove the van knew Andrew's name and usually gave him a free Coke. He was an errand boy for countless crews. He learned the names of tools that I'd never even seen.

My son loves to talk. He loves to pray. His two best friends come from a Korean- and a Spanish-speaking family. When he was five we had guests who worked on a mission field, and he asked to pray before the evening meal. We bowed our heads and he began to pray in an impeccable Spanish accent. Not a word or syllable was a real word, but his intonation was flawless. My son was praying in a foreign tongue of no known tribe. I could have died. The missionaries were not impressed, and there was a tense moment when he finished to see if I would discipline my son. Instead, my family went nuts, applauded, and asked him to pray again. He did. He is a wild boy.

What is his calling? Perhaps he will be a welcoming pastor in a charismatic church. Perhaps not. What does it matter? He thinks he would like to be a cartoonist. He loves to draw. I don't care if he makes a lot of money, goes to college, finds a career, or sells Fuller brushes door-to-door. I don't want him to be happy, nor do I merely wait for him to find his way. I want him to use all he is for the kingdom of God. And my task is to delight in his passion, promote his desires, let him fail, and sit quietly with him on the porch waiting for God to speak to us both.

God puts no premium on one job or another, formal ministry, or so-called secular employment. He only cares whether a heart desires to be part of his play. If we are on the healing path toward becoming more human, more unique, and more like Jesus, then he can use us to play an important role in other people's stories.

A radical life throws us daily into the lives of others. Not a day passes that is not entangled in story. Even if all we do is read a novel, we are still caught up in story. If we were to spend the day in silence away from people, books, music, and TV, we would still have plots and faces waltzing through our mind. We are surrounded and infiltrated by other people's lives, and we are called to interact with those people in radical ways.

So how are we to make use of our time as we sip a skinny latte with friends in a quiet coffee shop? Does the healing path compel us to converse in a particular way? The next chapter suggests ways to invite others to life through redemptive conversation.

CHAPTER 11

INVITING OTHERS
TO LIVE

W e converse daily with a number of people. Each person is brimming with what happened over the weekend or with new calamities that have complicated life. Often we listen merely to pay the requisite toll, which permits us to tell a related story. At times we are no different than third-graders, straining our arms to stretch higher than our peers', frantically fanning the air so we can offer our perspective. We are less overt and more sophisticated in our reserve, but if one could measure the heart's desire to be heard, we'd find we are no different than those children.

At a deep level, I'm torn in two by caring pursuit. I want someone who *wants* to hear me. Does hear me. Takes me seriously. Pursues me. Goes farther into my heart than the initial conversation might have indicated. But on the rare occasions someone does this, I panic and try to escape. I don't want to be taken too seriously or pursued too deeply; neither do I want the other person to quit or to be fed up. Usually I need not worry about feeling ambivalent, because few truly listen, are intrigued by me, or draw forth the implications of what is happening in my heart. Most conversations are like junk food—tasty and addictive, but not nutritious or life changing.

A person who lives a radical life, on the other hand, who is on the healing path toward becoming more fully himself and more essentially like Jesus, moves into the hearts of others with a redemptive purpose: to expose depravity and draw forth dignity. We are all a mixture of dignity (that which deeply desires what is good, lovely, and true) and depravity (that which refuses to confess that God is the sole good, beauty, and truth that our heart was made to desire—Psalm 73:25). Redemptive conversation delights in all that reflects dignity and disrupts whatever reeks of depravity. A radical life hears stories deeply enough to become a participant in another's life, an actor in a new story that God is telling on behalf of us all.

My wife and I had the opportunity to be in Scotland around the summer we both turned forty. We ended up staying in a glorious castle built in the fifteenth century. It was an eerie and awesome bed-and-breakfast that used a common table to feed its guests.

One night we went to dinner early, and another couple came down to sit near the blazing fire. We greeted each other and soon discovered where we were from and what we each did. The distinguished gentleman spoke with reticence and an air of world-weary finesse. He was neither looking for conversation nor opposed to interaction. He told me he was an emergency-room physician. I have known a few such warriors, and in an era prior to the television show *ER*, I was always impressed with the level of intense passion, intelligence, and high-level risk-taking involved in their art.

After a few minutes of interaction that had ambled through the demographics of our lives, I asked him when he knew he was meant to be a warrior. He looked at me quizzically, moved to sit down next to me, and asked, "What did you say?" I repeated my question, and his eyes blazed with incredulity. "Few know we are warriors. Even many in the field don't acknowledge our real calling. How did you know?" Thus began an evening that has been followed by a number of letters and phone calls.

The conversation eventually turned to the spiritual path God had used in each of our lives to draw us to himself. Our cultures and histories could not have been more different, but in that four hours God confirmed through another couple's story things he had been speaking to me for several months prior. God had been deepening my conviction that every moment of life is warfare, a battle against evil's hatred of glory. And every battle is won or lost to the degree our heart is open to the pleasure God has crafted for us to enter, embrace, and enjoy. Phrases the Spirit had spoken, thoughts that had been turning inside of me, embryonic and incomplete, were repeated by Jim and Rupal as they talked about their parenting and medical service, their love of good food, music, and literature, and their sacrifices for the sake of glory.

I met Jim and Rupal only once—but it was as if we were a long-lost family finally reunited. It was a jubilant night that enabled me to see the rich diversity, uniqueness, and similarity of calling God gives each of us. I still suspect that Jim and Rupal were angels, but I'm quite satisfied to accept it was a divine appointment that nourished me and inflamed my heart to live out my calling in spite of the cost or travail.

God sets us up for encounters that have the potential to change our lives. Some encounters are surprising but expected, as in significant conversations with a spouse or a good friend. Others are serendipitous rendezvous that leave us with a sense of destiny and wonder. Not every person or every conversation is meant to be life changing. If we attempted to make every conversation deep and eternally important, we would get little done and be a nuisance to most people we meet. Instead, we are to live with openness (faith) and expectancy (hope), invested in giving and receiving (love) from others as God so moves us.

How are we to enter the stories of others in a way that invites them to embrace the hunger of their heart (dignity) and their flight from God (depravity)? How are we to use a lunch hour or a plane flight to the glory of God? We have all participated in conversations that last for minutes and are profoundly deep; others can last for hours and barely scratch the surface. I make no value judgment about which is better. Some moments are ripe for quick and deep movement, while some relationships require decades of chit chat before a deep conversation can occur. What if it takes years to work toward discussing matters of the heart with a neighbor or coworker? Is that of any concern to God, the Master of time? Absolutely not, as long as we heed God's call to be available and engaged with the people he places in our lives.

Still, redemptive conversations follow a broad, common path, whether they occur during a two-hour plane ride or in a long-term relationship with a child, spouse, or friend. Conversation that has eternal impact enters the past that has shaped a person's faith, the dreams of the future that comprise their hope, and the people for whom they will sacrifice as they live out love. Conversations that enter the realm of faith, hope, and love will traverse four major stages.

(1) *Present to the Past.* We live in the present. Careful examination of what is happening right now in a person's life reveals their conflicts, desires, sorrows, and joys. We must join a person in joy and sorrow in the present or we won't be invited more deeply into his heart. Shared pain and desire serve as a doorway through which one can enter the matters of past betrayal, powerlessness, and ambivalence. The past clues us in to the ways a person has tried to make his life work apart from God.

(2) *Past to the Future.* We often repeat the past in the present; therefore the future is likely to be little more than a replay of our past. When past patterns of a person's flight from God are revealed, we can ponder the nature of her hope for the future. The future holds our dreams and our fears; therefore, understanding what a person desires and what she fears gives us a deeper sense of what controls her heart.

(3) *Future to the Present.* The future is the ground for reflecting on what a person wants to be to others, what legacy he wants to leave in the lives of

others. Reflecting on the future invites a person to consider his unknown, unformed potential to give and receive love. Movement from the future to the present challenges him to change and face whatever keeps him from loving and being loved.

(4) *Present to Eternity.* Love is always the doorway to the deepest existential questions of life and eternity. *Am I loved? Do I know perfect, unconditional love anywhere else other than in God? How do I live if I don't know this kind of love? How can I love others when they hurt and harm me if I don't know what it means to be forgiven?* By returning to a person's present struggles we can open the door for her to understand her need for deeper relationship with the eternal God.

Again, few conversations move through all four stages at one sitting. Some do, but they are rare and exquisite. Far more often we make a bit of headway in one area, then repeat it dozens of times over weeks and months with a person. But we need a vision of the whole vista we are called to traverse as we use conversation to grow glory in others.

Let me describe a map that can help you guide conversations beyond present concerns to matters of eternity. I'll use as an example a conversation that did move through all four stages in one sitting.

FROM THE PRESENT TO THE PAST

Exhausted and spent after teaching all weekend at a seminar, I boarded the Denver-bound plane in Chicago. I sat in my first-class seat, having upgraded as a frequent flyer from my coach ticket. As soon as I sat down, I put the stereo headset on and began looking for the classical music channel. There was no music on any channel, but I left my headset on expecting the music would come on momentarily and as a further buffer from being compelled to talk with anyone. My seatmate soon arrived, and I moved my legs to let him take the seat by the window. Like most frequent flyers, I am adept at cutting off conversation not only with the headset but by positioning my book to prevent any face-to-face contact.

I sat with my headphones on for ten minutes without any sound. A flight attendant eventually spoke over the loudspeaker, "We are sorry to inform you that our sound system is inoperative." I heard the announcement and rather sheepishly took off the headphones. My seatmate smiled and said, "Well, I guess you'll have to talk to me now." I smiled, agreed, and went back to reading my book.

As a flight lifts off I take personal responsibility to get the plane into the air. I grip the arms of my chair and pull us up. I couldn't both read and perform my feat, so I put my book down and white-knuckled the plane up off the tarmac. As soon as the book went down my seatmate began to chat. He was in his midthirties, already sporting a significant patch of gray and bifocals. He was a road warrior who was clearly violating the rules of the sky by talking. I was exhausted and didn't want to talk. But I heard the Spirit urge me several times, "Turn and look at him and talk." I said, "No." The Spirit did not confront me or get louder. He simply kept repeating the phrase, "Talk to him." I know the difference (usually) between a twinge of guilt and the Spirit's imploring. I realized soon that nothing would silence that insistent nudge, and so I turned and began to talk.

Usually conversations like this begin with banalities and then move to demographics. We both commented on how nice it was not to fight the small space of coach chairs and noticed we were being served the same dinner we'd had on other Chicago-bound flights. Junk-food conversation led the way to demographics. "Is Denver your home?" "What work do you do?" He told me that he was an electrical engineer. Internally, I grimaced. I thought to myself, "An anal retentive, left-brained scientist type. O Lord, why? Why not at least a writer, a typical businessman, or an older woman who might fall asleep?"

The Spirit kept calling me to talk, to care for the person God had put in the seat next to me. I finally said to him, "I know both words, electrical and engineer, but I have no idea what you do." He looked surprised but began a brief recitation of what he did. It made no sense to me. He told me again, and I still didn't understand, so I asked him, "Do you mind taking me through a typical day, let's say in fifteen- to thirty-minute increments?" He looked stunned. "Are you serious?" "Indeed, otherwise I won't have the slightest idea what you actually do."

He took me through his eight- to ten-hour day. It took about twenty minutes. I asked a few questions, but mostly I was silent. At the end, his work made a great deal of sense to me. I thanked him. He nearly gawked at me as he said, "I don't think anyone, including my wife, has ever asked me what I do during a day." It was my first opportunity to see how open his heart was to more meaningful conversation. I said, "That's sad. I think most of us live with people who assume they know what we do and don't really know." He stiffened and informed me that he didn't see that as a big deal. My first movement into disappointment and desire was thwarted.

We engage the present via small talk, expected questions, and demographic chatter. It is not meaningless or a waste of time. It is the initial dance to garner as much information about each other as can be learned without significant engagement.

What I look for as I try to meaningfully engage with someone's current situation is the style in which he or she speaks. If I were rummaging around a bookstore for a new novel, I would first try to learn what genre, or niche, it fits: mystery, science fiction, historical fiction, western. The style alerts me not only to the content I can expect but also to how to read the text. The same is true for human beings.

We each have a style, or a mode of interacting with our world. We use this style to regulate how close others may be to us and how far they may withdraw. If people get too close, we usually feel the awkward rise of shame; if they get too far from us, we often feel loneliness and loss. Our style of relating may be warm, friendly, and vague. By being warm and friendly, people are drawn to us; the shield of vagueness keeps people from getting too close while also exuding an air of mystery that keeps them from going too far away. On the other hand, our style might be cold, distant, and competent. Our competence keeps people from giving up on a relationship, but our cool demeanor assures that few will try to get too close.

The task required for redemptive conversation in the present is to look for a door, any door, that takes one from superficial data to matters of the heart. One of the best ways to find the door is to notice how the person draws you in or keeps you at a distance. The people who draw you in often fear loneliness more than shame. Those who keep you at a distance usually fear shame more than loneliness. Most people will draw and distance simultaneously. To find a door that might be entered, all one needs to do is not "give in" to the unstated instructions the person's style dictates.

Imagine a conversation between two women at a salon, one cutting the other's hair.

STYLIST: So your baby was born in March? When?

CUSTOMER: On the fourteenth.

STYLIST: My husband left for Korea on the thirteenth. He's been gone for a year.

CUSTOMER: What took him to Korea?

STYLIST: He's military.

CUSTOMER: I know that's hard. My dad was military and had to leave our family for a year when I was little.

STYLIST: He won't be back until August. Today's our anniversary. He called me this morning, and I hung up on him.

Many people would be at a loss as to what to say next. But all one must do is enter the terrain most angels fear to tread with an awareness of the push-pull of the other person's style. The stylist would not have mentioned the situation with her husband if she didn't want to talk. She is inviting conversation. But she does so abruptly and with some hostility, making it difficult to pursue her heart. If one is aware of the push (don't shame me) and pull (don't leave me), she can step into the middle terrain and invite an interaction. Perhaps like this:

CUSTOMER: You must miss your husband very deeply to be that angry and hang up on him. I don't know if you want to talk about something so important with a stranger, but if you do, I'd be honored to talk.

When expected patterns are disrupted, one is much more free to pursue the uniqueness of a person's character rather than ramble about the ordinary and predictable. If you look, you will almost always find a door to walk through. And the most important door creaks open when a person begins to talk about their core relationships. Listen to another conversation that one could have with a stranger.

A: Where are you from?

B: Pittsburgh.

A: Wow. Now there's a city that has changed its image.

B: That's for sure. It really is no longer an iron and steel town. The arts are flourishing. Going to downtown is a real treat.

A: I know. I used to hang out downtown in the early '70s, and it was a dump. What do you suppose brought about the change?

B: Well, I think enough people recognized that we weren't going to survive unless there was an economic change. That had to be preceded by a real commitment to the city itself, especially downtown.

A: As the cities go, so will the country. It is a strange era when we flee to the suburbs and let most of the cities turn into war zones.

B: Yeah, we're all mostly committed to little more than ourselves and our families.

A: For sure. My teenage daughter has helped me see that I'm a liberal in talk and a not-in-my-backyard conservative in attitude who doesn't want his property values or lifestyle affected by the world around me.

B: Kids. They can make your life miserable and wonderful. I've got two teenagers and they...

The conversation is off and running. It has moved from demographics and banter into relationships. Relationships hold the key to the human heart. If I am invited to hear about your important relationships, then I am off the porch and into your living room, closer now to what really matters. The "technique" for opening the door was a simple question and humble self-disclosure. Curiosity and vulnerability are our best tools for entering a person's heart. Once the door is open, then one must find the "tension point" or plot that is the current matter of concern to the other.

> My seatmate did not want to acknowledge disappointment or
> desire. I was rebuffed but not silenced. I looked for another
> door into his heart. I asked him, "So do most little boys want
> to grow up to be electrical engineers?" I asked how he got into
> his field in a way that avoided the demographic shuffle of
> where he went to school and how he got interested in engi-
> neering. By setting the question in the minor key of desire,
> dreams, and disappointment, I knew I was putting a big chunk
> of life on his tray table.

He took my bait. He laughed and said, "No. At least not me." The door was slightly cracked, and I asked, "Then what did you want to be before you gave yourself over to engineering?" He looked shocked again that I was interested and not talking about the weather. He said more quietly, "I wanted to be an artist until I was fourteen, then I gave it up."

There are gaps in every story. A gap is an unfinished bridge between two elements in a person's story that is probably significant to the development of a plot. A person may not tell it because he views it as incidental—or because it is too important. One will never know until the gap is entered. It's like spelunking in a cave: One cannot determine the depth or intrigue of an opening unless it is entered and interpreted. The only way to do so is to ask simple, apparently dumb questions like, "Adam, where are you?"

He'd quit at fourteen. I wanted to get more data before I entered that gap. I had my suspicions. And they were nothing more than a hypothesis: He was slightly, ever so slightly effeminate, a scientist who really wanted to be an artist. It doesn't take too much training to guess that someone, probably his father, had made it difficult for him to fulfill his dream. I didn't want to leap into that private space suddenly, but with sufficient light I wanted to enter the cave. Past betrayal, powerlessness, and shame are the formative, shaping influences that give direction to our flight from God. If I want to move into matters of faith, hope, and love, then I must enter a person's past stories.

I asked him, "What kind of art were you involved in?" He told me water coloring. I know enough about that process to know how difficult it is and how hard it is to learn. I asked when he began and what kinds of things he painted. Our discussion drew more passion from him and connection between us than any other moment. Passion is the guide to follow to know what matters to the heart.

I eventually said, "So what took you off your path to be an artist?" He looked at me and said, "My dad wasn't thrilled to have an artist for a son." He began to tell me about his father. He was a good, caring man who had a deep, abiding horror of the poverty he had experienced as a child. He wanted his son to have a good career and a secure income.

My seatmate told me what happened without telling me what happened. He told me the caption under the picture but did not let me see the picture. Our lives can be described without being illuminated. Our stories can be told without truly being told. I can say, "I was sexually abused when I was ten" or "I was divorced two years ago" and say little to nothing. But whole scenes can be pursued even when only captions are given.

We are to pursue the underlying narrative, but not quickly or with any sudden movement that would scare off our seatmate. It is none of our business as to what has shaped his life, but it is God's passionate business to send us into the stories of others. We have no right to push our way in, but if invited we have every right to be a good guest.

I asked, "So your dad made it difficult to continue with water coloring. That must have been one hell of a night." He looked at me as if someone had shot a gun off near his ear. "Yeah, how did you know? He came into my room and, in a fit of rage, broke every one of my brushes." The scene of shame, heartache, and rage unfolded before he knew what he was saying. When he realized he had told me more than he had ever said to anyone, he pulled his head back into his shell. He said, "Hey, I don't mean to ruin your meal with my personal tragedies. By the way, what do you do?"

His shift to me and my job was a panic move to get the conversation off his narrative. He was not sincerely asking, and I didn't want to get too far from his story so I said, "I'm a prophet." I don't know why the word popped into my head, but his look indicated he thought I was crazy. He said, "You mean like a biblical prophet type?" I smiled and said, "Sort of." He didn't know what to make of me and so he said, "How's the money?" I said, "Well, I am sitting in first class." We laughed and the conversation returned to neutral banter. The tension of the plot's development was lessened and we were good friends again, eating dinner and yapping away.

I let the shift continue for a while, but I was looking for another door. Finally, I invited the opportunity to go back to the story. I said, "You may not want to talk about it because it's too raw, but I'd love to know how you handled your father's rage and shame. I mean, that is a horrible thing to do to a kid. How did you deal with it?"

I wanted to gain access to his father's betrayal in order to invite him to see that he trusted few people, if anyone, after his father had left him powerless to dream. I wanted to understand what he had done with the artistic pulse he had shut down and how the shame of being seen as effeminate had hardened the arteries of his heart to love. I wanted to be invited into his struggles with faith, hope, and love.

A shift to the past can occur when the present plot and its conflicts are on the table. Our current conflicts reflect to some degree the themes and stories of the past. We repeat conflict; we replicate our themes throughout our lives. Once we get a glimpse of the current plot, we can begin to ponder how those matters were handled in the past. The past is joined when scenes of life-shaping influence are talked about in terms of what occurred and what it meant.

FROM THE PAST TO THE FUTURE

The past is the place we developed our deepest convictions about ourselves, life, and God. One cannot enter another's past merely by hearing the conclusions and convictions that resulted from it, but by being invited into the story itself. To enter the past one must ask permission. These life-shaping and raw scenes of life ought not be entered without invitation. When one is permitted into this terrain, the guest stands on holy ground.

Stories are made up of characters, plot, and setting. They have a beginning, middle, and end. The beginning usually involves innocence. The middle introduces tragedy, plot conflict, and the process of grappling with the "problem." The ending brings a conclusion, a resolution that usually involves meaning and an assessment of what one learned in spite of loss. The past requires more than one visit; it is a multifaceted structure that must be reentered many times to gain a greater understanding of its geography. But even one story gives a hint, a glimpse into the heart.

There is an ache in every soul. No matter how good life has been to us, we want what only heaven can provide. No matter how deeply we deny or attempt to escape our hunger for God, it can't help but haunt the narrative of our stories. It may not come to the surface as a clear and direct hunger for the transcendent, but our need for God is part of the genetic structure of every desire, whether legitimate and good or dark and decadent. We must develop the skill to hear and pursue desire, because desire reveals what the seeking heart most deeply pursues.

Desire lingers in most every discussion. Once pursued beyond a surface level, it will usually be met with some form of resistance. Resistance is
a block that often slows down the conversation's movement or entirely side-
tracks the discussion. Most resistance involves some measure of ambivalence: "I don't want to talk about something painful or deep; on the other
hand, I don't want you to quit pursuing me." Resistance requires an artistic touch that neither presses into what is being avoided nor backs away
from the story. Choice must be left up to the storyteller, not forced by the
story hearer. Listen to this interaction with my neighbor regarding his careful and intense bathing of his 1967 Mustang:

ME: Hey, John. Need any help washing your car?

JOHN: Are you kidding? You're a slob. I wouldn't let you touch my
baby. (Banter)

ME: Fine, but I'm going to bring a chair over and watch you caress
your true love. Do you mind? (Invitation)

JOHN: No. If you're that bored and have nothing else to do, come and
amuse yourself. (Banter)

ME: You know, I have never heard how you fell in love with this mistress. When did you get her? (Entry into story)

JOHN: I've had this car since '69. I bought her from a friend. My folks
had an extra garage, so after it became clear it was going to be a collector's
car, I kept it. (Effort to dodge his naked love for his car)

ME: Yeah, but you didn't keep it just because it was a collector's car.
(Gentle exposure of resistance)

JOHN: That's true. We have a lot of memories together. (Reentry into
story)

ME: I bet you do. I was teasing you before, but I know this hunk of
metal holds a lot of dreams and desires. (Testing accessibility to the heart)

JOHN: I suppose, but it is worth a good piece of change. (More
resistance)

ME: True, but you'd no more sell her than you would your soul. You just don't want to admit how much your car is like a picture album that holds a lot of your past memories and dreams. True? (Exposure of desire and invitation to pursue more)

JOHN: Yeah. I mean for years when I felt like a total dork all I needed to do was go cruise in my baby, and I felt better.

This conversation went no further. It didn't need to because it was only a first entry into what dearly mattered to my neighbor. His car held deep, personal memories that he had linked to feeling like a dork. In many ways, his honesty stunned me. I decided I'd gone far enough for the moment.

Many believers think a "redemptive" conversation must either be overtly spiritual or invite a person to make a decision to receive Jesus as Savior. The fact is, talking about Pearl Jam or a good veal piccata might be a profoundly "redemptive" conversation if it opens channels to knowing what stirs the other person's passion and delight. Patience in conversation allows us to make small entries without demanding we proceed beyond the natural potentiality of the moment.

The goal of redemptive conversation is not merely to move air or kill time, but to comprehend what the other loves. We all love someone or something. Resistance arises when we get too close to the scenes of the past that deeply matter. Resistance comes in too many forms and shapes to mention them comprehensively here, but three primary types usually emerge: abstraction, dismissal, or contempt.

Defensive abstraction involves a glossing over of details. The story-teller offers vague generalizations rather than gritty specificity. Abstraction is more than a gap. It is a fog that shields the eyes from a particularity that would be troublesome. For example, when you ask someone how he is and he answers, "Just fine," usually the word "fine" indicates absolutely nothing. It is a cloak word that says further conversation is neither desired nor necessary. Many vague statements are not actually a "no" to more conversation; instead they are boundaries, temporarily closed doors that will only open to gentle knocking.

Dismissal goes further. It owns up to a particular moment but dismisses its impact or meaning. For example, someone can say, "My father was a pretty mean guy." The speaker has been honest but left his remark vague. Notice the kind of poignancy that comes when specificity is added: "My father beat me with a thick belt until I quit crying. I usually couldn't sit for a couple days." The speaker is no longer abstract, but even specificity can be dismissed. Notice the potency of dismissal: "But he didn't know any better. His father broke his jaw when he was ten." This might be true, but the statement intends to dismiss the impact of his father's cruelty.

Resistance can turn even more hostile through a contemptuous assault against oneself or another: "I was a snotty kid who deserved to be beaten. Dad was just doing his best to get me to turn out right. I'm glad for the discipline today." It is common to deaden the pain of past harm and major losses by blaming oneself. Contempt might also be turned against the hearer: "I don't know why you're making such a big deal about stuff in the past. It's over and I forgive him." Instead of blaming oneself, it is easier at times to silence the questions of the one who hears what our stories have to tell. This story clearly says the storyteller experienced significant betrayal, powerlessness, and ambivalence in relationship with his father. At what cost? He probably struggles to trust others, refuses to surrender to big dreams, and fears intimacy. He would rather take the blame than face the loss involving his father; he would rather intimidate the one who sees than admit his pain.

Expect resistance. It is a tragic by-product of our fear of love and our memory of past betrayal. Our response to resistance should be to draw forth its implications by connecting two points in a story and coming to a sum factor. Implications ought to be stated tentatively with ample room to differ, clarify, or add more data. For example, implications could be drawn in this fashion:

A: Your father beat you, and to survive you learned to blame yourself.

B: I don't think so. I just don't see any good in rehashing the past.

A: Really. Then if the past is in such good shape, why are you tense and irritated at me?

B: Okay, so my life was not a piece of cake. But I learned to handle it, and I'm a lot different with my kids because of my past.

A: No question, my friend. You are a far, far better father to your kids than your dad was to you. But you continue to be extremely hard on yourself, which shows up when you get silent and disappear. You can't be reached. You're in another world. Your family is lonely for you.

The listener (A) connects points between the harm inflicted by B's father, B's self-blame, his good heart toward his kids, and his periodic withdrawals from the family. It is not elegant nor perfectly clear, but in connecting the dots a pattern begins to emerge. The listener's attempts to illuminate the pattern will either close down the conversation or grant passage through the defense. If the storyteller (B) embraces the pattern as (somewhat) true, then it may be possible for the listener to move him from how he has attempted to make his life work (faith) to a vision of glory (hope) that could become a dream greater than the way he is living now.

> When I asked my seatmate how he had dealt with his father's raging destruction of his brushes, he turned away from me, looked out at the passing clouds and said, "Not well. I did what he wanted. I studied hard and did well in science, but I would never let him see me happy with my grades or awards. I showed a total indifference and sort of made him pay for making me feel like crap."

We talked a little more and moved back and forth between the past and the present. It became clear that his marriage was in bad shape, he was a distant father, and he hated his work. After talking for about twenty minutes he looked at me again and said, "Really, I don't mean to bore you with my sordid life. What do you do?" This time he seemed to genuinely want to know. I said, "I'm a psychologist. At least that's how I make my living. What I really do is live as deeply and passionately as I am able for Jesus Christ. I am a Christian."

He looked at me as if I had just announced I was a terrorist who was going to hijack the plane. "No kidding. I would never have figured you for a Christian. In fact, I have never met a religious person like you before." Now it was my turn to be stunned. He had paid me a glorious compliment, but it also meant he had experienced a number of offensive encounters with other brothers and sisters in Christ.

There were many plates spinning in our discussion—his marriage, kids, job, father, Christianity, past offenses, and the flight attendant who was removing our trays and checking our dessert preference. He asked me how I had become a Christian. His question invited me to start talking abut my life. I told him about my relationship with my father. He had not taken my dreams from me; rather, I had failed to dream at all.

My story was different from my seatmate's in many ways, but I told him, without going into the specific details, that I had known other kinds of harm. And I made it clear that I'd handled the harm by trying to make life work without much risk of more pain. I admitted that I knew what it meant to be a desperate, frightened man.

Before telling him how I became a Christian, I asked if he

would answer a few very personal questions first. He smiled, "You know more about me than most of my friends. Shoot."

I said, "Am I right to say that your marriage, parenting, and job are on the rocks? Maybe not over, but not doing real well?" His face saddened, "Yeah. You're not far from the truth." "Then have you ever thought through how that commitment—or should I say 'oath'—when your father broke your dreams into bits, has shaped a lot of your life, including your relationship to your wife, kids, and job?" He replied, "I don't know what you mean by 'oath.'" I knew this was a crucial moment that would either take us into much deeper discussion or cause the conversation to taper.

No one can change without facing both the harm that has come from living in a fallen world and his own disastrous attempts to make life work apart from God. We change to the degree we see both the foolishness of our idolatry and the beckoning beauty of God's waiting heart. Forgiveness means little until we are exposed as adulterers and murderers. Forgiveness means much when we see what we deserve in contrast to the party that awaits if we merely go home.

I said, "I don't know if you made an oath at that moment consciously or unwittingly, given your prior history with your dad. But somehow you said, 'Never again, never will I ever want something so deeply. Never will I give myself to art, to beauty, to anyone who wants me to live with passion and freedom.' You were most alive when you painted, and when your dad crushed your heart, you took revenge on him—and unwittingly on every person who has ever loved you since. For some strange reason you have told me more than even your wife probably knows. I don't know if she is a good woman, but if she is, she is dying to know your stories and your very hidden heart. Am I in the ball park? If so, then I'd be glad to tell you about my far more decadent and vengeful heart."

By now you may be thinking, *Whoa—I don't have the ability to go that far in conversation, and even if I do, I don't want to be responsible to get that involved with people I know, let alone with strangers!* We do not have to carry on this kind of conversation every day or in every relationship. But the joy of rich involvement with another is far greater than the risk of being rebuffed. It is hard to state the next point loudly enough: *People in pain want to talk.* They are very forgiving of our errors as long as we are neither pushy nor arrogant. We can bumble and learn. The reward is enormous. Already, the privilege of involvement with my companion was well worth the time and energy.

His eyes were wet and he was eager to get the focus off of him and onto me. I obliged and told him a great deal of my journey. I talked about how my wife and I fought, wept together, and fought again—how redemption does not resolve conflict as much as it provides a safety net that enables us to go farther and do wilder tricks on the high wire than those who do not have the protection of God's grace.

The fifteen minutes I filled with my story gave him time to recoup and to process some of what I said. I continued to engage him by saying, "I am a mess, I know it, and I believe the God of the universe is involved in making me like himself. You are alone and caught up in at least twenty years of hatred and heartache. Do you want me to keep talking?" He lowered his eyes and said, "Yes."

Our conversation was now a dialogue. We had established a bond sufficient to allow movement between his past and his future and between my past and God's redemption of my future. The future is best entered through our disappointments and our fear to dream. As we dream, we also confess that we long for a future different from our past; we long to be different than we have been before. It is this desire for change that allows us to look at our present with different eyes.

FROM THE FUTURE TO THE PRESENT

We don't live in the past or the future; we live now. Life is daily, organized according to a structure we accepted without really reading the fine print. Mortgage payments. Retirement. College tuition. Investments. Vacation plans. New toys. Nothing is wrong with living an organized, predictable, middle-class life (or, for that matter, any-class lifestyle). The issue is choice—not the choice to make more money or become upwardly mobile, but the choice to reckon with life as it is and as it is meant to be.

Dreams disrupt our present commitments. My middle daughter, Amanda, wants to be a veterinarian, but she'd rather listen to music in her room and read novels than study science. I would like to lose weight, but I'm hungry now. The future beckons, but the present shouts.

When we invite others to live, we begin with the present and open the door to the past and the future. But we must always return to the present, where we embrace or flee truth and make decisions that will perpetuate our past or change the direction of our lives forever.

> We were fifteen minutes from landing. Our time was about finished, and my moment with this man was about to pass. I felt pressure. Should I ask him if he wanted to receive Jesus Christ as his Lord and Savior? Or should I give him a card and invite

further interaction? Should I trust the meeting would be followed by other divine setups and get ready to land the plane through my armchair-clenching heroics?

He solved my uncertainty by asking, "Have you written any books?" I said, "Yes, a few." He replied, "I'd like a couple of titles so I can look at your work." I had no idea why the word "No" popped out of my mouth, but by this point I doubt he would have been surprised by anything I said. He looked at me and said, "Now what?"

I said, "Remember what I said a half-hour ago? You are a man who asks no one for anything. You will not humble yourself to want anything from your wife, your kids, or, I suspect, from me. I'd love for you to ask God into your life, but I suspect the part of you that is willing to want and ask is still icy and hard. Right?" He nodded. "Then you are still, even now, making sure no one can get near your paintbrushes to break your heart. So ask me to send you a book."

His eyes never turned away, but it was clear he was in the middle of a titanic struggle. To ask was to violate his core commitment not to want or to make himself vulnerable. To not ask was to be exposed as even more icy and hard than he wanted to be. The moment seemed to last as long as the entire flight. His mouth opened and his eyes dropped, "Damn you. You are more right than I want to admit. But it is true. Okay. Would you send me a book?"

We were not two men involved in business negotiations, marking their territory and manipulating the terms of a deal to see who would win and who would lose. Rather, we were involved in a process that had to do with eternity and the heart. At the moment my seatmate asked for a book, he voluntarily lost and surrendered more than pride; he momentarily said "no" to a past that was ruining his future. He opened himself a little more to God.

I took his card and he asked, "What do I owe you?" I looked straight in his eyes with sufficient benevolent contempt to make him laugh. He said, "Okay, it's free." I replied, "Not exactly. Nothing is free, not even grace. What I want from you is one letter after you read the book telling me what you think. And I promise I will not hound you, plague you with more books, tracts, or Christian stuff unless you ask." He smiled again.

We were about to touch back to earth. I was so caught up in the lovely drama in which God allowed me to play a part that I forgot to land the plane. Nonetheless, we arrived at our gate safely.

FROM THE PRESENT TO ETERNITY

One of the most important skills we can develop is the ability to help others (most of all ourselves) discern what matters most. We always do what we want—even if it is hidden and unknown to us. Discernment requires us to summarize our life themes through the use of at least one dramatic scene. My seatmate's life theme was connected to the brush-destruction scene. He would not want nor ask for anything; instead, he lived an indifferent, closed life of duty—he was an unbelieving older brother (Luke 15). My summary of his life-defining theme and its relationship to his marriage, parenting, and work created a dramatic moment for him in the present: *Now what?*

As simple as it is to say, few people ask others, "Now what?" In order to yield fruit, conversation must invite the other to discard the life themes that rob him of joy; it must direct him to the provision offered through the Cross. Movement toward eternity usually involves decisions that bring the heart to a crossroads. The tension involved in such a moment is intense. All the figures have been put before you, your options clarified, and now you must decide if you want to buy the house or walk away from the offer. Even if you take an extra day to decide, it still boils down to a yes or a no. God is brilliant at putting us at a point where we must say yes or no. To join him in helping others walk the healing path, we must be willing to sit with a friend in the tension of asking, "Now what? What are you willing to invest for eternity?"

I would have been thrilled if my seatmate had asked, "How can I know the love of God through Jesus?" He didn't. Thankfully, a person's standing before God is never my personal burden; it is God's. My calling is to intrigue, disrupt, and invite the other person to consider his own heart. I was delighted that my companion shared his heart and invited me to share my story. All I wanted to do at the end was to see if the man desired any further contact. I wanted him to be faced with a decision, even if it was not a decision directly regarding his relationship with God.

My seatmate gave me his card. Within the week I sent him my book *Cry of the Soul*. I wanted him to grapple with the hard emotions and the questions they compel us to ask about ourselves and God. I did not harangue him, and I waited for his letter. It came six months later. It was brief and grateful. At the end of the letter he wrote, "If you want to further save my soul and marriage, send me the next book." I did. We have corresponded a number of times. It is not my burden to convert him or change him; I am merely called to be human and unique, a small picture of Jesus Christ to him through the gifts and opportunities I am given.

Eternity is rushing toward us. It is about to arrive like a speeding meteor that will one day hit this earth. I invite others to live in light of the eternity that is streaking toward us. I will do so more creatively to the degree I live with greater hope, more winsomely as I embrace my own story and live with more solid faith, more passionately as the love of God softens and shapes my heart. As I walk the healing path with greater faith, hope, and love, I invite others to walk the path as well.

Thankfully, I am not to walk that path as an isolated wanderer who trudges ahead, hoping a few may follow or that I might glimpse the backs of a few ahead of me. I walk alone often, but I also walk arm and arm with a few comrades who sojourn with me. Those few are the church, fellow aliens, and strangers.

What would it be like to be part of a pilgrim community, a sojourning family that knows what it means to bear my burdens as I share their laughter and tears? The final chapter reflects on walking the healing path with fellow travelers.

CHAPTER 12

CREATING A
COMMUNITY OF
SOJOURNERS

W here do faith, hope, and love lead as we live in community?
Gabriel Marcel defined community as the place where "I
hope in you for us." Imagine what would happen if I made
myself available to you, became responsible to enter your story, and committed myself to your glory? We would both be different—the transformation of our character and our calling would not be the exception, but
the rule.

A community of sojourners must leave the land of comfort and walk
the healing path toward a better city than we enjoy now. To join this apostolic band that incarnates Christ in a surprising and compelling fashion, I
must continuously leave the basic principles of my country, class, race, subculture, and family. I must cleave to this crew in the kind of relationship
that invites others to fight, surrender, and party for a larger purpose than
their own rights or pleasure. The result of leaving and cleaving will be a
form of weaving, a union of souls that leads to greater playfulness, service,
and worship.

Borrowed from the paradigm of marriage—to leave one's mother and

237

father, to join together, to become one flesh—this concept has application in every relationship and in all communities. Obviously there are differences (the most notable is the call for sexual purity in all relationships); nonetheless, we are to leave all to follow Christ, being in the world but not of it. We are to love one another deeply and from the heart and demonstrate the Father's love for his Son by the way we love one another. We are to know a pleasure and joy in communion, service, and worship that is the equivalent in marriage of becoming one flesh. Faith, hope, and love lead us to leave, cleave, and weave in community.

LEAVING THE BASIC PRINCIPLES

What are the basic principles of the world? They are the lists of dos and don'ts that rule most every social engagement and establish the boundaries for acceptable and unacceptable behavior. They are the conventions of respectability that announce you as a full member in good standing or, in their absence, mark you as a philistine, a poseur. Whether we are in third grade, at a trade convention, in the foyer of a church, or on a tennis court, we hate to wear the wrong clothes, say the wrong thing, or be dismissed for being different.

We all know that the rules are seldom (if ever) written and announced. The most powerful rules are unstated and assumed. We all know you don't wear white shoes before Memorial Day, and if you are a home boy, it would be utterly shameful to wear a pair of suede Birkenstocks. In some families, one knows never to bring up Uncle Al's alcoholism or to challenge Dad when he expresses a political opinion.

We long to fit in. We feel awkward when we are outsiders and shame when we were once inside but now are no longer accepted. What gets us in and keeps us inside? Following the rules—approving of those who are impeccable in their performance, viewing with derision those who are not.

As long as we align ourselves with the power base of whatever group we wish to enter, we receive the benefits of membership and avoid the liabilities of being a stranger.

But as Christians we are called to follow our father Abraham and by faith depart from our country, class, race, subculture, and family. We are to be in the world, but not wage life according to the basic human principles that determine good and bad, in and out. "In but not of" requires we belong while always retaining an awareness of our first loyalty.

Miroslav Volf writes,

> Christians can never be first of all Asians or Americans, Croatians, Russians, or Tutsis, and then Christians. At the very core of Christian identity lies an all-encompassing change of loyalty, from a given culture with its gods to the God of all cultures. A response to a call from that God entails rearrangement of a whole network of allegiances. As the call of Jesus' first disciples illustrates, "the nets" (economy) and "the father" (family) must be left behind (Mark 1:16-20). Departure is part and parcel of Christian identity. Since Abraham is our ancestor, our faith is "at odds with place."[1]

Does this involve a "leaving" that calls us to give up our very identity as constructed in the matrix of citizenship, class, race, subculture, and family? Yes. Does loyalty to Christ call us to be prophetic and disruptive to *every* group and person with whom we engage? No. We are called to a *particular* time, place, group, family, and person. Without an ability to enter the world of the particular others God has placed in our lives, however, we will never gain access to disrupt them and offer them a taste of the bounty of Christ.

God has shaped me to be in a particular situation in life, and I am to embrace my historical moment with honor and gratitude. If I am an American, I should cheer when my country wins a medal. If you are in a culture that reveres refined activities like shooting skeet, it is appropriate to be able to shoot two clays in one pull. On the other hand, if you are ministering to kids living in cardboard boxes, it would be ludicrous to wear a Laura Ashley dress or sport a conservative haircut.

We should strive to "fit in" almost every way that gives us access to those we are called to love, but without ever buying into the basic rules required to be a full-fledged, 100-percent, card-carrying member of a particular group. We should never blindly support any group or person—no matter if what brings the group together is a theological flag, moral issue, counseling orientation, or church denomination. Why? There is something wrong with every culture and group, and to affirm any as the basis of identity and the substance of life is to find a home rather than to live as a sojourner.

And yet in every culture and group (barring those overtly committed to hate, destruction, and intolerance) is something of God. No culture or group or person can completely eradicate the mark of being made in the image of God. No poet or philosopher, no matter how deeply they hate God and desire to destroy his presence on the earth, can live and work without making God known in some fashion. As the stars reveal the glory of God, so does every molecule made by God, including those who hate God but will one day bow their knee to his majesty.

Our calling is to delight in whatever reflects God in his glory, especially his sacrificial love. Only as we sit in a coffee shop and kibitz with the regulars, joining their joy and entering their sorrow, do we reverse the perception that Christians are those-who-are-against rather than those-who-love.

If we are strange and unpredictable, but we fit and can't be dismissed, then we have left our homes in Ur and are on the healing path. The path always leads to the center of the village.

A Church Without Walls

Where do we go when we start on the path of living for God? Sadly, for many the path leads to a building that is often referred to as a church. Missiologists tell us that when a person comes to Christ, he loses most of his friendships with unbelievers within the first year. Seldom does conversion lead back into bars, coffee shops, and jazz clubs. But this was never God's intent. We're meant to be a new community, a holy priesthood that returns to the insipid, cold world as salt and light, flavor and warmth. We cannot do so (and were never meant to do so) as a building that unbelievers occasionally visit or as a protest movement that merely lobbies for a Christian world-view. Instead, we are meant to be in the midst of society, conducting business, writing plays, selling paintings, drinking coffee, and infiltrating the world with faith, hope, and love.

In ancient Greek society, the central gathering place was called the *agora;* it was the "place of commerce, information, and ideas."[2] At the heart of the city, goods were sold, artisans interacted with others in their trade, and people gathered to debate political, philosophical, and theological matters. Most Western countries have no place comparable to the agora. It was not exactly the same as the shopping mall, boardroom, fitness center, Elks Club, bar, coffee shop, or jazz club; the agora was all these places combined.

We are to go to the "streets" (the word used in many English Bibles to translate the word agora) and invite to God's party any who will come (Matthew 22:9-10, Luke 14:23). Because there is no central agora today, we are to go wherever people hang out, conduct business, talk, eat, drink, dance, and gossip to invite others to taste the gospel.

But we fail to make the invitation incarnate, in the flesh, if we extend it solely with a tract, a bumper sticker, or a prefabricated one-size-fits-all gospel presentation. Just as there is nothing wrong with memorizing the chart of chemical elements to make progress in understanding chemistry, neither is there anything wrong in knowing numerous ways to present the gospel to someone who has never heard it. I am a faithful and supportive follower of Evangelism Explosion's methods. But to think of spreading the gospel as merely sitting next to a person in a coffee shop and asking in the first, or second, or twentieth interaction: "If you were to die tonight and were to stand before God, and he were to ask you…" negates the power and glory of incarnate story. So when *should* we ask the crucial questions? Simply when the stories of our lives intersect deeply enough that spiritual questions and conversation are part of the larger framework of knowing and delighting in each other.

Although we do not have an agora comparable to that found in Greek culture, any place can become an agora. We are to create agoras not merely for the sake of evangelism, but in order to celebrate the glory of the place, to fill it with life and delight that draws others to frequent it.

Where is your agora? Wherever your passion takes you. I love coffee, and I love to sit with old men and hear stories. It is in those contexts—sitting with a group of old men on a mall bench, where our wives have parked us so we don't ruin their shopping, or in a greasy spoon where men sip coffee and tell tall tales—that I listen, delight, ask questions, and probe the mysteries of the universe.

The agora is wherever your heart says, "Yes, I love it here," and "No, I won't let evil win. I will stand and fight the effects of the fall." Often the greasy spoon sponsors a donation jar for the high-school kid who was paralyzed in a car accident. Instead of merely dropping five bucks into the jar, why not put on a community talent show or car wash to raise money for the teen (or really go over the edge and do a dog wash)? Organize. Stick your neck out. Ask someone to help you, and serve someone unrelated to your church, your group, your small world.

Good friends who are in the leadership of Christ the Rock Church in Appelton, Wisconsin, heard that law enforcement agents conducting a search for a missing woman needed a central site to set up headquarters.

The church called and offered a Sunday school classroom. The search went on twenty-four hours a day for weeks. People in the church provided food, cots, and snacks, while helping families of the officers who could not get home for days at a time. The search was given local and national news coverage. As a result, the church gained a widespread reputation for its members' willingness to help and for their low-key but explicit heart for God.

The agora is Trout Unlimited, bowling leagues, golf outings, the ACLU, soccer leagues, literacy programs, food banks, AIDS work, civil rights, crisis pregnancy centers, suicide hotlines, rape-support counselors, sexual-abuse recovery groups, AA, Big Brothers, the Boy Scouts, and Special Olympics. A universe of opportunity waits for someone who can say yes to love and no to evil and longs not merely to do good, but to enter others' stories for the sake of glory.

The healing path is first and last about engagement. It is through engagement with you that I learn to hope more deeply for us. It is through hope that God slowly heals past brokenness on the basis of future promise. The healing path takes me from living as an "insider" to engaging in areas of burden and passion on the fringe of what most people view as the formal, structured local church.

But I am not to go alone. I am not meant to run a dog wash or prepare tasty meals for tired officers by myself. I am to sojourn with an apostolic band. We may occasionally walk alone, but we are meant to walk together.

An Apostolic Band

We walk the healing path alone and lonely at times. Moments specifically designed for each of us take us through the valley and into the desert, where God woos us with his strange, wild love. But the majority of our journey is meant to be traveled with a few others. The writer of Hebrews is clear about the importance of community. He writes:

See to it, brothers, that none of you has a sinful, unbelieving heart that turns away from the living God. But encourage one another daily, as long as it is called Today, so that none of you may be hardened by sin's deceitfulness.... Let us hold unswervingly to the hope we profess, for he who promised is faithful. And let us consider how we may spur one another on toward love and good deeds. Let us not give up meeting together, as some are in the habit of doing, but let us encourage one another—and all the more as you see the Day approaching. (Hebrews 3:12-13, 10:23-25)

We are indebted to one another. You cover my back. I watch yours. I must try to protect you from sin's deceitfulness and the resulting proclivity to harden your heart against God's tender call. We all stand in drying cement. If we don't keep moving on the journey we will become bound and enslaved to something or someone other than God.

I went on a steep fortieth-birthday mountain hike with ten other men. I was the second oldest and certainly the most out of shape. For the first several miles I led the way with three of my companions. By the end I was lumbering last in line, with a squadron of buzzards hovering overhead anticipating my demise. I noticed the group slowed its pace but without conceding to my exhaustion. They expressed sincere care and playful repartee. I knew I would not be left, but I also was "encouraged" to proceed rather than give in when part of me wanted to sacrifice myself to nature's hunger.

Mutual encouragement takes into account our history, continues to dream in spite of obstacles, and enters each other's hearts through sorrow and laughter, taking one more step toward the day. We are to gather together in churches, coffee shops, conference rooms, and on riverbanks to scan the horizon for the day. The Day of the Lord is ahead. Soon. Even if it doesn't arrive for another millennium, it is soon. And we are to band with a few mad watchers of the sky who know what it means to sip a good drink and send up a burnt offering of smoke as we reflect on today's spilt blood and tomorrow's battle. We need to count the day's losses and gains for glory. Accountability is little more than learning "to do math" with others as our comprehension of life's complex theorems deepens, and as we learn to figure the numbers we have been dealt.

The word *apostle* means "a sent one," or one who is to go forth to deliver a message. We are to be a community of "sent ones." Obviously, apostleship was once a formal office filled by twelve (the disciples), a thirteenth (Matthias), and then Paul; these men had a unique relationship with Christ and had authority given directly from him. But Scripture recognizes others who were also referred to as apostles. Jim Peterson discusses this differentiation:

> Paul wrote, "It was he who gave some to be apostles, some to be prophets, some to be evangelists, and some to be pastors and teachers, to prepare God's people for works of service, so that the body of Christ may be built up...." Paul is describing the functions that need to be present or available to the people of God if they are to discharge their calling.... You will need the apostle with his vision for the whole, and his ability to make new things happen. You will need the prophet with his special ability to interpret the times in the context of God's Word. The evangelist is necessary to help you in your own sowing and reaping. You're going to need the gentle, and sometimes not-so-gentle, care of the shepherd to stay encouraged and on track. And the teacher will help you live according to God's truth.[3]

We need visionaries who plunge into the unknown and direct us into battle—they are kings. We need people who interpret the times and the soul in light of the Word of God—they are prophets. We need encouragers who remind us of truth, draw near to offer support, and teach new paradigms of life—they are priests. We need a diverse group of people whose life stories, burdens, and training facilitate different aspects of disturbing, drawing, and directing others to Jesus. This motley, redeemed band is simply to go somewhere to say yes and no. Where? Anywhere. Who? Any two or more who share a burden and so link burden, gift, and calling to form a cohesive, deep, passionate relationship that mirrors a marriage.

People sit in church on Sunday morning. If they are really committed, they go to a Bible study or a small growth group. And if they are amazingly disciplined and committed, they will take on another ministry in the church like teaching Sunday school or helping out in a youth group. All these activities are wonderful. But what would happen if we also left the church as apostolic bands and entered the agora to join a fly-fishing club and visit a nursing home? What if we hung out in coffee shops and got involved in Big Brothers?

What would happen is we would immediately be in a mess. First of all, we wouldn't know what we were doing. Second, we wouldn't know how to talk with others in light of faith, hope, and love. Third, we wouldn't have the time. Fourth, we wouldn't get along. Our histories would conflict. Our dreams would not be the same. Our ways of engagement would ruffle each other's feathers. We would have to pray, confess, repent, forgive, and fight on with people as diverse as Matthew—who was a tax gatherer and a lackey of the state—and Simon—a zealot, a terrorist committed to the destruction of the government.

Why did Jesus stack his apostolic band with brothers from the same family, political enemies, and wild men? After all, one of the first basic principles of the world is "avoid conflict at all costs." Join with people who are like you, hold the same core values, know the right way to dress, and accept the rules, written and unspoken. Join a club. The gospel comes along and says, "You are meant to be fools. Strangers. Pilgrims and aliens. Reenter the world and witness to my love by loving those with whom you would not normally get along." We are to join with our motley crew members and enter the agora, intending to do more than merely have a good night out and kill some time.

What does entering the agora in company look like? Perhaps neighbors who attend the same or different churches start or join a book club. Reading and talking, drinking and laughing, month by month over years, they'll become part of each other's stories by hearing the tales that have led each person to perceive a book, a passage through certain kinds of eyes. But they can't do it as a "ministry," as one is normally conceived. One cannot genuinely engage in literature unless one loves fiction and good writing. They must be open to being moved and changed by the works they're reading, by the stories of the group. This "club" does not gather merely to critique, but to be transformed.

What would happen if a group of men who love to golf said, "Let's golf for God." Better your game. Take lessons. Hang out in the nineteenth hole afterward, swapping stories and watching the faces of men who are in the middle of tough times. Perhaps it will involve walking out to the car with a guy who is hurting and simply asking, "Are you okay?" When he answers, "Yeah. I'm doing fine," a response earned through hours of golf and kibitzing can be offered: "I don't think so. I won't press you, but I want you to know I will be praying for you. I'm warning you: In a couple days I will call so you can tell me again that you're doing fine. Okay?"

Rich people who like hanging out together ought to be asking, "How can we reach other rich people for God?" Men who regularly score above 180 ought to be asking, "How can we bowl for Christ?" Women who are mothers of preschoolers can use MOPS to get women together for a break and a time of reflection. People who are troubled by AIDS can go volunteer together.

The healing path takes us "on the road" with others who serve a vision, who serve each other, and who ultimately serve the glory of God. And this "leaving" together can be done only if we cleave together.

CLEAVING IN BATTLE

To cleave is to hold on to another for dear life. If we go to the same church, I might not even know your name, let alone your history, dreams, and calling. If I am in your small group, I may know a lot about you, but perhaps not the significant matters of your past, present, or future. We may like each other and spend time hanging out, but even then our commitment will be no deeper than the sacrifice we have made for each other. It is sacrifice, sorrow, and blood that bind the hearts of warriors and lovers together, not mere fraternity. If we don't bleed together, then when times are tough we will likely not cleave to each other.

War compels us to cleave and compels us to grow. The war must be bigger than our relationship, bigger than the wounds of failure, bigger than my comfort. Cleaving is, in other words, not suburban, middle-class camaraderie built around free time, convenience, and a break from routine. Am I implying that it's wrong to have a buddy with whom you play racquetball, chat for a few minutes, and then do not see until the next match? No, I am not. But the desire and the prayer for more ought to fill your car as you drive to the club. If an openness to cleaving is present, having coffee with friends, going to a movie together, or sharing a break is no waste of time. Cleaving in the war of life involves availability, responsibility, and accountability.

Availability and Faith

Opening our arms to each other is the most difficult, ongoing battle in any relationship. Over time I will hurt you, and you will hurt me. If we are mere acquaintances who chat superficially, then we can be friendly long enough to keep our mutual sin at bay. Church-foyer and potluck relationships require little more than civility. Friendly conversation can be a wonderful prologue to more meaningful engagement. It can also be a mockery of true community. Nothing is wrong with small talk as long as one's heart is alert enough to see cracks in the conversation that may allow for deeper entry into the other's heart.

Mutual investment in a burden greater than ourselves demands an investment in each other. The investment will be like a bucking stock that drops from forty-two dollars a share to three dollars and then slowly goes back up, falls, and grows. It will be tempting to sell early in order to cut our losses.

But true faith remembers. It remembers God's open arms waiting for us. Faith remembers the moments of embrace and the sweetness of reconciliation: As I have been loved, I am called to remain open to you. To open my heart to you is to be ready and willing to come to your aid with all that I have in order to do you good. It is also to open my heart to see how I have hurt you and failed to love you as well as I take care of myself.

Confession is an art of relationship that has been lost in our era. James tells us, "Therefore confess your sins to each other and pray for each other so that you may be healed. The prayer of a righteous man is powerful and effective" (James 5:16). Confession is twofold: first, opening our heart to God, admitting we are far from home and need his grace, and then saying to the other what we have already said to God. The word *confession* comes from a Greek word that means "saying the same thing as"—it is repeating what is obvious. I have stepped on your foot. Now I need to say, "I have stepped on your foot" and "forgive me." Confession releases pent-up fear and self-hatred. It also exposes the hidden part of my self-righteousness that says, "I would not have stepped on your foot if you hadn't gotten in my way."

Confession acknowledges failure, but more important, it admits desire: "I have failed you, we are divided, and I long to be restored." Confession remembers a day of intimacy and sees the current division in light of what was once a relationship of shalom. In asking for restoration we outstretch our arms to receive the blessing that can come only from one who knows the playful anticipation of forgiveness as well as we do.

Ultimately, availability is a hunger to be forgiven, and an openness to bless and forgive.

Responsibility and Hope

Responsibility is most often thought of as doing what one ought to do to fulfill one's word. A more accurate notion is that responsibility means one should be answerable for an act and its consequences. My children are responsible for keeping their rooms clean. I am responsible for taking out the trash on Wednesdays. A task can be measured as to its adequacy (were the clothes all picked up?) and who should complete the task if it is not properly done (the child whose clothes are on the floor). This judicial notion of responsibility is neither inaccurate nor wrong, but simply incomplete. So conceived, responsibility leads at best to greater civility and clarity in relationships. But there is more. Responsibility is truly a far wider and wilder concept.

To be responsible means to have the capacity to play. A ball is thrown high. If the one to whom it is thrown does not leap into the air, it will crash through a window. The one who leaps is responsible—that is, "response-able"—if he can make a quick decision, step back two feet, and then stretch high into the air to nab the ball. If the ball breaks the window, who is responsible? Primarily, the one who threw the ball high and out of control. But the one who chose not to stretch or react quickly, who chose to stand in a safe, passive position is also responsible. Every human interaction requires a response. The only utterly irresponsible act is not to act; an irresponsible person says, "I couldn't do anything; it's not my fault."

Is a mother whose son takes drugs responsible? No, he is accountable for his decision. He is not a mere product of his parents' failures or the licentiousness of the culture in which he lives. Nevertheless, every human being is responsible for the acts of every other person. A shooting in a school occurs in a distant state—am I "response-able"? Yes. I can weep. I can rage. I can pray. I can talk with my own kids. I can work for better communication in my school system. I can strengthen gun laws. I can help provide better adolescent counseling in my community. I can start a parents' discussion group. Instead, most of us watch the news as idle observers, grateful the harm has not come to our community or family.

Most of us are observers of life, like those who sit in the stands and watch *others* play. We feel something when we see television's images of shattered lives, but our emotions are drowned out by the next news story that passes our information-glutted eyes. To be "response-able" is to lean into the pending redemption that is hurtling toward us at increasing speed.

It is much like skiing. When I have taught people to ski, I have observed that their most common error is to lean back against the mountain. It seems safer to lean back than to shift one's weight toward the front of the skis. Though the skis are larger in front and provide greater control, the fear of falling draws one to lean back so our fall is less severe. The result, at best, is an awkward, nearly out-of-control stance and little speed. One may get down the slope alive, but it will not have been worth the time or energy.

On the other hand, leaning down the mountain, picking up speed, bending as one begins the turn, and then popping back up increases momentum. It feels frightening, but it is the way to attain both the greatest safety and the most fun. "Response-ability" means we glide into each moment, anticipating the change of terrain, the crowd of skiers on the right. We move into the shadows near the trees, enter powder, and alter our stance and turning radius to swoop through the snow rather than try to carve clean edges. We change our responses every moment as we lean into the future. We can't be fluid while skiing stiff.

To be fluid is to contour our lives elegantly to fit what we encounter on our life path, to be flexible as we keep promises to dispose ourselves toward a particular end. I promise my wife I will meet her at the base at 11:30. I plan my schedule to be there a few minutes early. A skier in front of me takes a terrible fall. I can ski by or assist him. I know what it means to have someone pick up my scattered skis and help me. I stop. The man is injured. My promise to my wife is now at odds with the implied "response-ability" to a fallen skier. Which has greater power? One can't be responsible merely on the basis of promise or moral categories; one must be playful. Fluid. Elegant. Open. Available and then "response-able" to the moment, within the larger frameworks of living out the love of God.

To be "response-able" is to live with our senses alive, to gather data given to us by others and then respond to it in terms of achieving the greatest pleasure and privilege known to humankind: growing glory. Hope makes us supple and playful. Our hearts are ready and anticipating the next moment. Hope frees us to respond—to be "response-able" to new data and new opportunities that lead to far greater joy than we normally associate with the concept of responsibility.

To live well we must respond freely to the good of others. It is playful to say to a friend: "I know you are hurting. I am exhausted and have little to give. Do you want to talk now or would you prefer I call you back when I'm less distracted?" If she refuses to be honest or turns away hurt and angry, it is not because you failed in your "response-ability." You heard her pain. You listened to the limit of your capacity to be involved. You gave a real alternative that promised response and engagement.

To be playful is to enter the battle of life for others just as you are, accepting your limitations while dreaming of the unlimited and redeemed. It is to engage in the present with your full presence for the sake of another's future.

Accountability and Love

To cleave is to cling to others by practicing availability and responsibility. Faith and hope always lead to love. Love is the greatest of the three; it is life. To love is to take into account your existence as the basis of discovering my own. I can't know myself, or know happiness, unless I know it through you. I am to cleave to you as to myself.

I have caught large trout single-handedly and felt the thrill of the chase and capture, the glory of seeing an angel of the water in her kaleidoscope of color and design. I have also caught small trout with a friend or watched a companion catch a fish, and the thrill of mutual participation in the moment is incomparable to any great catch made alone.

When we think of sojourning together for a common purpose, many Christians think only of "holding each other accountable"—making sure ("in love," of course) that everyone is doing their part for the kingdom. But accountability is not the process of chiding one another to be more faithful, nor is it merely encouraging others to be what they were meant to be. Rather, it is sitting back at the end of the day on a porch with other kingdom workers, laughing about Don's earlier efforts not to embarrass a man talking to him, who had a chunk of ravioli stuck to his tie. Or it is teasing Kirk for his college band outfit until tears stream down our faces and cause the retreat center's owners to look at us like we're mad. We are meant to weep together, marvel about each other, and with gratitude, let the sun set. Accountability means to recount the day together.

Each day is woven with ordinary thread. Some days have blazing gold intersecting the fabric; other sections of the cloth are stained and darkened by tragedy. In recounting the day the full tapestry needs to be considered.

It may become clear that one has worked too hard while another was slow and inefficient. If we are an apostolic band, then discussion must ensue. Not everyone can bring in the same number of bales, nor should they. Some are better drivers; others are better at getting a good price for the work. Our gifts are different, therefore our labor should not be the same. But our passion for the greater glory and the good of each person must shape the tone of our conversations. Accountability is storytelling in a round that brings each voice into play, ultimately forming a chorus that sings in praise of forgiveness, glories in the harvest to come, and rests in the gratitude of a day done.

As we make our way to our ultimate home and then cleave together along the way, we will experience moments of soul-transforming worship. Worship weaves our hearts together in wonder, gratitude, and service.

WEAVING IN WORSHIP

Human relationships should drive us to distraction and to worship. The more involved we are with any person, the more we need God. Our joint failures and sin will lead us either to divide or to cling to God more tenaciously. The more we cling to God, the more we will turn to each other—available and broken, "response-able" and playful, accountable and at rest. The more moments of rest we enjoy with others, the more we will be in awe of them, grateful for their love.

Awe and gratitude are the fundamental building blocks of worship. I am to look at you and scratch my head in wonder: "Why do you love me so well? Why have you not abandoned me? Why do you still like me, knowing me as you do?" I am to be in awe about your love and your faithfulness to me. And I am to go beyond admiring you, to thanking you for staying with me on the path.

Awe and gratitude must be expressed or they remain unplanted seeds.

Ironically, the more a friend has meant to me, the more difficult it is for me to tell him what he has brought to my life. Such inarticulate awe and gratitude for a human face and for companionship lead us to a new level of worship not for humankind, but for God. How can I thank you enough? I can't. The depths of awe and gratitude for a human embrace must either transcend the horizontal or taper off in quiet, wordless despair. We are either propelled to a vertical world or saddened that even the richness of the horizontal is still not enough. Horizontal, human awe and gratitude eventually will either become a self-indulgent demand for more or will drive us to peer into the heavens to rejoice in the invisible maker of all glory.

But God gives us a way to look one another full in the face while peering into the heavens. We can commune with him and with each other through communion. In the early church, communion was not a religious event held in a church; rather, it was a part of an ordinary meal, eaten together as a family but set apart as a time to lift the cup and divide the bread. Ingesting Christ's body and drinking his blood was distinct from the meal itself, but it took place within the context of ordinary gatherings for nourishment and conversation. We are to be in community with the world in a similar way, even while we remain compellingly different.

Savoring God's Love

We worship when we feast on God together in the past, future, and present. Jesus invites us to eat bread as his flesh as we anticipate the coming banquet. In hope we scan the future, holding the bread to the horizon, thanking him for his sustenance, and calling for him to return soon. Then we drink wine as his blood, in awe that we are marked by his life, just as the doorposts were covered to spare us from death. We drink—taking in the fragrance of the bouquet and the sweetness of the taste. Awake and aroused, we anticipate eating and drinking with him again.

This is the vision Jesus communicated to his band the night before he died. After celebrating Passover with his disciples and teaching them to remember him through bread and wine, Jesus gave them this stunning assignment:

> You are those who have stood by me in my trials. And I confer
> on you a kingdom, just as my Father conferred one on me, so
> that you may eat and drink at my table in my kingdom and sit
> on thrones, judging the twelve tribes of Israel.
>
> Simon, Simon, Satan has asked to sift you as wheat. But I
> have prayed for you, Simon, that your faith may not fail. And
> when you have turned back, strengthen your brothers. (Luke
> 22:28-32)

At that point, one would expect a moment of transcendent ecstasy to lift the disciples to the seventh heaven in Christ's presence. Instead they begin to bicker and boast: "I won't betray him. It is not me. I will die with him. In fact, recall how well I served him when we were in Galilee?" We dream and we remember and then we quarrel.

And, in response, Jesus serves. He takes the bowl and the towel and he washes our feet. He serves more food and drink. He does not confront or chastise. Instead, he disrupts his followers' hearts by looking directly at Peter and naming his betrayal, inviting him to return even before he departs.

Worship is an anticipation based on a remembrance that exposes our petty, quarrelsome, prideful hearts and then welcomes us to dine with him and feed our brothers and sisters. "When you have turned back, strengthen your brothers." There is no question: You will return. There is no question: He will receive you, empower you, and send you back to serve those you have harmed.

Body and blood swirling over our palate compel us to remember his body hanging limp and tortured. He was betrayed. He was powerless. He was ambivalent and put to shame. Yet he was faithful. He refused to despair. Instead he cried out to his Father and sacrificed himself in obedience to his calling for the sake of joy.

Worship is the prize for leaving our home and cleaving to our friends. Worship is eating and drinking and dancing at the party where we are the honored guests when we ought to be despised outcasts. Worship is the rest that strengthens us to serve.

It is time to set out, to pack up our stories, check our compass, and move together into a world of betrayal, powerlessness, and ambivalence for the sake of more stories, more awe and gratitude, and more God.

NOTES

Chapter 1: The Long Walk

1. Hannah Hurnard, *Hinds' Feet on High Places* (Wheaton, Ill.: Tyndale, 1986), 66.

Chapter 3: Embracing Life

1. The concept of embrace is a core concept that has been brilliantly developed by Miroslav Volf in his groundbreaking book *Exclusion and Embrace: A Theological Exploration of Identity, Otherness, and Reconciliation* (Nashville: Abingdon, 1996).
2. Toni Morrison, *Jazz* (Toronto, Canada: Knopf, 1992), 28-9.
3. Morrison, *Jazz*, 28-9.

Chapter 5: Powerlessness and the Loss of Hope

1. Toni Morrison, *The Bluest Eye* (New York: Plume, 1994), 39.
2. Albert Camus, *The First Man* (New York: Knopf, 1995), 80.
3. Frederick Buechner, *The Clown in the Belfry* (New York: HarperCollins, 1992), 98-9.

Chapter 7: The Wager of Faith

1. The categories of innocence, tragedy, imagination, and resolution that make a good story are drawn from the compelling work of Don Hudson in the *Mars Hill Review*, Volume 1, "Come, Bring Your Story," 73ff. For more information about the *Mars Hill Review* or this article call 1-888-WSS-2002.

Chapter 8: The Dream of Hope

1. Jacques Ellul, *Hope in a Time of Abandonment* (New York: Seabury Press, 1973), 177.

2. Gabriel Marcel, *Homo Viator* (Gloucester, Mass.: Peter Smith Publishers, 1978), 32,36.

Chapter 9: The Dance of Love

1. Emanuel Levinas, *Ethics and Infinity* (Gloucester, Mass.: Peter Smith Publishers, 1978), 92.
2. Marcel, *Homo Viator*, 187.
3. Marcel, *Homo Viator*, 187.
4. Marcel, *Homo Viator*, 189.

Chapter 10: Living a Radical Life

1. I have been profoundly influenced by Jim Petersen, *Church Without Walls* (Colorado Springs, Colo.: NavPress, 1992). His book has shaped my reflections on how the church is to enter a postmodern culture.
2. Mike Regele, *The Death of the Church* (Grand Rapids, Mich.: Zondervan, 1995), 182.
3. Regele, *The Death of the Church*, 177.
4. Ray Bowman, *When Not to Build: An Architect's Unconventional Wisdom for the Growing Church* (Grand Rapids, Mich.: Baker, 1992), 101.
5. Regele, *The Death of the Church*, 223.

Chapter 12: Creating a Community of Sojourners

1. Volf, *Exclusion and Embrace*, 40.
2. *The Interpreter's Dictionary of the Bible* (Nashville: Abingdon, 1962), s. v. "agora."
3. Petersen, *Church Without Walls*, 78.

About the Author

Dan B. Allender, Ph.D., received his M.Div. from Westminster Theological Seminary and his Ph.D. in counseling psychology from Michigan State University. He taught in the Biblical Counseling Department of Grace Theological Seminary for seven years, then was a professor in the master of arts in biblical counseling program at Colorado Christian University.

Currently, Dr. Allender serves as professor of counseling at Western Seminary–Seattle. He is the author of *The Wounded Heart* and has co-authored two books with Dr. Larry Crabb: *Encouragement—The Key to Caring* and *Hope for the Hurting* (Zondervan). With Dr. Tremper Longman he has coauthored four books: *Bold Love* and *Cry of the Soul* (NavPress) and *Intimate Allies* and *Bold Purpose* (Tyndale).

Dr. Allender and his wife, Rebecca, live with their three children, Anna, Amanda, and Andrew, in Washington.